"The Oly[illegible] biggest sporting even[illegible] in the world. I think everyone is watching the Olympics"

USAIN BOLT, p6

"Every British athlete has got to be wildly excited. It's a once-in-a-lifetime opportunity"

PHILLIPS IDOWU, p102

"There is a special sense of togetherness at the Olympics. You're all going on this journey together"

CHRSTINE OHURUOGU, p140

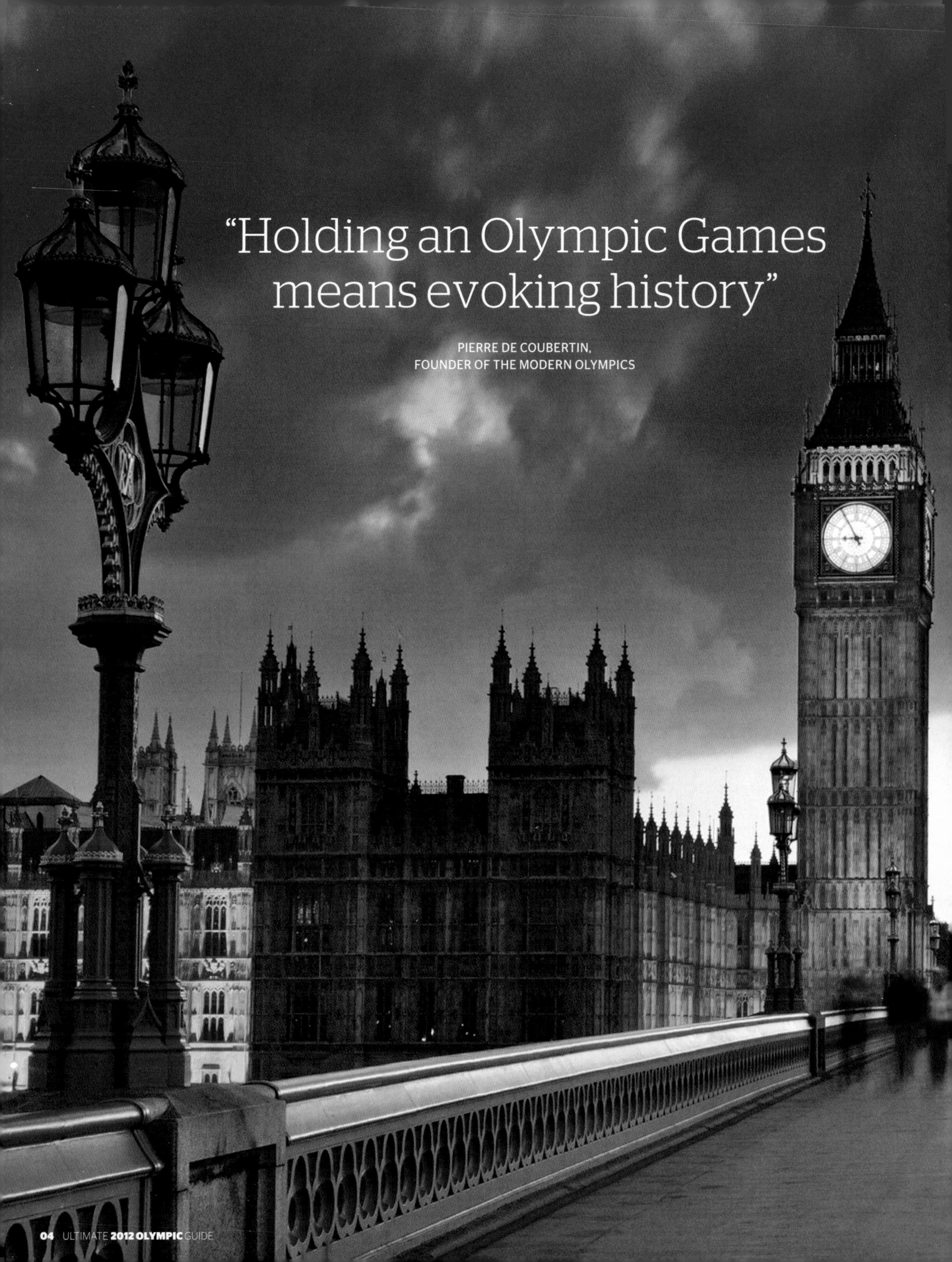

“Holding an Olympic Games means evoking history”

PIERRE DE COUBERTIN,
FOUNDER OF THE MODERN OLYMPICS

ULTIMATE **2012 OLYMPIC** GUIDE

Welcome to your Guide to the London 2012 Olympic Games. With nearly 15,000 athletes from 205 countries taking part in 26 sports, 302 gold medals up for grabs and 5 billion people expected to tune in across the globe, it's safe to say that London 2012 will be the biggest sporting event the city, and indeed the world, has ever seen.

Naturally, some of the disciplines on the Olympic programme are more popular and less complicated than others. In front of 80,000 fans in the new Olympic stadium in Stratford, Usain Bolt (interviewed overleaf) and Chrstine Ohuruogu (p140) just have to run from one point to another faster than their opponents – easy, eh? But what about the ins and outs of Beach Volleyball or the particulars of the Modern Pentathlon?

Starting on p16, our exhaustive A-Z Olympic Guide highlights the history of the 39 different disciplines on offer, their rules, intricacies and when in the programme you can apply your newfound knowledge.

In order to appreciate the enormity of the event and the special aura which surrounds it, we have also produced a huge Olympic History guide with all the big statistics and stories from Athens in 1896 through to Beijing in 2008. Can you believe Fanny Blankers-Koen won four gold medals in 1948 whilst pregnant with her third child? Or that the USA's basketball 'Dream Team' of 1992 won the gold medal without calling a single timeout throughout the whole tournament?

Just two of many illuminating anecdotes that await you over the next 145 pages. Enjoy the occasion, and your ULTIMATE **2012 OLYMPIC** GUIDE.

Stuart Messham, Editor

THE FASTEST MAN ON THE PLANET

There is no one quicker and no athlete in more demand than Usain Bolt. He tells us what it's like to be the Fastest Man on Earth.

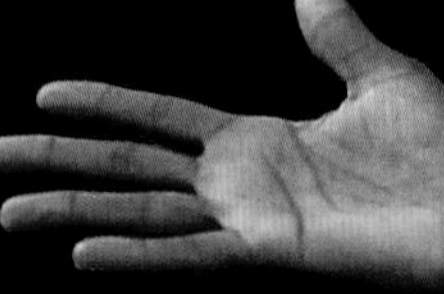

What does it feel like to run as fast as you do?
It feels good – I like winning races and running fast!

What first got you interested in athletics?
My cricket teacher advised me to try sprinting because he saw I was fast in my run-up when I was bowling.

What single thing makes you turn up for training every day?
I want to defend my world and Olympic titles.

Who was your athletic hero as a youngster – your inspiration?
In athletics, it was Don Quarrie and Michael Johnson who I wanted to run like – they were at the top in the 200m.

In 2002, you became the youngest gold medallist at the Junior World Championships in Kingston, Jamaica, winning the 200m in front of your home crowd. How special was that?
That was amazing. I was so nervous I almost put my shoes on the wrong feet. To win in front of my own people was very special.

Talk us through a day in the life of Usain Bolt. How much work and how much play?
At the moment, it is all work. We are in the middle of the track season and I am solely focused on training and racing. I normally train in the morning and evening, and just chill out in between.

You're known for being incredibly laid back, chilled even. How does this help in such an explosive sport?
I tend to run better when I am relaxed. I don't see how getting all tense and stressed would help me run faster.

When you smashed the 100m world record, were you shocked or did you know you could be that quick?
I broke the 100m world record three times. I didn't even realise I did it the first time, until after my victory lap. Beijing was great – my aim was to win the race and I wasn't thinking about times. In Berlin, I knew I was in good shape and we had all predicted a fast time so I wasn't shocked about that one.

You were criticised for disrespecting your opponents by celebrating so early during your 9.69-second 100m race in Beijing. What's your response to that?
It was only one person who criticised me and I think he has changed his mind since.

If you hadn't celebrated, your time would have been quicker. How fast can you go?
I don't dwell on times. My aim is to win races.

In Beijing, you were apparently on a diet of chicken nuggets. Has your approach to food changed or are they still top of your list?
I eat a healthy diet when I am at home in Jamaica, but in a country where I am not familiar with the food, I tend to stick to the things I know. I knew nuggets in Beijing!

How will you celebrate if you add to your gold medal tally at London 2012? And what if you break the World Record again?
I will be extremely happy if I can defend my titles in London. I hope there will be a big party!

Will anything other than gold be regarded as a failure?
I am aiming for gold.

What is so special about the Olympic Games for you?
It's the biggest sporting event in the world. I think everyone is watching the Olympics.

What other events at the London Olympics will you be most interested in and why?
The problem is, I have to run almost every day, so I don't get much time to do anything else. I will probably watch some football and basketball on TV.

You're a massive football fan and not bad in front of goal. Tell us about your football ambitions – Sunday league? Premier League winners? World Cup with Jamaica?
When I retire from track & field, I would like to play for a team. I don't know if that will be Sunday league or at a higher level, but I want to give it a shot. I tell everyone I want to play for Manchester United – that would be a dream!

You are an idol and an inspiration to many people in this country. What's your message to them for London 2012?
Thanks for all the support so far and I will try my best to put on a good show in London. ■

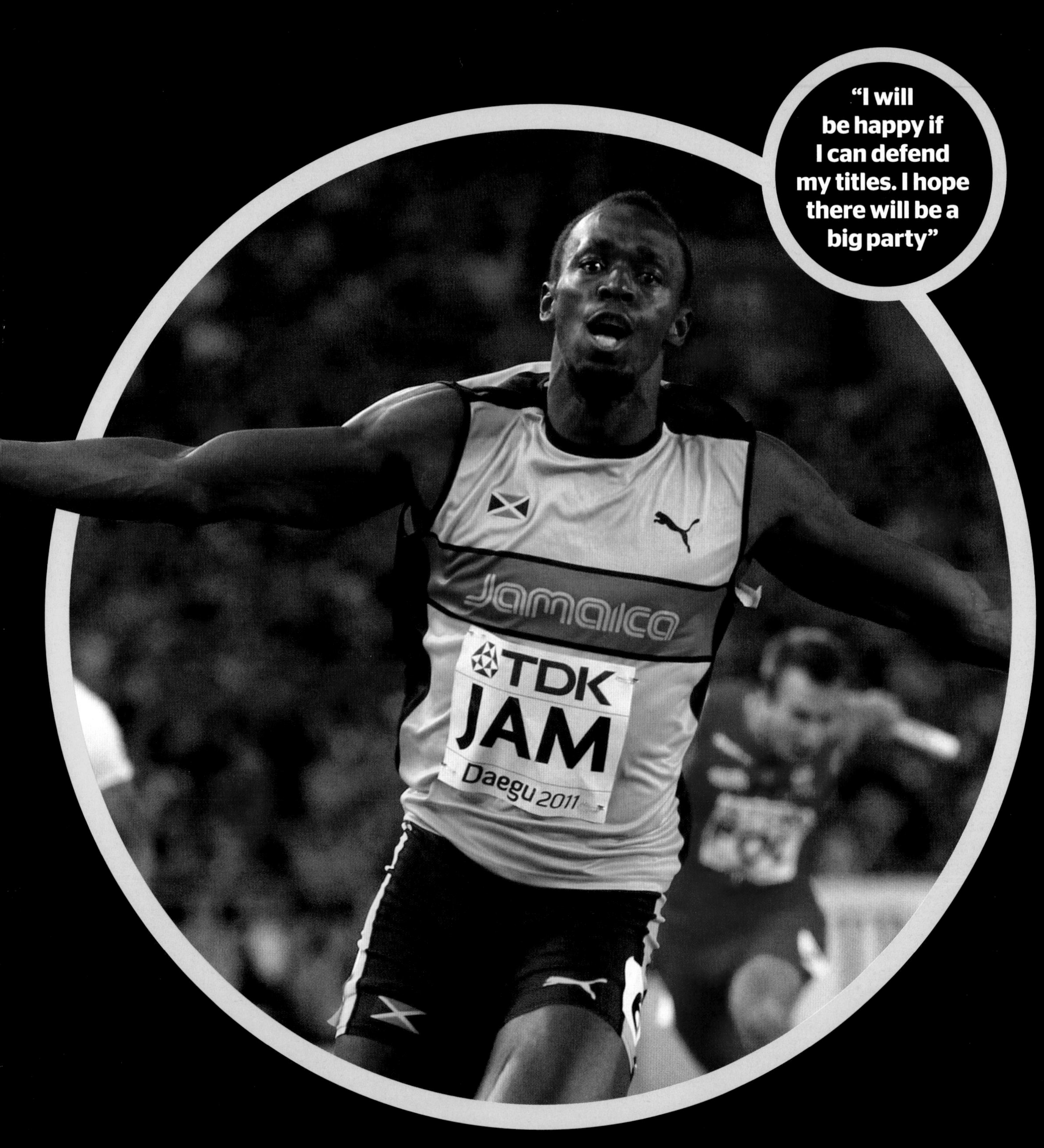

"I will be happy if I can defend my titles. I hope there will be a big party"

THE **OLYMPIC GAMES**

HISTORY

1896 Athens (Greece)

Ancient Greece being the birthplace of the Olympics, Athens was seen as the perfect starting point for the inaugural Modern Games, the event opening at the foot of the Acropolis. A local shepherd and post office messenger called Spiridon Louis won the marathon and became a household name, but famously declined the hand in marriage of the Games financier's daughter straight after finishing. A lot of the athletes had to fund their own travel, so were selected on the basis of whether they could actually get to the Games rather than on their ability. Bob Garrett, who won gold in the discus, had never even seen a discus before arriving in Athens. Women were not allowed to compete in the 1896 event.

Stadium: Panathinaiko Stadium **Competing nations:** 14 **No. of sports:** 9 **No. of events:** 43 **No. of athletes:** 246 **Top medal-winning nation:** Greece (47) **Did you know?** Given the financial cost of actually getting to Athens, some of the competitors turned out to be well-to-do tourists who were holidaying in Greece at the time.

1900 Paris (France)

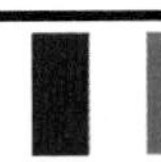

Despite having the honour of staging the second Olympic Games, Paris didn't organise an opening or closing ceremony, and conditions for the athletes and spectators were said to be appalling. The city was concurrently hosting the World Exhibition, so a lot of practical and administrative errors occurred – athletes running on grass tracks, swimmers having to negotiate sewerage in the Seine and some athletes not even aware they were competing for real. Most winners did not receive medals, but were given cups or trophies – and some were given silver medals for coming first. Britain's Charlotte Cooper became the first female Olympic champion in tennis, but it was all a bit of a shambles really.

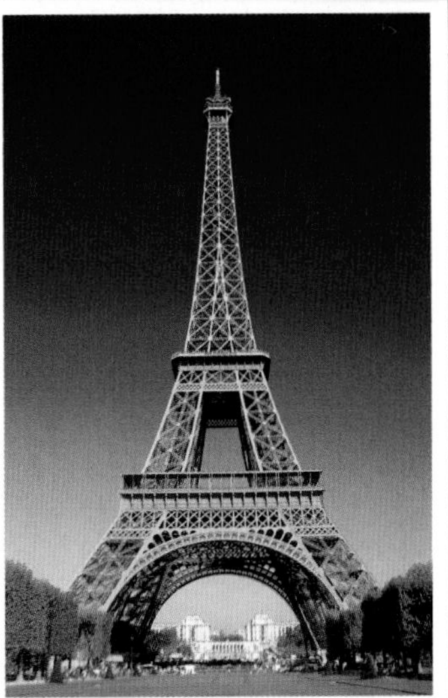

Stadium: Vélodrome de Vincennes **Competing nations:** 24 **No. of sports:** 18 **No. of events:** 95 **No. of athletes:** 1,225 **Top medal-winning nation:** France (102) **Did you know?** Some unusual events were contested at an Olympics for the only time, including motorcycle racing, cricket, croquet, Basque pelota, the 200m swimming obstacle race and underwater swimming.

1904 St Louis (USA)

At the request of US President Roosevelt, the Games were switched from the city of Chicago, Illinois, to St Louis, Missouri, which was hosting a World's Fair at the same time. But the Olympics suffered the same drawbacks as in Paris, four years earlier – the more popular exhibits of the World's Fair rather overshadowed the athletic showpieces, which were spread out over four months. Unfortunately, as well as being somewhat of a sideshow, the Games' geographic location restricted many European athletes from taking part. Only about 100 of the 645 competitors were from overseas. The USA took advantage by winning 80% of the medals, the St Louis Games being the first to hand out gold, silver and bronze medals.

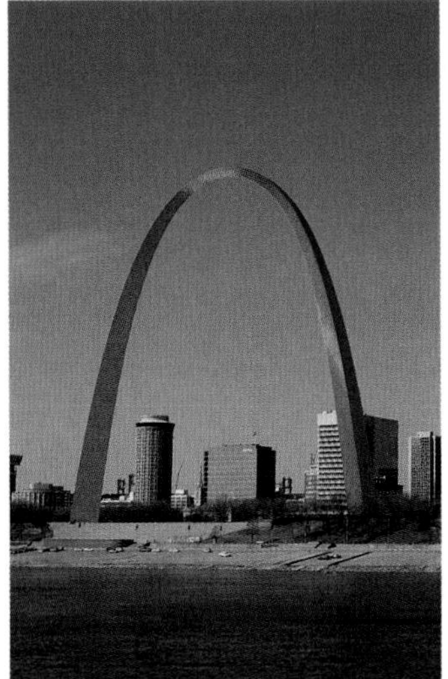

Stadium: Francis Field **Competing nations:** 12 **No. of sports:** 17 **No. of events:** 91 **No. of athletes:** 645 **Top medal-winning nation:** USA (238) **Did you know?** Tswana tribesmen Len Tau and Jan Mashiani became the first African Olympians. They were in St Louis as part of the Boer War exhibit at the World's Fair, but decided to enter the marathon while they were there!

1906 Athens (Greece) unofficial

Not officially recognised as an Olympic Games – and now referred to as the 'Unofficial' or 'Intercalated' games – a huge debt is owed to the Athens event of 1906 for saving the entire movement from extinction. Such was the poor organisation and subsequent fallout from the two previous Games that the notion of Olympic gatherings had been put at risk. But, in 1906, the International Olympic Committee's tight organisation and crisp event format – competitions didn't drag on for months – was to prove instrumental in prolonging the life of the Olympic movement.

Stadium: Panathinaiko Stadium **Competing nations:** 20 **No. of sports:** 14 **No. of events:** 79 **No. of athletes:** 877 **Top medal-winning nation:** France (40) **Did you know?** Most participants in the 1906 event thought they were competing at the Olympics but, in 1949, a three-man commission headed by future IOC president Avery Brundage, concluded the Athens games were not official. Even so, they were the first to limit entries to athletes sent by national committees and the first to have a Parade of Nations.

1908 London (GBR)

After the Italian government decided to divert Olympic funds to the rejuvenation of Naples after an eruption of Mount Vesuvius on 7 April 1906, London replaced Rome as the destination of the (now accepted) fourth Modern Olympics. The technological marvel that was White City Stadium was built – with a swimming pool placed within the non-standard, three- laps-to-a-mile running track – and Bishop Ethelbert Talbot gave a sermon at St Paul's that was later adapted by Baron Pierre de Coubertin to form the Olympic Creed. It reads: "The important thing about the Olympic Games is not to win, but to take part, just as the important thing in life is not the triumph, but the struggle. The essential thing is not to have conquered, but to have fought well."

Stadium: White City **Competing nations** 22 **No. of sports:** 19 **No. of events:** 110 **No. of athletes:** 2,008 **Top medal-winning nation:** GBR (145) **Did you know?** A new marathon distance (still adhered to today) of 26 miles 385 yards was established for the London Games so the race would finish in front of the Royal Family's viewing box in the White City Stadium.

1912 Stockholm (Sweden)

The one time the Olympics have been held in Sweden was a huge success. These were the first Games to be staged within a two-month period and the first to attract large media interest. Newspapers in the UK and USA ran front-page stories from Stockholm: Jim Thorpe (USA) winning the pentathlon and decathlon; Portuguese runner Francisco Lazaro dying from a heart attack during the marathon (the first athlete to die at an Olympic Games) and Sir Steve Redgrave's rowing predecessor, Ewart Horsfall, winning his first two gold medals. Electric timing devices were introduced for track events and the front crawl technique was pioneered by Hawaiian swimmer Duke Paoa Kahanamoku.

Stadium: Stockholm Olympia-stadion **Competing nations:** 28 **No. of sports:** 14 **No. of events:** 102 **No. of athletes:** 2,407 **Top medal-winning nation:** Sweden (65) **Did you know?** 1912 was the last time Olympic winners were issued with solid gold medals.

1916 NOT HELD

1920 Antwerp (Belgium)

The 1916 Berlin Games were cancelled because of World War I and, four years later, the Olympics were awarded to Antwerp to honour the atrocities it suffered during that conflict. These were the first Games at which the Olympic Flag was flown: the five rings representing the five continents, their connection symbolising unity and their colours on every national flag the world over. The brilliantly named Nedo Nadi won five fencing golds and runner Paavo Nurmi won three of his nine distance golds.

Stadium: Olympisch Stadion **Competing nations:** 29 **No. of sports:** 22 **No. of events:** 154 **No. of athletes:** 2,626 **Top medal-winning nation:** USA (95) **Did you know?** Sweden's Oscar Swahn, 72, won the team '100m running deer double-shot' shooting event. He is the oldest person ever to win an Olympic gold medal.

1924 Paris (France)

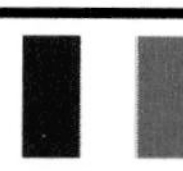

With the impending retirement of Modern Olympics founder Baron de Coubertin as IOC president, the Games were held in Paris in his honour. They were supposed to be held in Amsterdam, but the old boy insisted and eventually got his way, plus the French wanted to make up for the shambles that was 1900. They did this by building the rather splendid 60-000-seater stadium at Colombes, an Olympic village and a new swimming complex. The film *Chariots of Fire* was based on the exploits of Britons Harold Abrahams (100m gold) and Eric Liddell (400m gold) at Paris 1924, and the Olympic Motto was introduced at this Games, as was the custom of raising the flags of the IOC, the host nation and the next host nation at the closing ceremony.

Stadium: Stade Olympique **Competing nations:** 44 **No. of sports:** 17 **No. of events:** 126 **No. of athletes:** 3,089 **Top medal-winning nation:** USA (99) **Did you know?** Johnny Weismuller won two gold medals at swimming on July 20 and would later star in 12 Hollywood Tarzan movies.

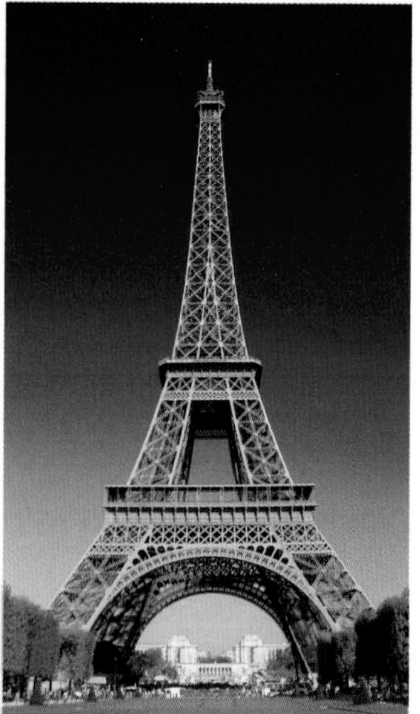

1928 Amsterdam (Netherlands)

After 20 years of economic instability and war, the Amsterdam Olympics proved a global meeting of peace and harmony. The Games also signalled the emergence of Asia and women in the Olympics, the former winning its first gold medals and the latter now with places in gymnastics and track & field. However, exhausted female runners at the end of the 800m final was enough to persuade anti-feminists and the IOC that women should be banned from running races of more than 200m, a measure that was enforced for 32 years at the Games.

Stadium: Olympisch Stadion **Competing nations:** 46 **No. of sports:** 14 **No. of events:** 109 **No. of athletes:** 2,883 **Top medal-winning nation:** USA (56)

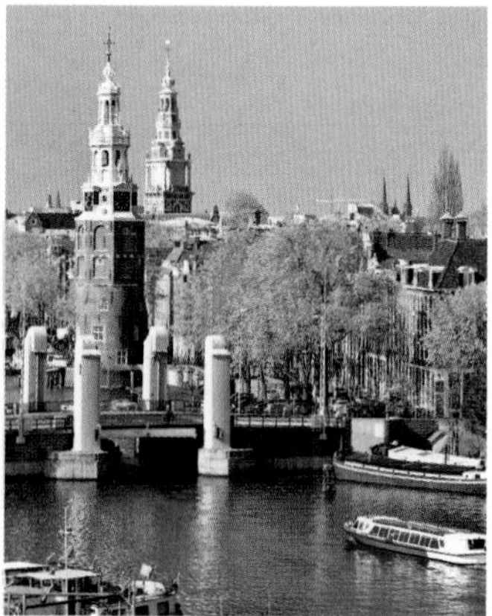

Did you know? Halfway through his quarter-final single sculls race Australian rower Henry Pearce stopped to let a family of ducks pass his boat. He still won the race and, eventually, the gold. He was later refused entry to race at Henley because he was a carpenter.

1932 Los Angeles (USA) 

It may not have been a good idea to have the X Olympiad on the west coast of America in the midst of The Great Depression, but Los Angeles was the only city that applied. The result was less than half the number of athletes that attended Amsterdam 1928 – and the football tournament was cancelled. But crowd numbers were huge and the Games returned a $1m profit. American 'Babe' Mildred Didrikson was the heroine of the Games, qualifying for all five track & field events and being allowed to compete in three, winning gold in javelin and the 80m hurdles, and setting world records in the hurdles and the high jump. Sweden's Bertil Sandström finished in second place in the equestrian dressage, but was demoted to last place for communicating with his horse via 'clicking noises'!

Stadium: Los Angeles Memorial Coliseum **Competing nations:** 37 **No. of sports:** 14 **No. of events:** 117 **No. of athletes:** 1,332 **Top medal-winning nation:** USA (103) **Did you know?** The United States government briefly lifted Prohibition so Europeans could slurp wine at the Games.

1936 Berlin (Germany)

The rise to power of Adolf Hitler and his Nazi Party had been unforeseen when the Games were awarded to Berlin in 1931, but – despite international condemnation of his anti-Semitic politics – the Olympics went ahead. The Nazi war song *Horst Wessel Lied* was played more than 500 times during the event and athletes were instructed to shout 'Sieg Heil' and salute Hitler when they passed him at the opening ceremony (the Americans refused). But Hitler's desire to use the Games to prove the superiority of the Aryan race was widely undone, especially by the performances of Jesse Owens, who won four gold medals and publicly befriended German rival Luz Long during the long jump competition. Despite Hitler's dreadful politics, the spirit of sportsmanship endured.

Stadium: Olympic Stadium **Competing nations:** 49 **No. of disciplines:** 19 **No. of events:** 129 **No. of athletes:** 3,963 **Top medal-winning nation:** Germany (82) **Did you know?** Germany's Toni Merkens was adjudged to have impeded Arie van Vliet, of Holland, in the cycling sprint final, but instead of being disqualified he was fined 100 marks instead!

1940 Not held

1944 Not held

1948 London (GBR) 

Japan's invasion of China and subsequent involvement in World War II put paid to Tokyo 1940 and, after the Soviet Union invaded Finland, its replacement, Helsinki 1940, was also scuppered. London 1944 suffered the same fate, but despite the country being very poor and ravaged by war, the British Olympic Association accepted the honour of hosting the first Games in 12 years. No new facilities were built, athletes were housed in army barracks and the record 59 competing nations were asked to provide their own food and rations. Japan and Germany were banned from competing. 'Flying Housewife' Fanny Blankers-Koen, of Holland, was the stand-out performer, winning all four sprint events she was allowed to enter.

Stadium: Wembley Stadium **Competing nations:** 59 **No. of sports:** 17 **No. of events:** 136 **No. of athletes:** 4,104 **Top medal-winning nation:** USA (84) **Did you know?** American Bob Mathias won the decathlon at just 17, having only been doing the sport for four months. He remains the youngest winner of a track & field event in Olympic history.

1952 Helsinki (Finland)

These Games were deemed to be such a success, both in terms of organisation and discipline, that some observers advised they should be held in Scandinavia from here on in. Finnish legends Paavo Nurmi and Hannes Kolehmainen carried the Olympic Torch during the opening ceremony and, although segregated from fellow competitors, the Soviet Union made their Olympic bow, proving particularly formidable in the team gymnastics. Alexsandra Chudina was the greatest all-rounder of the Games: she won silver medals in the javelin and the long jump, and a bronze in the high jump.

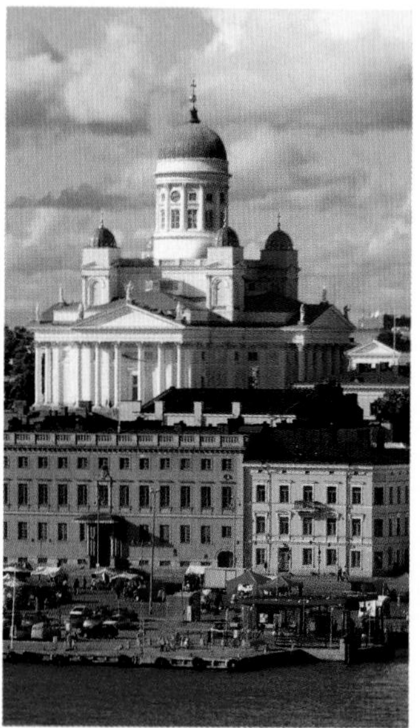

Stadium: Olympic Stadium **Competing nations:** 69 **No. of sports:** 17 **No. of events:** 149 **No. of athletes:** 4,955 **Top medal-winning nation:** USA (76) **Did you know?** Czech Emil Zátopek retained his 1948 5,000m and 10,000m titles, and also won the Olympic marathon by two-and-a-half minutes. It was the first time he had ever run the distance.

1956 Melbourne (Australia)

Winning the Games by one vote from Buenos Aires, Melbourne hosted the first Games to be held outside of the USA or Europe. Quarantine laws meant the equestrian events had to be held five months earlier, in Stockholm. The Suez Canal crisis forced out Lebanon, Iran and Egypt, while Holland, Switzerland and Spain boycotted in protest at the Soviet invasion of Hungary. The USSR and Hungary met in the now infamous water polo semi-final, which had to be abandoned after a headbutt caused a near riot. Al Oerter won the first of his four consecutive gold medals in the men's discus, swimmer Dawn Fraser took the first of her three consecutive 100m freestyle golds and László Papp became the first boxer to win three golds.

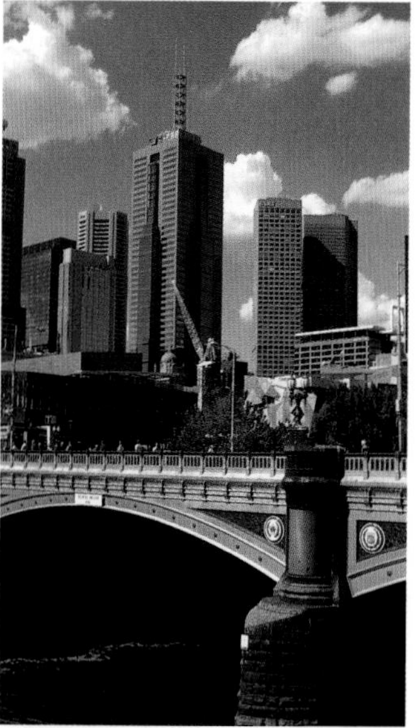

Stadium: Melbourne Cricket Ground **Competing nations:** 72 **No. of sports:** 17 **No. of events:** 145 **No. of athletes:** 3,314 **Top medal-winning nation:** USSR (98) **Did you know?** These were the latest ever 'summer' Games, held from 22 November to 8 December.

1960 Rome (Italy)

The Rome bid team finally got their Olympic wish, 54 years after the eruption of Mount Vesuvius put paid to the Italian Games of 1908. The USA's grip on coxed-eights rowing, men's 4x100m track relay, and springboard and platform diving was broken by an emerging Germany, and India, after 30 consecutive field hockey victories, were beaten 1-0 in the final by Pakistan. Rome 1960 also featured a boxer who would build on his Olympic gold to become the world's most famous sportsman, Cassius Clay. Ghana's Ike Quartey became the first black African medallist, with silver in light-welterweight boxing, and fencer Aladár Gerevich earned his sixth consecutive gold medal.

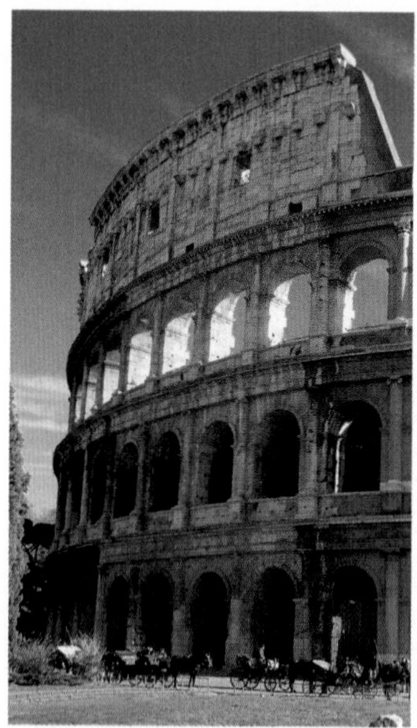

Stadium: Stadio Olimpico **Competing nations:** 83 **No. of sports:** 17 **No. of events:** 150 **No. of athletes:** 5,338 **Top medal-winning nation:** USSR (99) **Did you know?** The USA's Wilma Rudolph could not walk properly until she was nine because of childhood polio, but won 100m, 200m and 4x100m golds in Rome.

1964 Tokyo (Japan)

The first Games in Asia, the first to be telecast via satellite to America and Europe, and the first from which South Africa were banned because of apartheid. Gymnast Larysa Latynina won two medals of each colour to bring her Olympic tally to an unequalled 18 and Abebe Bikila became the first athlete to retain the marathon title, despite having his appendix out six weeks earlier. Before the Games, Dawn Fraser was in a car crash that killed her mother, but she still retained her 100m freestyle title. She was later caught stealing the Olympic Flag from the Imperial Palace and banned from swimming for 10 years, ending her Olympic career.

Stadium: Olympic Stadium **Competing nations:** 93 **No. of sports:** 19 **No. of events:** 163 **No. of athletes:** 5,151 **Top medal-winning nation:** USSR (96) **Did you know?** The USA's Billy Mills beat Tunisia's Mohamed Gammoudi in the 10,000m. Both were virtual unknowns, but each knocked 45+ seconds off their PB.

1968 Mexico City

The only Games held in Latin America nearly didn't take place when, 10 days before the opening ceremony, Mexican police opened fire on student protestors, killing 250 people and wounding 1,000. After the assassinations of Robert Kennedy and Martin Luther King, plus the Soviet invasion of Czechoslovakia, the world was in turmoil again. It wasn't just the political backdrop that affected the outcome of these Games, though: Mexico City's high altitude (30% less oxygen than at sea level) proved ruinous in the endurance events, but profitable in the sprints. Five athletes broke the triple jump world record and Bob Beamon's spectacular long jump would last for 22 years.

Stadium: Estadio Olímpico Universitario **Competing nations:** 112 **No. of sports:** 20 **No. of events:** 172 **No. of athletes:** 5,516 **Top medal-winning nation:** USA (107) **Did you know?** Vera Caslavska, a Czech gymnast, was in hiding before the Games, but emerged to win four golds, two silvers and get married, to the joy of spectators.

1972 Munich (Germany)

The biggest Olympic Games to date, with 195 events and competitors from 121 nations, was indelibly marred by the capture and subsequent execution of 11 Israeli athletes by eight Palestinian terrorists. They wanted the release of 234 Palestinians being held in Israel, but were all killed – along with their hostages – in a failed rescue attempt. A memorial service was held in front of 80,000 people in the Olympic Stadium and the Games were suspended. 34 hours later, IOC president Avery Brundage announced "the Games must go on" – and go on they eventually did. Mark Spitz won seven golds in the pool and then fled the country under instruction; his status as an American Jew making him another terrorist target.

Stadium: Olympic Stadium **Competing nations:** 121 **No. of disciplines:** 23 **No. of events:** 195 **No. of athletes:** 7,134 **Top medal-winning nation:** USSR (99) **Did you know?** Gymnast Olga Korbut became such a star at the Games she had to hire a clerk to deal with all her fan mail.

1976 Montreal (Canada)

Chosen as hosts by the IOC because Canada is not a superpower, thus limiting the potential for boycotts, Tanzania still stayed away from the Games because of New Zealand's antecedent rugby tour of South Africa. The fact South Africa were still banned from the Olympics because of apartheid and that rugby had no affiliation with the movement whatsoever didn't seem to deter the Tanzanians, and more than 20 other African nations followed suit, as did Iraq and Guyana. Fourteen-year-old gymnast Nadia Comeneci achieved the first perfect 10 score, on the parallel bars, and earned six more on her way to three golds. From nowhere, East Germany's women dominated in the pool, winning 11 of 13 events in the calendar. Suspicions that they were using prohibited drugs were later found to be true. The USA's Sugar Ray Leonard won boxing gold.

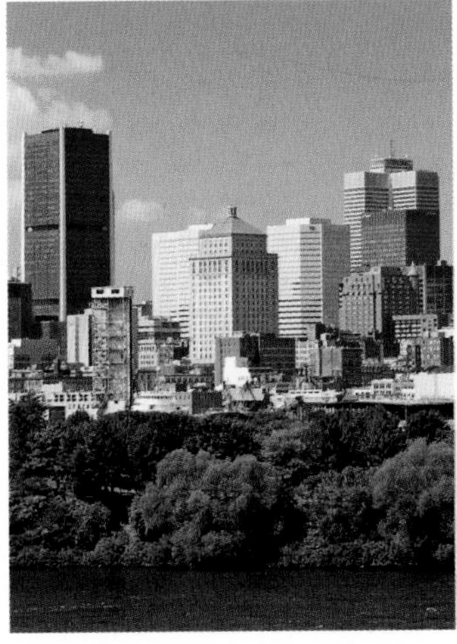

Stadium: Olympic Stadium **Competing nations:** 92 **No. of sports:** 21 **No. of events:** 198 **No. of athletes:** 6,084 **Top medal-winning nation:** USSR (125) **Did you know?** Princess Anne, in GB's equestrian team, was the only female athlete in Montreal not to have to submit to a sex test.

1980 Moscow (USSR)

Only 80 nations competed in Moscow, the lowest number since 1956. This was largely because of American president Jimmy Carter's protest against the Soviet invasion of Afghanistan. He threatened to revoke the passport of any American athlete who attended the Games and forcibly cajoled weaker nations into following his lead. In all, 65 nations turned down their invitations, 80% as a result of Carter's persuasions. Russian Aleksandr Dityatin earned a medal in every men's gymnastics event, Cuban heavyweight boxer Teófilo Stevenson became the first to win gold in the same weight division at three consecutive games and the intense rivalry between Britain's middle-distance athletes Seb Coe and Steve Ovett captured the world's attention as each won gold in the other's considered speciality.

Stadium: Grand Arena of the Central Lenin Stadium **Competing nations:** 80 **No. of sports:** 21 **No. of events:** 203 **No. of athletes:** 5,179 **Top medal-winning nation:** USSR (195) **Did you know?** The 1980 Olympic Games were the first to be staged in Eastern Europe.

1984 Los Angeles (USA) 

In retaliation for the American-led boycott four years earlier, 14 Eastern Bloc countries, including Cuba, the Soviet Union and East Germany, stayed away from the Olympics in 1984. But a record 140 nations did compete and athletes broke ranks during the opening ceremony to join in with some spontaneous dancing, reflecting the apparent goodwill. Los Angeles 1984 were the first Games not to be government-financed and a profit of $223m was made. The sponsor-led financial model for all future Olympic Games had been established. Rower Sir Steve Redgrave, the greatest endurance Olympian ever, won his first gold medal in the coxed four and track athlete Carl Lewis matched his USA compatriot Jesse Owens' feat of 1936 by winning the 100m, 200m, the long jump and the 4x100m relay.

Stadium: Los Angeles Memorial Coliseum **Competing nations:** 140 **No. of sports:** 23 **No. of events:** 221 **No. of athletes:** 6,829 **Top medal-winning nation:** USA (174) **Did you know?** O.J. Simpson was one of the Olympic Torch-bearers who crossed 33 States, from New York to LA.

1988 Seoul (South Korea) 

South Korea became democratic in order to host the Games and 76-year-old Sohn Kee-chung (winner of the 1936 marathon, which he entered under a Japanese name because South Korea was still occupied) ran the Olympic Torch into the stadium. Table tennis made its Games debut, the host nation sharing the spoils with China. Unfortunately, drugs came to the fore in Seoul: Kristin Otto, of East Germany, who took four golds, was later proved to be on a diet of prohibited drugs, and Canadian Ben Johnson's emphatic 100m victory over Carl Lewis, in a world record time of 9.79secs, was overturned after his positive drug test. On a happier note, Steffi Graf added tennis gold to her record.

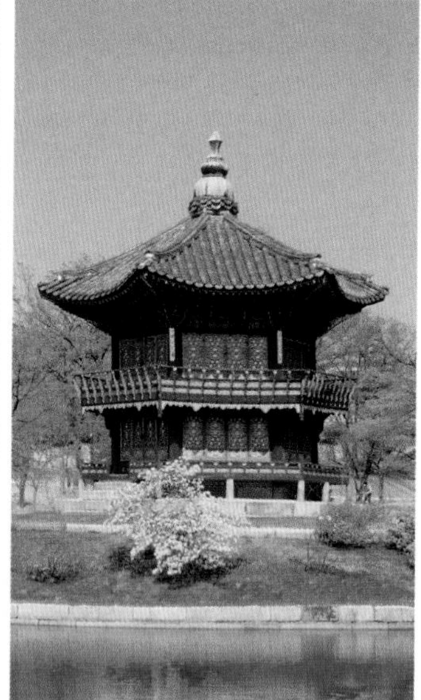

Stadium: Olympic Stadium **Competing nations:** 159 **No. of sports:** 25 **No. of events:** 237 **No. of athletes:** 8,391 **Top medal-winning nation:** USSR (132) **Did you know?** Christa Luding-Rothenburger was the first athlete to win summer (track cycling, Seoul) and winter (speed skating, Calgary) Olympic medals in the same year.

1992 Barcelona (Spain) 

Global political change had a huge effect on the 1992 Olympic Games. South Africa repealed apartheid and were allowed back in; the Berlin Wall fell and East and West Germany were reunited; and the Soviet Union broke into 15 separate countries after the collapse of communism. For the first time in 20 years, all nations were represented, though controversy remained around Yugoslavia because of its recent military aggression. Men's basketball was opened up to professionals, resulting in the USA 'Dream Team' including Magic Johnson, Michael Jordan and Charles Barkley. Gail Devers won the women's 100m gold, two years after nearly having her feet amputated because of radiation treatment for Graves' disease.

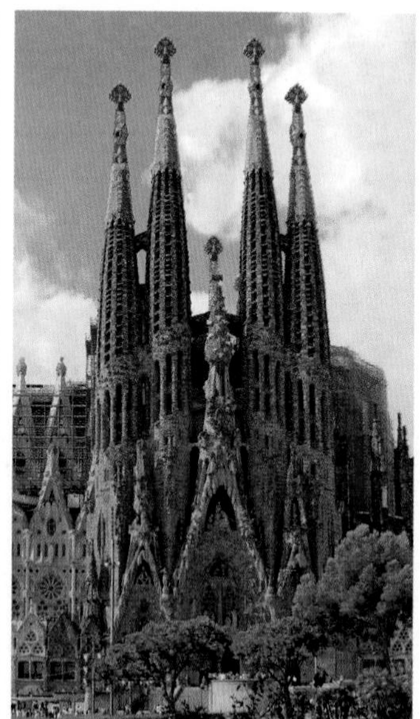

Stadium: Estadi Olímpic Lluís Companys **Competing nations:** 169 **No. of sports:** 28 **No. of events:** 257 **No. of athletes:** 9,356 **Top medal-winning nation:** Unified (112) **Did you know?** At 32, Linford Christie became the oldest 100m champion by four years.

1996 Atlanta (USA) 

Unofficially known as the Centennial Olympics, the 1996 Games helped turn Atlanta into the cosmopolitan city it is today. Muhammad Ali lit the Olympic Flame and beach volleyball, mountain biking, lightweight rowing, women's football and softball made their bow. Marie-José Perec and Michael Johnson did the double in the women's and men's 200m and 400m, and Carl Lewis's long jump gold made him only the third person in Olympic history to win the same event four times. Nigeria beat Argentina in a great football final and Birgit Schmidt won her fifth kayaking gold, 16 years after her first Olympic victory. A record 79 nations won medals and 53 nations won gold.

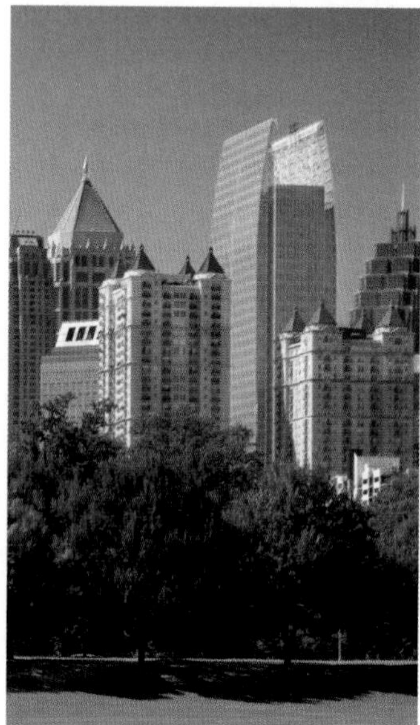

Stadium: Centennial Olympic Stadium **Competing nations:** 197 **No. of disciplines:** 26 **No. of events:** 271 **No. of athletes:** 10,318 **Top medal-winning nation:** USA (101) **Did you know?** On 27 July 1996, a bomb exploded in the Centennial Olympic Park killing one person. Why? It has never been solved.

2000 Sydney (Australia) 

These were the largest Olympics yet, with 300 events scheduled. Birgit Fischer, of Germany, triumphed in the canoeing to become the first athlete to win gold medals 20 years apart and British rower Steve Redgrave became the first to win gold at five consecutive Olympics. Haile Gebrselassie pipped Paul Tergat in a thrilling 10,000m race and 17-year-old Ian Thorpe smashed Olympic record after world record in the pool. Michael Johnson defended his 400m title, but the heroine of the games was Marion Jones, who became the first woman to win five track & field medals at one Games. Sadly, she was later at the centre of a drugs scandal which saw her stripped of her medals.

Stadium: Stadium Australia **Competing nations:** 200 **No. of sports:** 28 **No. of events:** 300 **No. of athletes:** 10,651 **Top medal-winning nation:** USA (97) **Did you know?** Aboriginal Australian Kathy Freeman lit the Olympic Flame and won gold in the women's 400m.

2004 Athens (Greece) 

The Olympic Flame travelled through every continent on its way to the birthplace of the Olympics. Despite fears the Greek government would not complete organisational and building work on time, the Games were a huge success and a fitting tribute to an Olympic-mad nation. Kelly Holmes brought gold to Britain with an historic double in the women's 800m and 1,500m, but emphatic favourite Paula Radcliffe had to pull out of the women's marathon with less than five miles to go. Birgit Fischer won again to become the first person in any sport to claim gold at six different Olympics, while Hichem EL Guerrouj, of Morocco, became the first runner since Paavo Nurmi to win the 1,500m and 5,000m at the same Games.

Stadium: Olympic Stadium **Competing nations:** 202 **No. of sports:** 28 **No. of events:** 301 **No. of athletes:** 11,099 **Top medal-winning nation:** USA (103) **Did you know?** Argentina put an end to the USA's dominance of men's basketball by beating them 89-81, then overcoming Italy in the final for gold. They also won the football.

2008 Beijing (China) 

Becoming the 18th nation to hold a summer Olympic Games, the Chinese played host to 43 world records and 132 Olympic records - and an incredible 86 different countries secured medals. The largest television audience for any Olympics saw Usain Bolt unequivocally claim the title of 'World's Fastest Man', smashing the 100m and 200m world records by previously unthinkable margins. Swimmer Michael Phelps also broke the record for most gold medals won at one Games, winning an astonishing eight pool events. It is estimated that as much as $40bn was spent on Beijing 2008, which would make it the most expensive Olympic Games by a huge margin. It is generally regarded as a ground-breaking Games, though, and one that truly put Beijing - and China - on the sporting and political maps.

Stadium: Beijing National Stadium **Competing nations:** 204 **No. of sports:** 28 **No. of events:** 302 **No. of athletes:** 11,028 **Top medal-winning nation:** USA
Did you know? The magnificent centrepiece of the 2008 summer Olympics was the Beijing National Stadium, which was nicknamed 'The Bird's Nest' because of its skeletal, nest-like structure.

2009 GOYANG
2009
TOYOTA
DIBABA
Daegu
JAPAN
TOYOTA
NIIYA
Daegu 2011
MENS
GBROWINGTEAM

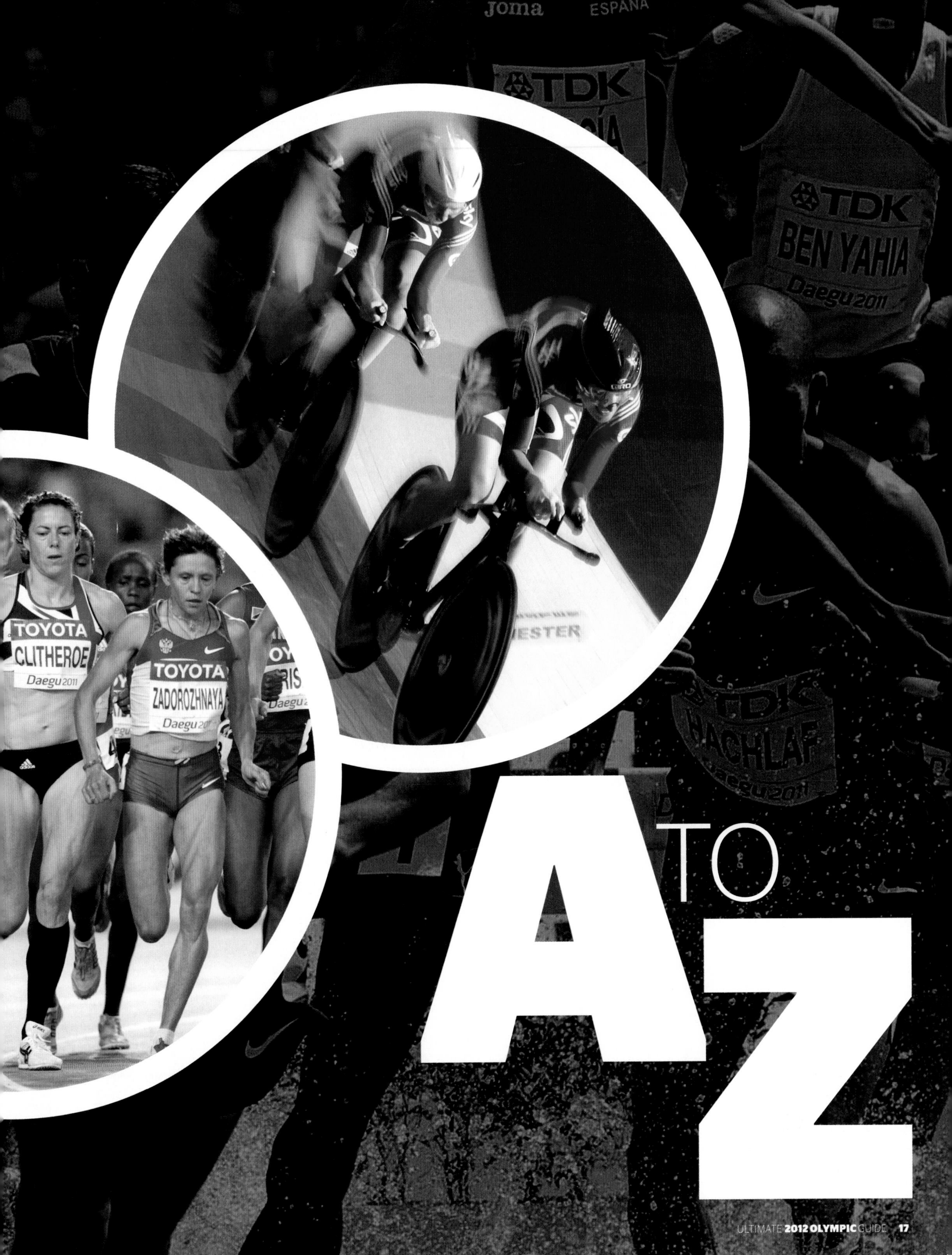
Joma
ESPAÑA
TDK
BEN YAHIA
Daegu2011
TOYOTA
CLITHEROE
Daegu2011
TOYOTA
ZADOROZHNAYA
Daegu2011
TDK
CHLAF
A
TO
Z

ARCHERY

The earliest evidence of archery can be traced back around 10,000 years, when human beings used the skill for hunting and survival. But it was first recognised as a sport in medieval England, where Archery was considered so important to the nation's defence that males aged between seven and 60 years were required by law to take part in competitions.

However, Archery has had a bit of a rocky time of it at the Olympics, first appearing in Paris in 1900, but then being dropped from the 1920 programme because of too many rules and equipment variants between competing nations.

The sport found itself out of favour with the International Olympic Committee for 52 years until it was re-introduced to the Games in Munich, in 1972, by which time international standardised laws for Archery had been agreed.

Since then, it has remained a highly competitive and popular discipline at the Games, with two stand-out nations.

South Korea have been the most successful since 1972, winning 16 golds and 30 medals in total. Their closest rivals are the USA, with eight golds and 13 medals overall. The rest of the world trail way behind these bowing behemoths, with no other country winning more than one gold medal.

If you're a betting man or woman, we suggest putting your money on the Korean women's team in 2012. They currently have the world's three top-ranking women on their team.

Archery is an easy event to get your head around: the men's and women's individual and team competitions have a knock-out format from the first arrow until the last.

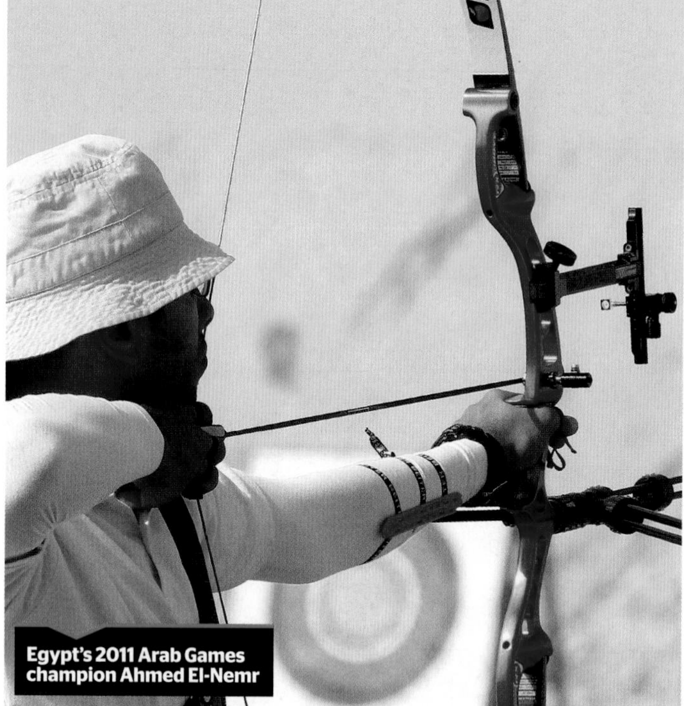

Egypt's 2011 Arab Games champion Ahmed El-Nemr

In the team event, there are three archers per team and countries compete against each other in a best-of-24-arrows match.

The target - which has a diameter of 1.22m and a gold, centre ring measuring 12.2cm across - is set at a distance of 70m for all archers, male and female. A maximum 10 points are awarded for hitting the centre ring, with one less point awarded for each ring outside of it.

Matches at London 2012 will be the best of five sets, with each set consisting of three arrows per archer. Competitors have 40 seconds in which to release each arrow.

It is a fitting tribute to the ancient activity that the 2012 competition is being held at one of London's oldest sporting grounds - Lord's Cricket Club (est. 1816).

Hitting the bull's-eye is worth 10 points

DID YOU KNOW?

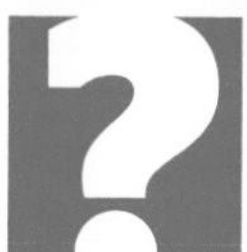

If an arrow hits the line between two scoring circles, the higher score is awarded ■ Each arrow shot travels at roughly 150mph ■ An archer's initials must be engraved on each of their arrows ■ The first organised Archery competition took place in London in 1583 - 3,000 people attended ■ Archer Neroli Fairhall of New Zealand made history in 1984 by being the first athlete in a wheelchair to compete at a 'regular' Olympics ■ To split the arrow of a competitor with your own arrow is known as a 'Robin Hood'

Archers take aim in a London 2012 test event at Lord's cricket ground

OVERALL MEDAL TABLE
TOP THREE NATIONS

1. SOUTH KOREA

GOLD	SILVER	BRONZE
16	9	5

2. UNITED STATES

GOLD	SILVER	BRONZE
14	9	8

3. BELGIUM

GOLD	SILVER	BRONZE
11	6	3

Factbox

Where: Lord's Cricket Ground
When: Friday 27 July - Friday 3 August
Medal events: 4
Athletes: 128 (64 men, 64 women)

REASONS TO WATCH

1) BALANCE AND SKILL

This isn't like throwing discarded paper in the wastebin at work. Archers are aiming at a 1.22m target from a distance of 70m - and the centre ring is just 12.2cm in diameter, so finding that takes a tremendous amount of skill! Hitting the bull's-eye three times is gold-winning mentality.

2) EXEMPLARY NERVE

In no other sport does a competitor's nerve have such an effect on their medal chances. The slightest twitch can cost an archer valuable points.

3) RACE AGAINST TIME

Each archer's shot-clock ensures the sport is played at a high tempo, with the last arrow often winning or losing a match. Who can remain the most calm under the most pressure?

ATHLETICS – TRACK

The most famous and popular of all Olympic events, Track Athletics always comes with an immense amount of excitement, expectation and pressure, as millions of eyes turn to see what will happen in the new Olympic Stadium.

It is a Blue Riband competition and athletes from around the world will be expected to perform over and above their very best – jumping longer and higher, running faster and throwing farther, busting every sinew of their being to achieve the ultimate sporting prize: Olympic gold.

Of course, winning isn't everything and the gathering of people from a range of cultures inside the Games' centrepiece arena will generate an atmosphere unlike any other – of unity and congregation, as well as rivalry.

As the Modern Olympics founder, Pierre De Coubertin, said: "The most important thing in the Olympic Games is not winning, but taking part; the essential thing in life is not conquering, but fighting well."

With 2,000 athletes taking part in 24 events – 12 for men and 12 for women – ranging in distance from 100m to 10,000m, some including hurdles, there will be plenty of opportunity for athletes to "fight well" in the hope of standing atop the winner's podium.

The programme is completed by the marathon and race-walking events, which will bring Olympic excitement onto the streets of central London.

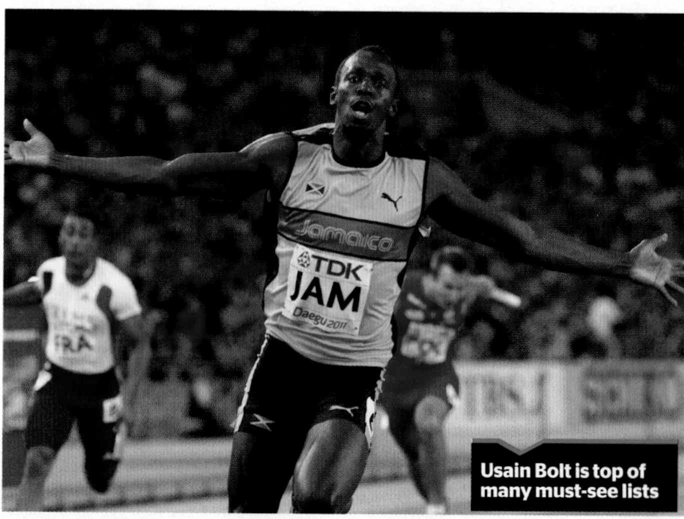

Usain Bolt is top of many must-see lists

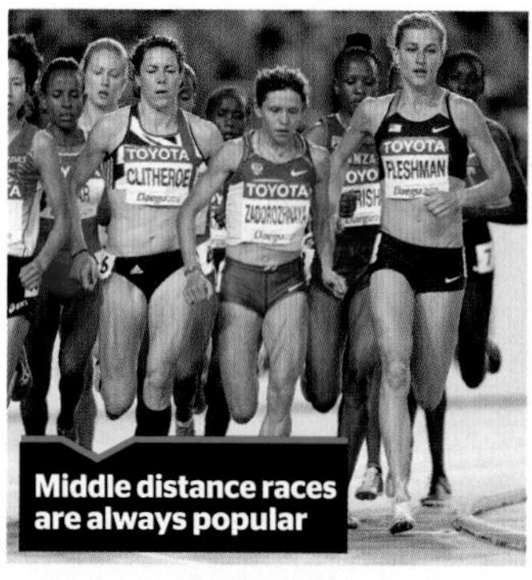

Middle distance races are always popular

Records could fall in the Olympic Stadium

Host nation Britain expect to do well

One chance to shine after years of slog

Steeplechase is a real test of endurance

Jamaica win medals to match their kit

DID YOU KNOW?

Women were banned from running races of more than 200m at the Olympic Games between 1928 and 1960 ■ Frenchman Joseph Guillemot's heart was on the right side of his chest and he smoked a pack of cigarettes a day – but he still won the 5,000m in Antwerp in 1920. Before the final, his coach gave him a mysterious concoction to drink, claiming it would make him unbeatable. It was water, sugar and rum ■ In the first Olympic relay (the men's 4x400m) in 1908, runners touched hands instead of passing a baton

Athletes have many obstacles to clear on their way to gold

Factbox

Venue: Olympic Stadium – Olympic Park (track, field and combined events); The Mall (road events)
When: Friday 3 August – Sunday 12 August
Medal events: 47
Athletes: 2,000

REASONS TO WATCH

1) ANCIENT LINEAGE
Track athletes at the Olympic Games are the latest incarnation of a racing tradition that can be traced as far back as 776BC.

2) VARIETY PACK
What other sport can offer spectators the blistering power, feats of endurance and tactical intrigue that come from races that last for less than 10 seconds or for more than two hours? There's never a dull moment!

3) HISTORY BEING MADE
You'll want to tell your grandchildren you saw the fastest man on earth/a double-gold medal victory/the upset of the Games… some of the best London 2012 stories will happen on the track.

The sprint relays always throw up a fair amount of drama

The Ultimate Olympic A-Z

ATHLETICS – FIELD

When the eyes of the world are not focused on the track in 2012, there will be plenty going on in the Field disciplines to divert their gaze.

Some of the most famous names in Olympic history have been Field athletes: Jesse Owens, Bob Beamon, Dick Fosbury, Carl Lewis – the list goes on, and there'll be plenty more action and drama in the Field of London's Olympic Stadium.

"Every British athlete has got to be wildly excited. It's a once-in-a-lifetime opportunity," says Great Britain's world champion triple jumper Phillips Idowu (interviewed on p102). "Being born and bred in east London, I can't think of a more inspiring Olympic scenario to be competing at. For me, it's quite simply the biggest sporting event in the world."

The 16 Field events for men and women at the summer Games fall into two categories – throwing (shot put, javelin, discus and hammer) and jumping (pole vault, high jump, long jump and triple jump).

While the training and preparation for these events is gruelling and complicated, the events are not. Simply jump higher, jump farther or throw farther than your opponent and you win.

An Olympic Field athlete will have spent years of torturous hard work in the gym and at the training track, and it will all boil down to a couple of moments in the Olympic Stadium.

"It was all-consuming. Every part of every day of my life was focussed on being the best at triple jump," said Britain's Jonathan Edwards (in a recent interview), who won gold in Sydney in 2000 and who was the first athlete to legally jump more than 18m.

"When I finished my session, everything I would do before starting my next session would be focussed towards just that. So it was the waiting and the dieting, and getting to bed early every night that was probably the hardest part of the challenge."

All the events have a qualification stage, with the leading athletes moving into the final to compete for the medals. It's at this stage that the imposing new Olympic Stadium will be filled with the kind of atmosphere only Field athletics can truly muster.

Holding 80,000 spectators, it's going to be loud and imposing, and provide the perfect stage for the world's brightest sporting stars.

"I think it's a triumph of construction, I really do," said Edwards. "It will be equally as impressive as anything we achieve on or off the track in 2012. It's a whole new part of London and the way they have delivered it within such a tight time-frame is fantastic."

Ultra-talented athletes and a magnificent new stadium, packed to the rafters with noise and celebration – there's myriad reasons to be looking forward to the Field athletics in 2012.

DID YOU KNOW?

Field events that have been dropped from the Olympic programme for various reasons include standing long jump, standing triple jump, standing high jump, 56lb weight throw, two-handed shot put, Greek discus, two-handed discus throw, freestyle javelin and the two-handed javelin throw. ■ Guinn Smith, of the USA, was the last pole vaulter to win Olympic gold using a bamboo pole. Bamboo was replaced by aluminium in the early 1950s, which in turn was replaced by fibre-glass in the late 1950s

Field athletes will either be flying through the air...

...or making an object fly through the air at London 2012

OVERALL MEDAL TABLE
TOP THREE NATIONS

1. USA

GOLD	SILVER	BRONZE
311	238	189

2. SOVIET UNION

GOLD	SILVER	BRONZE
64	55	74

3. GREAT BRITAIN

GOLD	SILVER	BRONZE
49	78	61

Factbox

Venue: Olympic Stadium - Olympic Park (track, field and combined events)
When: Friday 3 August - Sunday 12 August
Medal events: 47
Athletes: 2,000

REASONS TO WATCH

1) AUDIENCE INVOLVEMENT

A lot of Field athletes stir up the crowd before making their effort, bringing a real sense of involvement for the fans. When 80,000 people clap in unison, the atmosphere is pretty special.

2) LOCAL LAD

Hackney-born triple-jumper Phillips Idowu will be competing for gold in his backyard. All of the home fans will enjoy massive support, but for local-boy Idowu the occasion will be extra-special.

3) TRADITIONAL SPORTS

Field events hark back to the Games of Ancient Greece and perfectly echo the Olympic Motto 'Citius, Altius, Fortius', which translates as Swifter, Higher, Stronger.

The Ultimate Olympic A-Z

BADMINTON

Badminton was first played at the Olympic Games in 1972, in Munich, where it was one of two 'demonstration sports' (along with waterskiing). It took another 20 years for the International Olympic Committee (IOC) to realise they actually quite liked the sport and to make it an official fixture of the Barcelona Games, in 1992. They haven't looked back since.

Badminton is a British military adaption of the game Battledore and Shuttlecock, which was first played around 2,000 years ago in Ancient Greece. The aim of the game was for two players to use their battledore (racket) to keep the shuttlecock off the ground for as many hits as possible.

During the 19th century, British military officers based in India introduced a net and an alternative scoring system to the game – transforming it from Battledore and Shuttlecock into the sport of Badminton we know today.

When officers returned home from India, the game was introduced to the upper classes and rapidly developed, with the first official laws of the game being drawn up in 1873 at the Duke of Beaufort's Gloucestershire residence, Badminton House. The sport became known as the Game of Badminton.

There will be five Badminton competitions in 2012: men's singles and doubles; women's singles and doubles; and mixed doubles. All of the 15 medals on offer at the 2008 Beijing Games were shared between only four nations – China (eight), Indonesia (three), South Korea (three) and Malaysia (one).

World number 1, Malaysia's Lee Chong Wei, lines up a smash

China's Gao Ling is Badminton's all-time leader in terms of winning the most Olympic medals. In 2000 and 2004, she won two gold medals (in mixed doubles), one silver and one bronze (both in women's doubles).

One to watch at the 2012 Games, however, is her fiery countryman Lin Dan, who – on his way to winning the men's singles gold medal in Beijing, in 2008 – ruffled feathers by squaring up to one of his opponent's coaches after a line call upset him.

Lin's got previous, too, because, earlier in the Games, it was reported he punched his own coach during a training session.

However, Lin loves bringing out his A-game on the big occasions and he did so again in 2011, when he won Badminton's first one-million dollar tournament, the Korea Open.

Badminton equipment has come a long way since the days of Battledore and Shuttlecock, when the battledore was little more than a wooden paddle and the shuttlecock a complex weave of animal guts attached to several pieces of parchment, which, in turn, were attached to a small, lightweight base of cork.

The rackets have also dramatically transformed, from their heavy wooden origins to today's professional carbon fibre ones that only weigh between 70 and 95 grams.

The elite players choose carbon fibre rackets because they offer an impressive strength-to-weight ratio, as well as having superb kinetic energy transfer – which can make a huge difference in the modern game.

DID YOU KNOW?

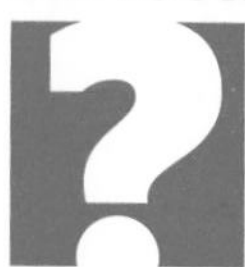

The fastest recorded shot in Badminton was by China's Fu Haifeng, for his whopping 206mph smash in the 2005 Sudirman Cup ■ China are the most successful Olympic Badminton nation with a total of 30 medals since the sport debuted in 1992 ■ Legend has it that the best shuttlecocks are made from 16 feathers plucked only from the left wing of a goose ■ More than 1.1 billion people watched the first official Olympic Badminton competition – in Barcelona in 1992 – on television

Men's doubles is one of five Badminton events at the Games

OVERALL MEDAL TABLE
TOP THREE NATIONS

1. CHINA

GOLD	SILVER	BRONZE
11	6	13

2. SOUTH KOREA

GOLD	SILVER	BRONZE
6	7	4

3. INDONESIA

GOLD	SILVER	BRONZE
6	6	6

Factbox

Where: Wembley Arena
When: Saturday 28 July – Sunday 5 August
Medal Events: 5
Athletes: 172

REASONS TO WATCH

1) FIERCE RIVALRY
Malaysia's Lee Chong Wei is world number one, but has yet to win a World Championship or Olympic gold medal – unlike China's world number two Lin Dan, who has won both and who defeated Lee in a very one-sided men's singles final in Beijing in 2008.

2) GREAT ATMOSPHERE
Etiquette dictates that, during a Badminton rally, the crowd should be silent, to allow the players to concentrate. Invariably, though, spectators get far too excited for etiquette and the 'oohs' and 'ahhs' are amplified by the indoor arena and reach a crescendo when an important point is won.

3) CONTROVERSIAL CALLS
The frantic pace of the sport means line judges are susceptible to getting a call wrong now and then. Player protests aren't quite in the John McEnroe league, but when melodramatic body language begins, and the crowd turn up the volume, the spectacle almost tops the badminton.

BASKETBALL

Basketball is one of the few Olympic sports the origins of which can be traced back to one man – and with an accurate date. In December 1891, James Naismith, a physical education teacher at the YMCA School, Springfield, Massachusetts, came up with the rules for basketball as a vigorous sport to keep his students occupied and fit during the New England winters.

Naismith gave his students an association football to play with and nailed pear baskets (that had to be emptied after each point) to the wall. The sport stayed like that for years.

The fast-paced dribbling that we are all familiar with today only became part of the game as recently as the 1950s. It owes its place in the game to the advance of modern technology and the creation of a perfectly cylindrical ball, with no laces (such as association footballs had at the time) to hinder the bounce and, therefore, the control of the ball.

Basketball was introduced as an Olympic event for men in 1936 and, since its inclusion, the USA have been the team to beat.

But they have not enjoyed a flawless record; the Soviet Union have twice denied them gold (in 1972 and 1988), while Yugoslavia have also helped themselves to the Olympic title, at the 1980 Games. In Athens in 2004, the USA were trumped by Argentina (gold) and Italy (silver).

Women have played Basketball at the Games since 1976, when the Soviet Union won gold from the USA. They took gold again in 1980, but the USA have won every Games since then, bar Barcelona 1992, when they finished third behind a Unified team of former Soviet republics and China.

When the sport's governing body FIBA approved a rule that NBA players could represent their nations at the Olympics, the USA fielded a men's 'Dream Team' at the 1992 Barcelona Games. The squad of 12 players included 10 who would be named in the 1996 '50 Greatest Players in NBA History'. The team possessed such legends of the sport as Michael Jordan and Magic Johnson.

Basketball at the 2012 Games will be played at the purpose-built, 12,000-capacity Basketball Arena in London's Olympic Park and North Greenwich's O2 Arena.

The men's and women's events will each feature 12 nations and the USA again looks likely to field a star-studded men's team for the London Games, with the likes of LeBron James, Kobe Bryant and Dwyane Wade all confirmed and eager to retain their country's gold medal.

300 basketballs will be used during the competition

DID YOU KNOW?

There are 3,395 dimples on a Spalding basketball ■ The USA 'Dream Team' of 1992 won the gold medal without calling a time-out during the whole tournament ■ In the original rules of Basketball, there was no such thing as a three-pointer. All baskets scored one point, no matter from where the shot was taken ■ The backboard was invented to stop fans in old viewing galleries from interfering with the ball on its way to the basket ■ The current tallest professional basketball player is China's Yao Ming at 7ft 6in tall

LeBron James is just one of the star names in the USA squad

OVERALL MEDAL TABLE
TOP THREE NATIONS

1. USA

GOLD	SILVER	BRONZE
19	2	3

2. SOVIET UNION

GOLD	SILVER	BRONZE
4	4	4

3. YUGOSLAVIA

GOLD	SILVER	BRONZE
1	5	2

Factbox

Where: Wembley Arena
When: Saturday 28 July – Sunday 12 August
Medal Events: 2
Athletes: 288

REASONS TO WATCH

1) WORLD-CLASS TALENT
Basketball in 2012 will feature some of the most talented and skilful athletes in the world, and the Olympic Games in London is the only place in the world you'll see the likes of Kobe Bryant, LeBron James and Dwight Howard compete on the same team!

2) RAISED INTENSITY
An already fast-paced sport will pick up more speed at the Olympics as the match time has been cut from 12-minute quarters to 10-minute quarters. The raised intensity level will add an extra dimension for the viewer.

3) MIGHTY SCALPS
Every country in the world will raise their game tenfold against the United States, so don't expect this to be a cakewalk. In fact, there may well be a nasty surprise in store for the USA's superstars in 2012...

The Ultimate Olympic A-Z

BEACH VOLLEYBALL

At London 2012, the Beach Volleyball will be played on 3,000 tonnes of sand deposited on the Prime Minister's doorstep at Horse Guards Parade, with 48 male and 48 female competitors battling for the gold medals.

Twenty-four teams will take part in the men's and women's events, with the preliminary stages incorporating four groups of six, who all play each other once. From this phase, 16 teams then go on to a knock-out competition.

The court is the same size, 16m x 8m, as for indoor volleyball, but is covered in sand – and teams comprise two players, as opposed to six. Contestants wear less and the winners are decided by a best-of-three set contest. The first team to 21 points wins a set but, if a deciding set is needed, this can be won with 15 points. However, a set must be won by a two-point margin.

Teams switch court after every seven points during sets one and two, and every five points during set three. When the total number of points is 21 (adding the scores of both teams), there is a technical time-out.

Part of the game involves looking at your partner's bottom. Not in a crude way, of course, but to understand what kind of play to pursue for the next point. Block signals were created by player Randy Stoklos in the early 80s and are now widely used in the game. They are displayed using a different number and combination of fingers, held behind the bottom so the opposing team cannot see them.

On the subject of bottoms, Britain's Denise Johns claims the regulation women's uniform – a two-piece bikini – is intended to be "sexy" and to draw attention, rather than be of benefit to the athlete, and her argument has drawn some support and attention.

Slogging away on sand is exhausting

Such rules, while not entirely detrimental to the sport's audience figures, suggest a reluctance to shake off Beach Volleyball's history on the sun-drenched Californian beaches of Santa Monica. But these athletes are no beach bums, they are some of the most dedicated in sport and toiling on sand for three gruelling sets can be exhausting, especially when you consider no substitutions are allowed.

Naturally, countries with abundant sandy beaches appear to be the most successful, with Brazil expected to be among the medals in the men's and women's events.

No matter which nation prevails in 2012, fans will be hoping the sun stays out between Saturday 28 July and Thursday 9 August.

Brazil are hot tips to win medals in 2012

DID YOU KNOW?

No substitutions or replacements are allowed during Olympic Beach Volleyball matches. Once you start, you cannot stop ■ In Southern California, where the sport began, naturists/nudists still play on Black's Beach. Whether this is an agreeable sight is, we guess, a matter for the spectators involved ■ Beach Volleyball made its Olympic debut at Atlanta in 1996. It has become one of the most popular spectator sports at the Games

The USA is the most successful Olympic beach volleyball nation, having won 5 gold in total

OVERALL MEDAL TABLE
TOP THREE NATIONS

1. USA

GOLD	SILVER	BRONZE
5	1	1

2. BRAZIL

GOLD	SILVER	BRONZE
2	5	2

3. AUSTRALIA

GOLD	SILVER	BRONZE
1	0	1

Factbox

Where: Horse Guards Parade
When: Saturday 28 July – Thursday 9 August
Medal events: 2
Athletes: 96 (48 men, 48 women; 24 teams in each event)

REASONS TO WATCH

1) OUTDOOR EVENT
Grab some rays while you watch the action in Horse Guards Parade.

2) BOTTOM SIGNALS
Learn more about block signals by staring at some of the finest derrières at the Games!

3) TOIL AND ELEGANCE
It's hard enough manoeuvring in sand without having to keep a ball in the air, right? These athletes do it with enviable elegance, which has to be applauded.

The Ultimate Olympic A-Z

BOXING

The squared circle will be the scene of much interest in London 2012, not only because of the wealth of talent in the men's contest, but also because, for the first time, women will be allowed to take part in an Olympic Boxing event.

Thirty-six women will vie for gold in three categories: flyweight (48-51kg), lightweight (57-60kg) and middleweight (69-75kg), boxing for four two-minute rounds.

Men will fight across 10 divisions: light flyweight (46-49kg), flyweight (up to 52kg), bantamweight (up to 56kg), lightweight (up to 60kg), light welterweight (up to 64kg), welterweight (up to 69kg), middleweight (up to 75kg), light heavyweight (up to 81kg), heavyweight (up to 91kg) and super heavyweight (+91kg), for three three-minute rounds.

Fighters score points for every head and upper-body punch landed. Judges have a console in front of them and, whenever they deem a boxer to have connected with a scoring punch, they hit a button. If three of the five judges push their button within one second, the fighter is awarded the point and it is displayed in the arena and on TV screens. When boxers trade blows in a flurry of fighting, where no full-force punches land, the judges wait until the end of the exchange and award a point to the boxer who got the better of it.

If, at the end of a bout, the boxers have the same number of points, the judges decide a winner by assessing such factors as which of the two took the lead and showed better style and better defence. The fighter who has the most points at the end of the allocated number of rounds wins.

All Boxing events at London 2012 will be unseeded and contested in knock-out format. The winners of the two semi-finals in each weight category will fight for the gold medal, while the losers of the semi-finals will each be awarded a bronze.

Three eight counts in a round is game over

Fighters wear mandatory protective headgear and a boxer who has been knocked down may not resume fighting until the count of eight. Three eight counts in one round, or four in a fight, results in defeat for that boxer. A single 10 count ends the fight and the referee can stop a bout if he feels one fighter is taking excessive punishment.

Some of the most famous boxers started at the Games, including Joe Frazier, George Foreman, Lennox Lewis, Wladimir Klitschko, Oscar de la Hoya and Muhammad Ali. It is the only Olympic sport that will not allow professionals to take part.

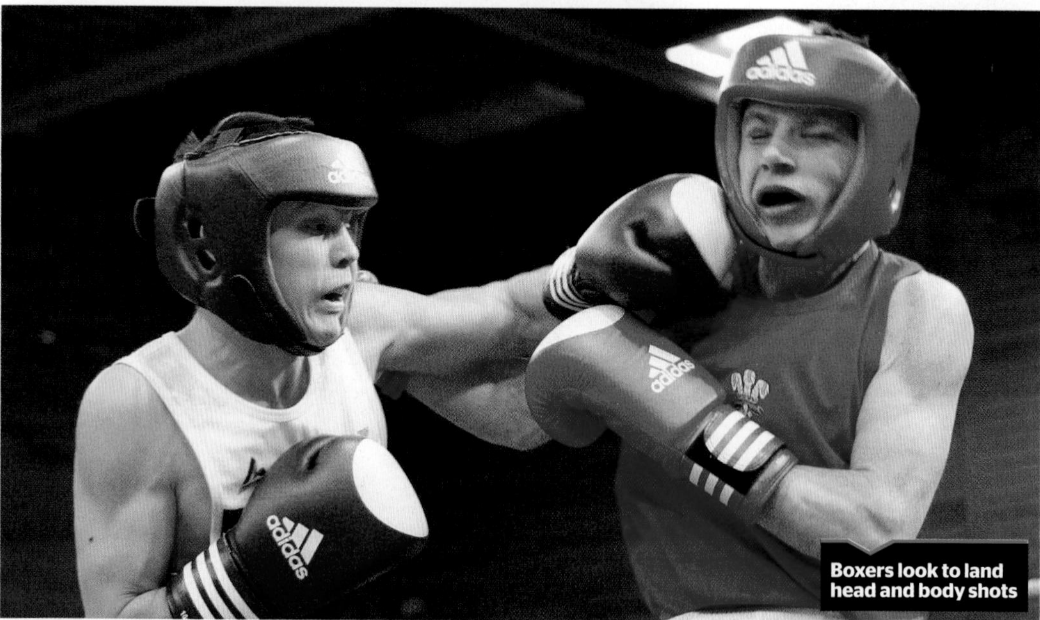

Boxers look to land head and body shots

DID YOU KNOW?

Until 1936, weights were measured in pounds, but from 1948 onwards, they were measured in kilograms ■ After some controversial judging decisions at the 1988 Olympic Games in Seoul, the International Amateur Boxing Association brought in new regulations, including daily alcohol tests for referees and judges ■ Boxing featured at the original Olympics in the 7th century BC, when opponents fought with strips of leather wrapped around their fists

OVERALL MEDAL TABLE
TOP THREE NATIONS

1. USA

GOLD	SILVER	BRONZE
48	23	38

2. CUBA

GOLD	SILVER	BRONZE
32	19	12

3. ITALY

GOLD	SILVER	BRONZE
15	13	16

Factbox

Venue: ExCeL
Dates: Saturday 28 July – Sunday 12 August
Medal events: 13
Athletes: 286 (250 men, 36 women)

REASONS TO WATCH

1) ULTIMATE CONTEST
There's nothing quite like Boxing to test the character of its combatants and whet the appetite of the crowd. Desire, power, strength and courage will all be on show in the ExCeL arena.

2) UNSEEDED DRAW
All competitors are amateur and no one is seeded, meaning you can get some big match-ups way before the medals are being contested, guaranteeing excitement from the very start.

3) HISTORY OF CHAMPIONS
Patriotic Cubans aside, most fighters use the Games as a springboard to going professional. We might see the new Muhammad Ali at London 2012, so keep your eyes peeled!

Women will compete in Boxing for the first time at London 2012

The Ultimate Olympic A-Z

CANOE – SLALOM

First demonstrated at the Paris Games, in 1924, Canoeing and Kayaking became an official part of the Olympics in 1936, at the Berlin Games. However, the slalom event didn't make its debut until the next time Germany hosted the Games, in Munich in 1972, and didn't become a regular feature of the Olympics until the Barcelona Games in 1992, when its all-action, dramatic nature won the sport an army of fans.

At the 2012 Games, there will be three disciplines on show: men's and women's single kayaks (K-1); men's single canoe (C-1); and men's doubles canoe (C-2). The difference between a kayak and a canoe is based on traditional Inuit styles of canoeing – where paddlers use a double-ended paddle, that is referred to as 'Kayaking', while a single-ended paddle is used in 'Canoeing'.

To complete the slalom course, paddlers must pass – in order – through a series of numbered gates, going through green gates downstream and red gates upstream.

The Olympic format of the sport is slightly different to the smaller slalom competitions, where competitors only use their best run from two attempts for qualification.

In the Olympic slalom, paddlers have to complete two runs of the same course and their times are added together for qualification. Once both runs have been completed, the fastest paddlers are entered into the semi-finals, which take place on a different course, and previous times have no bearing.

Competitors have only one attempt at the semi-final run and the 10 with the best times make it through to the final, where they have to tackle the semi-final course again.

Double gold winner, Stepanka Hilgertova

The winner is the competitor with the best combined time from the semi-final and final.

The sport owes a lot of its drama to the strict penalty system that is in place; the slightest mistake can incur a heavy penalty that can ruin a paddler's medal chance.

Two-second penalties are given if any part of the boat, competitor's body or paddle, touches the gate – and there are 50-second penalties if a gate is missed completely, a gate is missed at a 45-degree angle, a paddler goes through a gate upside-down or a gate is passed in the wrong order.

The evolution of equipment in this sport has been incredible. In the 1960s and 70s, the boats paddlers used were roughly three times as heavy as they are today.

As technology has developed, boatmakers began using a mix of Kevlar, carbon fibre and fibreglass cloth to make the boats as light, but as rigid as possible.

The result was that wealthy nations with the resources to make or buy light boats developed a significant advantage over other competing nations. The sport's governing body therefore introduced minimum weight and size specifications to help to equalise competition.

At the 2012 Games, these are: K-1 boats – length 3.50m, width 0.60m and weight 9kg; C-1 boats – length 3.50m, width 0.65m and weight 10kg; C-2 boats – length 4.10m, width 0.75m and weight 15kg.

DID YOU KNOW?

The Lee Valley White Water Centre was built for the 2012 Olympic Games and cost £31m to construct ■ A 250-year-old Native American birch-bark canoe was recently found in a barn near Penryn, Cornwall. It was brought to the county by Lt John Enys after fighting in the American War of Independence in 1776 ■ 200 gate poles need to be painted red and green for the 2012 Canoe-Slalom course ■ In the early days of competition, Canoe-Slalom events were held on flat water, but later switched to white-water rapids

There are penalties if a competitor touches the slalom gates

GB's Campbell Walsh won silver in the K-1 event in Athens

Factbox

Where: Lee Valley Water Centre
When: Sunday 29 July - Thursday 2 August
Medal Events: 4
Athletes: 82

REASONS TO WATCH

1) HIGH INTENSITY

Each trial lasts between 80 and 120 seconds, and the paddlers have to give it 100% from start to finish.

2) HIGH DRAMA

At any time, the slightest of mistakes can ruin any chance a competitor has of winning a medal.

3) HIGH SPEED

Medals will be won and lost because of what can happen within a fraction of a second.

Men's double canoe (C-2), one of three disciplines in 2012

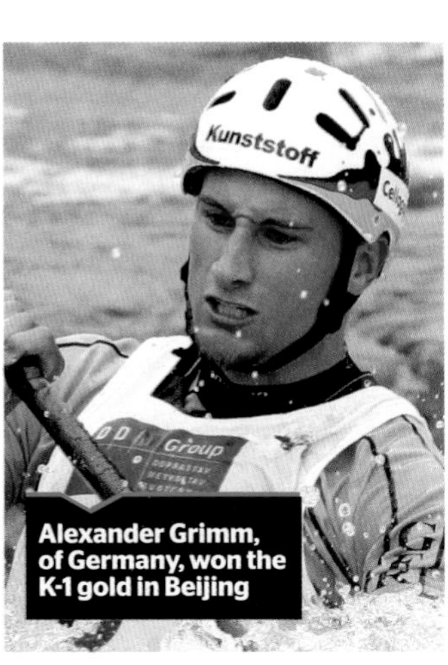

Alexander Grimm, of Germany, won the K-1 gold in Beijing

The Ultimate Olympic A-Z

CANOE – SPRINT

Making its first appearance – as a demonstration event – in the Olympic Games of 1924, Canoe-Sprint became a fully fledged Olympic event in Berlin, in 1936. The sport is now divided into two distinct parts: the kayak and the canoe. In the kayak class, the paddler is in a fixed seat and uses a double-ended paddle, whereas canoe competitors must kneel and propel themselves forward with a single-ended paddle.

The canoe event features only single and double disciplines, but the kayak competition is battled out in one-, two- and four-man boats.

For men, both events used to be contested over 500m and 1,000m of still water but, at the London Games, the former race distance will be scrapped and replaced with an explosive 200m challenge. The women only compete in the kayaking class, over a distance of 500m.

When the sport was first introduced to the Games, a hellish-sounding 10,000m race was included, but these long-distance marathons were abandoned at the Melbourne Games of 1956 in favour of the shorter, far more exciting ones we see today.

The rules are as straightforward as they get: in all events, nine canoes race in a row across a stretch of water and the boat that crosses the finish line first is the winner.

Somewhat refreshingly, it has always been a sport in which the traditional Olympic powerhouses of the USA and China have been outdone by the Central or Eastern Europeans. Though the Germans, Hungarians and Russians have ruled the roost in the past, less prolific nations – such as the Czech Republic, Romania and Sweden – have done their countries proud in the event. There has even been a notable late burst from much smaller nations such as Belarus in recent Games and World Championships. Will there be a power play from outside Europe in London 2012? We shall see.

Women compete in kayaking, over 500m

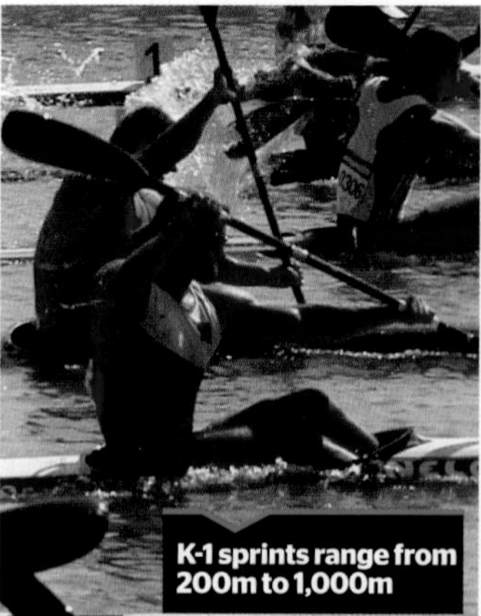
K-1 sprints range from 200m to 1,000m

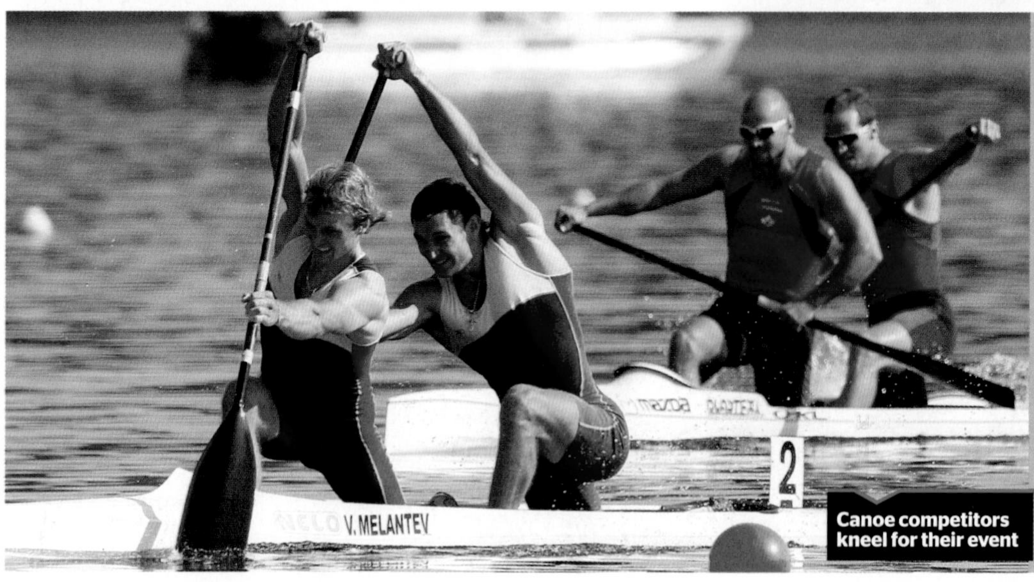

Canoe competitors kneel for their event

DID YOU KNOW?

Each event in Canoeing is defined by a code that includes a letter, denoting the type of competition, and a number, denoting how many people are in the boat. (eg K-1 for single kayak, C-2 double canoe) ■ The oldest canoe club in the world, the Royal Canoe Club of London, was founded in 1866 ■ Cornwall kayaker Jeff Allen and his paddling partner Harry Whelan set the world record for the fastest circumnavigation of Ireland when they achieved the feat in 24 days, 10hrs and 15mins. The previous record was 33 days

Hungary's K-4 women are tipped for glory at London 2012

OVERALL MEDAL TABLE
TOP THREE NATIONS

1. SOVIET UNION

GOLD	SILVER	BRONZE
29	13	9

2. GERMANY

GOLD	SILVER	BRONZE
25	14	16

3. HUNGARY

GOLD	SILVER	BRONZE
19	27	25

Factbox

Where: Eton Dorney
When: Sunday 6 August – Saturday 11 August
Medals Events: 12
Athletes: 246

REASONS TO WATCH

1) STUNNING LOCALE
All the Canoe-Sprint events will take place at Eton Dorney, one of the best stretches of still water in the world – and only a stone's throw from historic Windsor Castle.

2) EDGE-OF-YOUR-SEAT STUFF
The nature of the discipline is such that it's all over extremely quickly (with the 200m race expected to last about 30 seconds), promoting an atmosphere akin to the most exciting track events.

3) A NEW FIRST
For the first time, the men's 500m distance will be scrapped in favour of a new 200m course at the London 2012 Games. Regardless of what the result is, history will be made.

The Ultimate Olympic A-Z

CYCLING – BMX

Having made its debut just four years ago, BMX is the undisputed baby of the Olympic scene, planning to bring a youthful injection of recklessness and cool to the London 2012 games.

Gaining traction in California in the late 1960s, BMX's popularity was boosted by the rise of motocross in the USA. It was this sport that provided the inspiration for the pedal-powered pastime we know today.

With the discipline's various rules becoming more unified in the late 1980s, it achieved official recognition from the International Cycling Union in 1993 and, a decade later – to the delight of many – BMX achieved Olympic status.

Five years after that, at the 2008 Beijing Games, the world witnessed a genre of cycling as exciting as it was hazardous.

With bikes built with a solitary gear and only one brake – not to mention wheels about two thirds of the size of an ordinary road bike – this isn't a discipline for the safety conscious.

All the races at the London 2012 Games will unfold on a short, outdoor track – starting on an eight-metre-high ramp – with hairpin bends and an assortment of jumps for contestants to traverse at breakneck speed. In groups of eight, riders will hurtle down the short, steep slope, before negotiating the circuit's tight turns and jumps.

The men's and women's events will begin with a seeding phase, in which each rider will attempt to complete the track once, within a set time of 40 seconds, to determine their allocated position for the next round. The quarter-finals then lie in wait, held over five races in groups of eight riders.

What follows is essentially a knock-out contest, after which the top-placed riders progress to the finals and potential medal glory.

As BMX was only showcased on the Olympic stage for the first time in 2008, a 'Hall of Champions' has not yet been established – though the USA set out their stall in Beijing, with their men and women claiming three of the six medals available.

Australia and New Zealand, consistent advocates of the world's more extreme sports, will no doubt consider themselves contenders, and British hopes are alive in Shanaze Reade, who was unlucky to miss out on a medal in Beijing after an accident right at the death.

The London Games competition will be watched by 6,000 fans at a specially constructed track next to the Velodrome at the Olympic Park.

BMX is a fast and furious sport

London 2012 will be BMX's second Olympics

DID YOU KNOW?

■ The International BMX Federation was founded in April 1981, with the first world championship held a year later ■ The rider who takes the lead after the start of a race is called the 'holeshot' ■ Anne-Caroline Chausson, of France, and Maris Strombergs, of Latvia, claimed the inaugural BMX Olympic gold medals in Beijing in 2008 ■ Injuries are an occupational hazard for BMX riders and Britain's Shanaze Reade has had her fair share, including broken metatarsals, wrists, elbows and fingers, and a fractured knee

OVERALL MEDAL TABLE TOP THREE COUNTRIES

1. FRANCE

GOLD	SILVER	BRONZE
1	1	0

2. USA

GOLD	SILVER	BRONZE
0	1	2

3. LATVIA

GOLD	SILVER	BRONZE
1	0	0

Factbox

Where : BMX Track – Olympic Park
When: Wednesday 8 – Friday 10 August
Medal events: 2
Athletes: 48

REASONS TO WATCH

1) UNKNOWN QUANTITY

Having featured in only one Olympics before London 2012, even the most knowledgeable of Games aficionados doesn't know what to expect. A big hit at Beijing in 2008, BMX promises to attract an excitable young crowd to the London Games.

2) ONE SHOT AT GLORY

Only one rider per country will be allowed to compete in the women's and men's events at London 2012. With an entire nation's expectations on one pair of shoulders, the pressure to perform will be absolute.

3) URBAN THRILLS

In the absence of skateboarding or roller-blading from the Olympic programme, BMX is the only event in the Games that has a huge extreme-sports following. It really is a one-of-a-kind event and should be a great watch. There may even be a few wipeouts for the more sadistic sporting spectators to enjoy.

After the games the BMX track will be open to the public

The Ultimate Olympic A-Z

CYCLING-MOUNTAIN

Mountain Biking is an Olympic sport as far removed from the Ancient Games as you're likely to see in 2012 – and that's why you should embrace it. The sport's extreme, challenging and dangerous nature is a symbol of how far the Modern Games have come since their birth in Athens in 1896.

The key to Mountain Biking is balance: not just the sort required for a rider to stay on their bike, but balance of strength and stamina, speed and agility, and – most importantly – the balance of a bike's durability and lightness.

Such is the importance of having a lightweight machine, that bikes suffer in terms of their robustness. As riders push them to the limit during the 100-plus-minute races, they often sustain punctures and mechanical problems, so every rider carries a tool kit to make repairs along the way.

However, these are sometimes not enough, so there are also official assistance zones for bigger problems, which, naturally, have a detrimental effect on a rider's race time. All of this combines to make Mountain Biking one of 2012's must-see events.

The format of Mountain Biking is straightforward. There is one race for each sex – 50 male athletes and 30 female athletes – and all of the riders start together, with the first person to finish awarded the gold medal. Competitors have to complete several laps of a trail, with traditional course lengths being 40-50km for men and 30-40km for women. Racers are eliminated if they are lapped by the leader or if their bikes are damaged beyond repair.

Balance is key to Mountain Biking

The London 2012 Mountain Biking event will take place at Hadleigh Farm, in Essex, where a challenging, purpose-built trail has been constructed, over a 550-acre site, complete with a top-to-bottom escalation of 70m for riders to gruellingly pedal up and down.

Mountain Biking first came on the scene in the 1970s, but was local to the hills of northern California. The first World Championship took place as recently as 1990 and, soon afterwards, the International Olympic Committee adopted the sport and made it an official part of the programme at the Atlanta Games, in 1996.

At London 2012, France's Julien Absalon will be looking to complete a hat-trick of gold medals, having won the men's event at Athens in 2004 and Beijing in 2008.

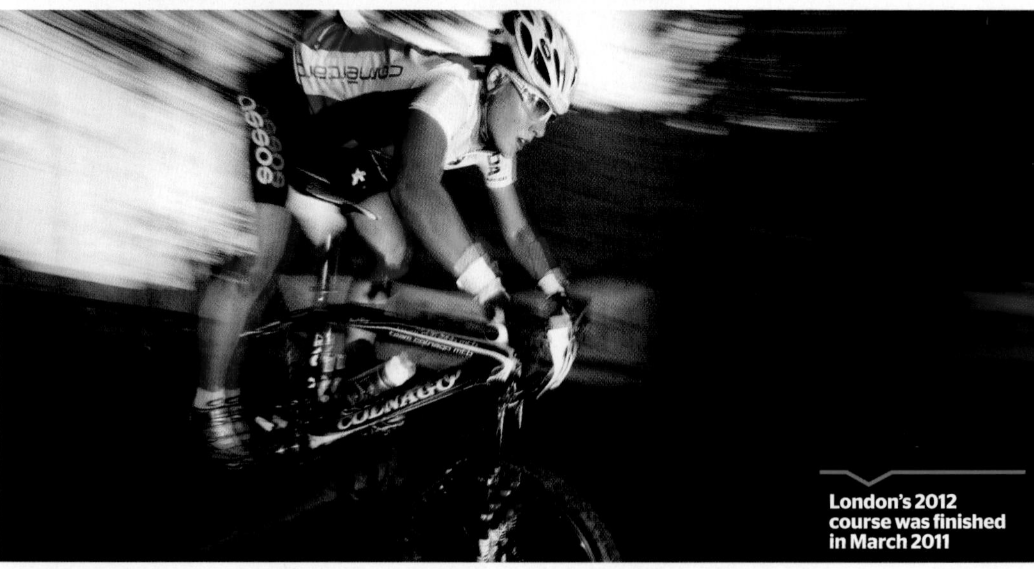

London's 2012 course was finished in March 2011

DID YOU KNOW?

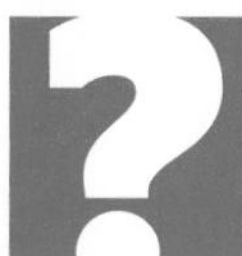

Fifty riders started the men's race in Beijing 2008, but only 28 finished the course ■ An Olympic mountain bike weighs less than 10kgs ■ The average speed of the 2008 men's gold medalist was 23.6kph. The winner, France's Julien Absalon, took 1hr 55mins 59secs to complete the 36.8km course ■ Bart Jen Brentjens of the Netherlands won the first Mountain Biking event at the Atlanta Olympics ■ Mount Tamalpais is generally regarded as the first mountain on which the sport was contested

Germany's Sabine Spitz has a Beijing 2008 gold to defend

Mountain Biking throws up thrills and spills for spectators

Factbox

Venue: Hadleigh Farm, Essex
Dates: Saturday 11 – Sunday 12 August
Medal events: 2
Athletes: 80 (50 men, 30 women)

REASONS TO WATCH:

1) THRILLS AND SPILLS

This is possibly the most bone-crunching sport at the Games, as riders hurtle down unforgiving terrain with little more than a helmet and thin gloves for protection.

2) RIDER EQUILIBRIUM

A competitor's chance of winning a gold medal can be crushed by riding too fast and too hard, with punctures a common and costly occurrence in the sport.

3) ONE CHANCE ONLY

There are no second chances in Mountain Biking because the medals are determined by one race, and one race only.

The Ultimate Olympic A-Z

CYCLING – ROAD

Cycling is one of the most popular events at the Olympic Games. It debuted at the inaugural Modern Olympics in Athens, was surprisingly ditched in 1900, 1904 and 1908, but has been a staple event since 1912.

There are four gold medals on offer at London 2012 for the Road Cycling events, two each for the men and women in the road race and the time trial for which 145 men and 67 women will compete.

Sacrificing any kind of comfort for pure speed, every racer will be trying to achieve the perfect aerodynamic form to shave seconds off their time and increase their performance.

The road race (250km for the men, 140km for the women) has a mass start with the first person to reach the finish line capturing gold. The time trial competitors start 90 seconds apart, cycle their hardest around a set course (44km for men, 29km for women) and the rider with the fastest time wins the gold.

The Olympic Cycling Road races (along with the Olympic and Paralympic marathons) will start and finish in The Mall, go south west through the capital across Putney Bridge, through Richmond Park, past Hampton Court Palace, into Surrey for some gruelling circuits around Box Hill (nine for the men, two for the women) then doubling back through Leatherhead and Kingston to Richmond Park and then back to The Mall for the finish.

Unusually for the Olympic Cycling time trial event, the London 2012 course is one single lap and also takes its route through south-west London.

Good aerodynamics equal good times

Riders will begin at Hampton Court Palace, navigate punishing parts of Richmond, Kingston and Surrey and head back to Hampton Court Palace to the finish line.

Great British support will be guaranteed along the routes, especially with the formidable Nicole Cooke defending her road race gold from Beijing 2008 and the incomparable Mark Cavendish in action for the men. And they'll certainly not be the inherent problems of pollution that were all-too apparent in Beijing.

All about speed, intensity and pure stamina, the Road Cycling will be one of the most competitive events in the XXX Olympiad.

Mark Cavendish will take some beating

DID YOU KNOW?

Miguel Indurain, who won five consecutive Tour de France titles (1991-1995) had a lung capacity of 8 litres, a heart circulation of 50 litres per minute and a resting heart beat of 30bpm ■ Nicole Cooke won the BBC Wales Sports Personality of the Year in 2003. She is also the first woman to become the road race World Champion and Olympic gold medallist in the same year ■ Along with St. James's Palace, Hampton Court Palace is one of only two surviving palaces out of the many owned by Henry VIII

A rider's positioning in the pack is vital for a chance at victory

OVERALL MEDAL TABLE
TOP THREE NATIONS

1. FRANCE

GOLD	SILVER	BRONZE
40	24	22

2. ITALY

GOLD	SILVER	BRONZE
32	16	8

3. GREAT BRITAIN

GOLD	SILVER	BRONZE
18	24	21

Factbox

Where: The Mall (Road Race); Hampton Court (Time Trial)
When: Saturday 28 July - Wednesday 1 August
Medal events: 4
Athletes: 212 (145 men, 67 women)

REASONS TO WATCH

1) SCENIC LONDON
The XXX Olympiad may have constructed some wonderful stadia but there's nothing like the streets of London, and we'll be seeing plenty of them in the Road Cycling.

2) PURE STAMINA
There'll be no greater test of endurance in the entire Olympics than the Road Cycling and we'll be able to watch it tested up close and personal!

3) MASS START
Is there any more exciting and eventful start to a race at 2012 than the Road Cycling mass start? We think not.

The Ultimate Olympic A-Z

CYCLING – TRACK

Track cycling is more popular than ever right now and there promises to be an electric atmosphere in the 6,000-capacity Velodrome during the London 2012 Games because the host nation dominated the sport in Beijing, picking up seven of the 10 golds on offer, plus three silver and two bronze medals.

The research and technology on show at the Track Cycling will be among the most sophisticated you will see at the Olympics. There isn't another sport at the Games for which being as light and as aerodynamic as possible holds as much importance.

Take the bike on which Britain's Sir Chris Hoy won three gold medals in 2008, for example. It weighed a puny 7kg and (like all other track cyclists) he had no gears or brakes fitted to his machine because they weigh too much and would have slowed him down.

For London 2012, Track Cycling has dropped a few of its formats to even out, at five each, the number of medals on offer to men and women. The disciplines that remain are:

The Sprint: This is a race for two cyclists, who start next to one another on the track and then attempt to be the first to complete three laps. It sounds straightforward, but is anything but. The riders do not sprint the whole race because, inevitably, one would sit in their opponent's slipstream and save energy for the final lap. So, for roughly half of the race, they take it extremely slowly around the track, until one competitor is confident they can outpace the other for the rest of the race. Cue an explosion of pace and high drama as the cyclists go hell for leather to the finish line. The Sprint event can be won or lost in the blink of an eye.

Keirin: This is approximately a 2km race featuring up to seven riders, who start in a line (riders draw lots for bank positions) and then follow a pace-setting motorbike until there is only 700m left to race. The motorbike starts the pace at a deliberately slow 25kph and exits the race at 50kph. It is then simply a matter of which cyclist is first to cross the line. Expect to see plenty of crashes in this format.

Omnium: London 2012 will be the first Olympic Games to feature the omnium. It contains six sub-formats and riders are scored depending on how they finish in each section. Points are awarded in reverse order, so the winner of each event gets one point, second place two and so on. The winner of the omnium is the rider with the least points. The six omnium events are: 1. A timed flying lap; 2. A point's race; 3. An elimination race; 4. Individual Pursuit; 5. Scratch Race; 6. Time trial. Think of it as a Track Cycling Hexathlon.

London 2012 will not feature the Madison...

Team Sprint: This is a three-lap race around the velodrome, in a head-to-head format between two teams that each have three riders. Each team starts with all three of their riders on one side of the Velodrome. After the first lap, the leading rider peels off and lets the second rider lead the team for the second lap, and, on the final lap, only one rider from each team is left to sprint for the finish. Nations who want to do well in this event will select their sprinter with the best endurance for the all-important final lap.

Team Pursuit: The final gold medals up for grabs at the Olympic Velodrome will be for teams of four (for men) and three (for women), and can be won in two ways. The conventional way is to complete the distance (4km for men, 3km for women) before your opponents do. However, because teams start the race on opposite sides of the track, a victory is also awarded if one team overtakes the other before the full distance is completed.

...but fans will still see the Team Pursuit

DID YOU KNOW?

The track at the London 2012 Velodrome is made from 56km of sustainable Siberian pine and was fixed into place with 300,000 nails ■ In 2008, Chris Hoy became the first British athlete to win three gold medals at a summer Games since swimmer Henry Taylor bagged himself three in the London 1908 Games ■ Indoor cycling first took place in Britain in the 1870s. The sport was brought indoors to make it easier to charge spectators and to race during the winter

Britain dominated Track Cycling at the Beijing Games

OVERALL MEDAL TABLE
TOP THREE NATIONS

1. FRANCE

GOLD	SILVER	BRONZE
40	24	22

2. ITALY

GOLD	SILVER	BRONZE
32	16	8

3. GREAT BRITAIN

GOLD	SILVER	BRONZE
18	24	21

Factbox

Where: Velodrome
When: Thursday 2 – Tuesday 7 August
Medal Events: 10
Athletes: 188 (104 men, 84 women)

REASONS TO WATCH

1) EXTREME SPEED
Sprint cyclists can cover ground at the rate of 20 metres per second. Not even Usain Bolt can travel that fast without an engine being involved!

2) STEEP LEARNING CURVE
At its steepest, the bank of the track is 44°, meaning crashes are not only commonplace, but rather brutal when they do occur.

3) HOME CROWDS
Track Cycling offers the home crowd one of the best chances to see medals being won by British athletes – so you can bet the 6,000-capacity Velodrome will be rocking from start to finish.

The Ultimate Olympic A-Z

DIVING

Diving is one of four aquatic events at the Summer Games, along with swimming, water polo and synchronised swimming. At London 2012, there will be two boards from which divers will compete – the 3m springboard and the 10m fixed platform – and there will be four events for both men and women, with eight medals up for grabs in total. These events – unchanged from Beijing in 2008 – are the 3m springboard, 10m platform, 3m synchronised springboard and 10m synchronised platform.

Divers are scored, on a one to 10 scale, by a panel of judges, and points are awarded for the difficulty and execution of each dive. In the synchronised events, judges also place significant emphasis on the level of synchronisation displayed by the competing pair.

Diving has been a feature of the Olympics since it was introduced to the Games in St Louis in 1904, when the sport was called 'Fancy Diving'. The two competitive disciplines back then were the 'Fancy High Dive' and the 'Plunge for Distance'.

The Fancy High Dive is not dissimilar to the diving of today, but the Plunge for Distance event was essentially an odd, aquatic long jump. Divers had to perform a standstill dive from water level and try to submerge themselves as deep as possible into the water. There was an added element of difficulty because divers had to remain motionless once they hit the water – and they had a maximum of 60 seconds in which to finish their plunge.

In 1904, the USA's William Dickey won the gold medal and still holds the Olympic record with his plunge of 19.05m – but this is because the Plunge for Distance was dropped from the Games after 1904, it being deemed too boring.

Points are awarded for synchronicity as well as difficulty

Britain's Tom Daley is a 2012 medal hope

In Beijing 2008, China dominated the Diving event, winning seven of the eight available gold medals and, in recent years, they have been by far the most successful nation. But the most decorated nation overall is the USA, with a hugely impressive 48 golds and 131 medals in total, which easily eclipses any other nation's Olympic tally.

However, this table has to be treated with caution because the sport's current top nation, China, has only been allowed to compete in the Diving events since 1984. Before then, the sport's governing body, FINA, refused to allow the Chinese to compete because of their government. China has topped the Olympic medals table in all but one of the Summer Games since the ban was lifted.

Diving is going to be one of the most popular events at the London 2012 Olympic Games, thanks to the host nation's popular teenage star – and firm medal hope – Tom Daley.

Daley made his first Olympic appearance in Beijing in 2008, at the age of just 14. He came away empty-handed, but has since won two gold medals at the Commonwealth Games and is the current FINA World Champion on the 10m platform.

DID YOU KNOW?

At the 1988 Olympics, American diver Greg Louganis banged his head on the 3m springboard during a dive in the preliminary rounds. He suffered concussion, but still went on to win the gold medal ■ China have only been allowed to compete at Diving in seven Olympic Games but in that time, have won 27 gold medals and are currently the second in the medals table ■ Synchronised Diving was only added to the event in Sydney 2000 ■ 180,000 tiles were used to line the pools in the Olympic Aquatic Centre

China dominate the current Diving scene

OVERALL MEDAL TABLE
TOP THREE NATIONS

1. USA

GOLD	SILVER	BRONZE
48	41	42

2. CHINA

GOLD	SILVER	BRONZE
27	14	8

3. SWEDEN

GOLD	SILVER	BRONZE
6	8	7

Factbox

Where: Aquatics Centre at the Olympic Park
When: Sunday 29 July – Saturday 11 August
Medal events: 8
Athletes: 136 (68 men, 68 women)

REASONS TO WATCH

1) STRIVING FOR PERFECTION
Divers can (and often do) lose medals by the tiniest of margins. The smallest splash of water or over-rotation can be the difference between a gold and silver medal.

2) TOTAL DISCIPLINE
Divers have to have extreme discipline and dedication to reach Olympic standard without looking rigid and robotic in their dives. The levels of skill and concentration involved are truly enviable.

3) BEAUTIFUL SHAPES
The manoeuvres, shapes and rotations that divers manage to pull off within a matter of seconds from board to water are truly breathtaking to behold.

The Ultimate Olympic A-Z

EQUESTRIAN - DRESSAGE

The Paris Olympics of 1900 introduced Equestrian events to the Games and - apart from in St Louis in 1904 and London in 1908 - they have been a fixture ever since. Dressage, as we know it today, was not part of the original Olympic Equestrian format and was only added when the sport was reinstated to the Games in Stockholm, in 1912.

When Dressage first appeared in the Olympic Games, only 21 riders from eight countries took part, and the sport was split into three categories; flat test, jumping test and obedience test.

The flat test took place in a 20m x 40m space - which is now referred to as the 'small arena' - and lasted a maximum of 10 minutes, with extra points being awarded for riding one-handed.

In the jumping test, riders tackled four 1.10m-tall fences and one fence with a three-metre spread.

Finally, the obedience test examined how riders controlled their horses while riding close to objects that were considered spooky or unnerving for the animals. Competitors were scored on a scale from nought to 10.

The Netherlands' Edward Gal in action

Today's Equestrian Dressage is a little different and is one of the few sports in which men and women compete on equal terms.

Every participating nation enters all of their riders into the first round - known as the grand prix - and they must all complete the same manoeuvres. Each rider and horse pairing are given a score and the 25 highest-scoring progress to the next stage, the 'grand prix special'.

This is a shortened version of the grand prix, but with emphasis on two manoeuvres. Firstly, the 'piaffe', which is a trotting movement performed almost on the spot, and, secondly, the 'passage', a slow and animated performance of the trot. Medals are then awarded to the teams with the highest scores.

The individual Equestrian Dressage event is called the grand prix freestyle and the riders are selected from the 18 highest-scoring competitors in the grand prix special.

In this event, the riders and their horses have to perform and impress the judges with their own freestyle routine set to music. Riders are marked on their performance and the three highest-scoring individuals are then awarded the gold, silver and bronze medals.

Dating back to 1433, Greenwich Park - London's oldest Royal Park and a World Heritage Site - will be the venue for the 2012 Games' Equestrian events, while the spectacular National Maritime Museum building will provide a fitting backdrop for this historical and elegant sport.

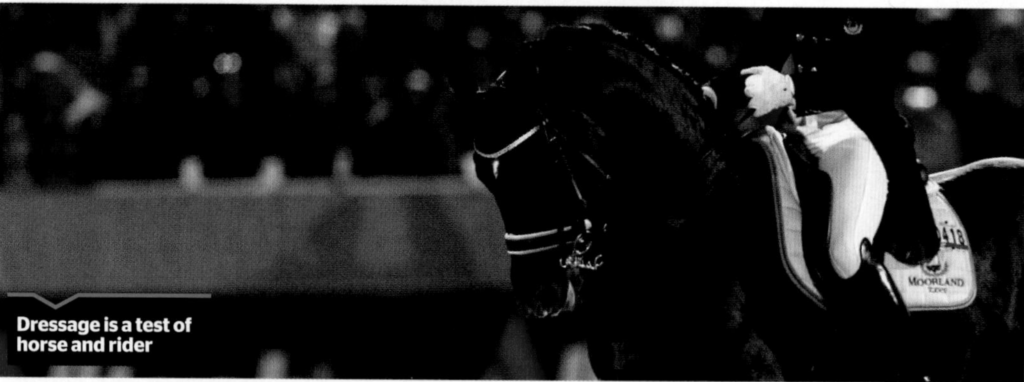

Dressage is a test of horse and rider

DID YOU KNOW?

Only male cavalry officers were allowed to compete in Olympic Equestrian Dressage up until the 1952 Games in Helsinki ■ The origins of Equestrian Dressage can be traced back 2,000 years, to when the Greeks used it to prepare their horses for war ■ At the Helsinki Games, Denmark's Lis w won silver in Dressage despite being paralysed below the knees ■ The word 'dressage' is French and is most commonly translated as 'training'

Men and women compete on equal terms in Dressage

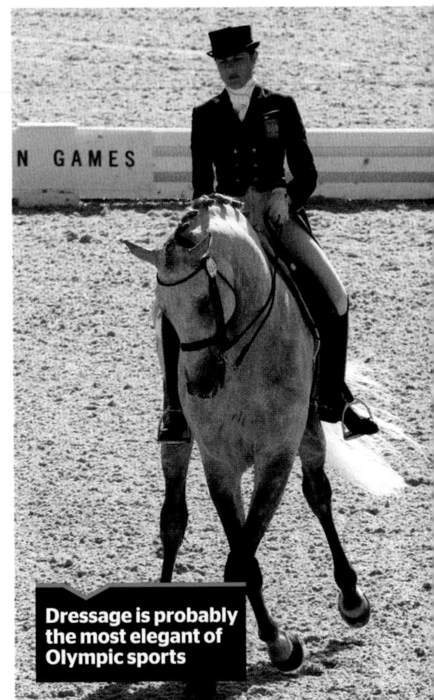

Dressage is probably the most elegant of Olympic sports

Factbox

Where: Greenwich Park
When: Thursday 2 August - Wednesday 8 August
Medal Events: 2
Athletes: 50

REASONS TO WATCH

1) POISE EQUALS POINTS

The rider's formal clothing and the horse's grooming and manoeuvring make this the most elegant sport at the Summer Games.

2) MAN V BEAST

Dressage is the ultimate test of a rider's ability to control a horse.

3) CRACKING LOCATION

The sport's rich heritage has met its match in its London 2012 venue. Greenwich Park's National Maritime Museum is a breathtaking backdrop for the Equestrian Dressage and will provide a memorable setting for more historic performances.

The Ultimate Olympic A-Z

EQUESTRIAN – EVENTING

Eventing will be the pinnacle contest for horse and rider at the London 2012 Games, where they must hone their symbiotic relationship across all three equestrian disciplines – dressage, cross country and jumping.

Introduced to the Games in 1912, in Stockholm, Eventing has been a staple of the summer Olympics ever since. With a high chance of injury – and seconds and centimetres the difference between competitors – Eventing is brutal and demanding of commitment in equal measure.

Dressage displays the wondrous understanding between Olympic athlete and Olympic steed; cross country tests the speed, courage and fortitude of both parties; and the tense finale on the jumping circuit will be an examination of timing, skill and precision under pressure.

A test of courage, speed and fortitude

As with all equestrian competitions, men and women battle it out on equal terms in Eventing, and the four-day competition features individual and team events.

The first two days of competition involve dressage. The horse is considered as much of an athlete as the rider and the panel of judges' scores are converted to penalty points that carry over to the next event.

On day three, it is time to tackle the ultra-challenging cross country course, which has been beautifully crafted in London's Greenwich Park. As with the dressage, riders can accrue penalty points – for jumping errors and time blunders – which are added to their dressage score.

The culmination of Eventing is on day four, with the show-jumping. Again in front of enthusiastic support in London's oldest Royal Park, horse and rider will have to address a tricky sequence of jumps in the quickest possible time. They will incur penalties for obstacles refused or clipped, and for being over time. The first jumping test will determine the team medals and the second the individual winners.

Water jumps make a great spectacle

In Beijing, Germany triumphed in the individual (Hinrich Romeike on Marius) and the team events, and are expected to put up a strong defence of their Olympic titles in London. But they can expect stiff competition from the USA, Sweden and Great Britain, for whom the Queen's granddaughter, Zara Phillips, is hoping to qualify after missing out in 2008 because of injury to her horse, Toytown.

DID YOU KNOW?

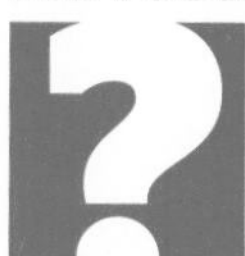

There are two age limits for Olympic Equestrian events, one for the riders (18 years or over) and one for the horses (at least seven years of age) ■ In 1960, in Rome, Australia's Bill Roycroft suffered concussion and a broken collarbone in the team Eventing cross country. Knowing his team could not win gold unless he continued, he discharged himself from hospital to complete his show jumping and help Australia to their first Olympic title ■ The cross country course in Eventing is between 5,700m and 6,840m long

Cross country jumps are a test of nerve for rider and horse

Factbox

Where: Greenwich Park
When: Saturday 28 July – Tuesday 31 July
Medal events: 2
Athletes: 75

REASONS TO WATCH

1) NO HIDING PLACE
With up to 45 jumps, the gorgeous but tricky cross country course is an uncompromising way to separate the wheat from the chaff on day three. Screw this up and your medal chances fritter away.

2) ANIMAL ATTRACTION
Such a powerful: partnership between man and beast is something to behold. To see the size of the obstacles at Greenwich is to understand just how dangerous Equestrian can be.

3) NERVE-JANGLING
With the number of obstacles – and, therefore, penalties – rider and horse must negotiate, you can't take your eyes off the action for a second. By the third day, Eventing really does become a nail-biting test of nerve – and that's just for the spectators!

The Ultimate Olympic A-Z

EQUESTRIAN – JUMPING

Jumping (more commonly known in Britain as 'show jumping') was the earliest of the three Equestrian disciplines to feature in the Olympics and its origins hark back to the days of enclosure, when adaptations had to be made to 18th-century horseback hunting.

Before the arrival of fences in the British countryside, hunters could gallop unopposed across fields in pursuit of foxes. But with new wooden obstacles in their way, horse and rider had to adapt – thus jumping was born.

The sport has been a feature of the modern Olympic programme since the early 1900s, but entry to Equestrian events was initially limited to the military. It was not until the Helsinki Games of 1952 that the competition was widened to include civilian riders, too. This, in turn, allowed women to make their mark in the sport and they entered the Olympic Jumping scene at the 1956 Games, in Stockholm.

As a result, Equestrian became one of the very few Olympic sports in which men and women compete against one another.

The event has been dominated by Europeans (in both the individual and team competitions) and the only nation from outside this sphere to mount a serious Olympic challenge has been America. Over the past 40 years, their riders have amassed an impressive tally of medals and they'll be eager to mount the podium again at the 2012 Games.

Taking place in an arena housing up to 14 fences of varying difficulty, the aim of Jumping is for rider and horse to successfully negotiate their way around the course without collecting faults and within the allotted time – if they do this, they achieve what is known as a 'clear run'.

Faults are awarded if the horse knocks over any of the jumps, stops at any of them (called a 'refusal') or finishes outside the set time. Should two or more riders complete the course and incur the same number of faults, there is a 'jump off', in which competitors must jump a shortened course as fast as possible, without knocking down any fences.

As with Dressage and Cross Country, Jumping is divided into team and individual events.

At London 2012, a total of five rounds will be contested, two of which will determine placings in the team event, whereas all five will play a part in determining the outcome of the individual competition.

Horse and rider must clear up to 14 fences

DID YOU KNOW?

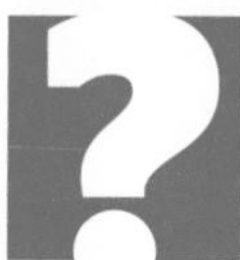

Canada's Ian Millar, who won a team Jumping silver at the 2008 Beijing Games, was the oldest athlete competing in any event that year, at 61 ■ In team Jumping, countries may have any mix of male and female athletes. They are not required to have minimum numbers of either sex, they simply choose the best riders ■ Jumping obstacles may include parallel rails, triple bars, water jumps and simulated stone walls. A triple combination is three fences close together, with only a few steps in between

Jos Lansink won team gold with The Netherlands in 1992

OVERALL MEDAL TABLE: TOP THREE COUNTRIES

1. GERMANY

GOLD	SILVER	BRONZE
21	10	11

2. SWEDEN

GOLD	SILVER	BRONZE
17	10	14

3. FRANCE

GOLD	SILVER	BRONZE
12	12	10

Factbox

Where: Greenwich Park
When: Saturday 4 August – Thursday 9 August
Medal events: 2
Athletes: 75

REASONS TO WATCH

1) NICE SPOT FOR A PICNIC
All the Equestrian events will be held at Greenwich Park, one of the most picturesque – and certainly the oldest – of London's Royal Parks.

2) GENDER RIVALRY
There are very few sports in which men and women compete on an equal basis – but Equestrian is one of them. So when riders enter the Jumping arena, there is an added dimension to the rivalries between nations.

3) NAIL-BITING STUFF
It may not look like it to the casual observer, but Jumping provides many a nerve-shredding conclusion – with the width of a pole or split-second of the clock often the only thing separating rider and horse from glory in the 'jump off'.

The Ultimate Olympic A-Z

FENCING

There are three forms of Fencing at the Olympics and each discipline is named after the sword used: foil, épée and sabre. The principles for each are essentially the same, but there are subtle differences.

Individual bouts are split into three rounds of three minutes or last until one fencer scores 15 points. In team Fencing, teams of three fencers compete against their opponents over nine bouts and a maximum of 45 points can be won. All Fencing events at the Summer Games are in a knock-out format.

Foil: This is the lightest and quickest sword used in Olympic Fencing. The foil must have a blade that is no longer than 90cm and no heavier than 500g – although 100g is the weight most fencers opt for. The sword is equipped with an electronic button at its tip and a Fencer only wins a point when the button is depressed with a force of at least 4.90 Newtons for at least 15 milliseconds.

The scoring area for foil Fencing is restricted to an opponent's torso – the scoring area is covered in a conductive material called lamé, which sounds an alert to let officials know when a point has been scored.

There is a 'right of way' system in foil Fencing, so if both competitors score a hit at the same time, the point is awarded to the fencer who initiated the exchange. A fencer's 'right of way' is lost when an attacking action misses, falls short or is successfully parried – the 'right of way' is then passed over to the opponent.

Foil fencers aim for their rival's torso...

...while footwork is important in sabre

Épée: Épée Fencing was created in the 19th century by a group of French students who sought a less regulated and more free-flowing form of the sport. The blade is heavier and the hit area is extended to the entire body of an opponent.

Épée has no 'right of way' in terms of scoring a point and, in the event of simultaneous hits landing within four milliseconds of each other, both fencers are awarded a point – unless it is a point to decide the bout, in which case no points are awarded.

As with the foil, the épée is fitted with a push button on its tip and a point is only scored when the tip is depressed for 1 millisecond, with a force of at least 7.35 Newtons.

Sabre: This sword appeared at around the turn of the 20th century and was traditionally used as a cutting weapon, it being shaped with a double-edged blade.

In the sabre event, points are awarded when any part of the blade makes contact with the opponent anywhere above the waist. Sabre Fencing has a 'right of way' scoring system and greater emphasis is placed on skilled footwork because of the ease with which fencers can register a hit.

There are 10 Fencing gold medals up for grabs at the 2012 Games. For men they are individual foil, épée, sabre, plus team épée and sabre. While, for women, they are individual foil, épée, sabre, as well as team foil and sabre.

Italy and France are the historical powerhouses in the sport, so keep an eye out for them when they inevitably meet.

DID YOU KNOW?

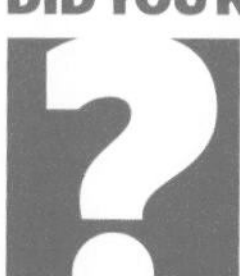

Italy's Nedo Nadi is the only fencer to have won gold medals with all three swords at one Games, in Antwerp in 1920 ■ Confrérie de Saint-Michel is the oldest fencing club in the world. Located in Ghent, Belgium, it was founded in 1613 ■ There are an estimated 1.5 million active fencers in the world ■ Hungarian fencer Aladar Gerevich is the only Olympian to win gold medals at six consecutive Games. He was a sabre Olympic champion in every Summer Games from 1932 to 1960

OVERALL MEDAL TABLE
TOP THREE NATIONS

1. ITALY

GOLD	SILVER	BRONZE
45	38	31

2. FRANCE

GOLD	SILVER	BRONZE
41	40	34

3. HUNGARY

GOLD	SILVER	BRONZE
34	22	26

Factbox

Where: ExCeL
When: Saturday 28 July – Sunday 5 August
Medal events: 10
Athletes: 212

REASONS TO WATCH

1) SWORD PLAY
Fencing is the only way you're legally going to witness sword fighting in today's world.

2) OLYMPIC HERITAGE
It is one of only a few core sports that have featured in every Summer Olympic Games since 1896.

3) MERCILESS GRACE
Few other sports require such balletic athleticism and total concentration as Olympic Fencing.

The whole body is a target in the more free-flowing épée

The Ultimate Olympic A-Z

FOOTBALL

The most popular sport on the planet is enjoying a renaissance at the Olympic Games and the eyes of the world will be on both the men's and the women's tournaments, with medals fought for at six stadia.

First introduced as a medal sport for men at the 1908 London Olympics, football has appeared at every Games since then, except for Los Angeles in 1932. The first women's tournament was played in Atlanta in 1996.

Because of the sport's popularity, the Olympic Games has often clashed with the domestic leagues of the footballing superpowers (Western Europe and South America). It wasn't until 1992 that all professionals aged under 23 were considered eligible to play in the Games and it was 1996 before the IOC allowed three players over that age to be enrolled in the 18-man squads. The women's event has no such age restrictions.

USA beat Brazil in the 2008 women's final

At London 2012, both sexes will play 90-minute matches in the group stages, while the knock-out stages will feature 30 minutes of extra-time and penalties if neither team scores a winner in open play.

Teams of 11 will fight it out on standard pitches (105m x 68m), with standard goals (24ft x 8ft), and three substitutions per game will be allowed.

The men's tournament will feature 16 teams and the women's 12, with eight teams from each qualifying for the knock-out phases. Winning semi-finalists will fight it out for the gold medal at Wembley and the two losing semi-finalists will play-off for the bronze.

The men's Olympic top-scorers list makes for interesting reading, with Romário (seven, Brazil, 1988), Bebeto (six, Brazil, 1996), Hernán Crespo (six, Argentina, 1996), Iván Zamorano (six, Chile, 2000), and Carlos Tevez (eight, Argentina, 2004) painting a picture of recent South American dominance.

In Beijing in 2008, Argentina retained their Olympic title and beat Brazil 3-0 on their way to a final victory over Nigeria, Real Madrid's Angel Di Maria scoring the only goal in the final.

All the big European countries will be fielding their strongest men's teams in UEFA Euro 2012, which finishes only three weeks before the Olympics, so don't expect to see anyone from these squads lining up in London.

The women's holders are the USA, who beat Brazil in the 2008 final thanks to a goal from Carli Lloyd in the sixth minute of extra time. A crowd of 51,612 watched that final, while 89,102 attended the men's gold-medal game in the National Stadium.

Lionel Messi won gold in Beijing

Brazil's Ronaldinho won bronze in Beijing

DID YOU KNOW?

Before their victory in 2004, Argentina had never won an Olympic football championship and had not won an Olympic team sport since the polo tournament of 1936 ■ Several historically strong men's football nations have unimpressive Olympic records. The Netherlands won bronze in the first three tournaments, but have not reached the podium since – and Brazil's two silver medals in the 1980s are the best they have achieved

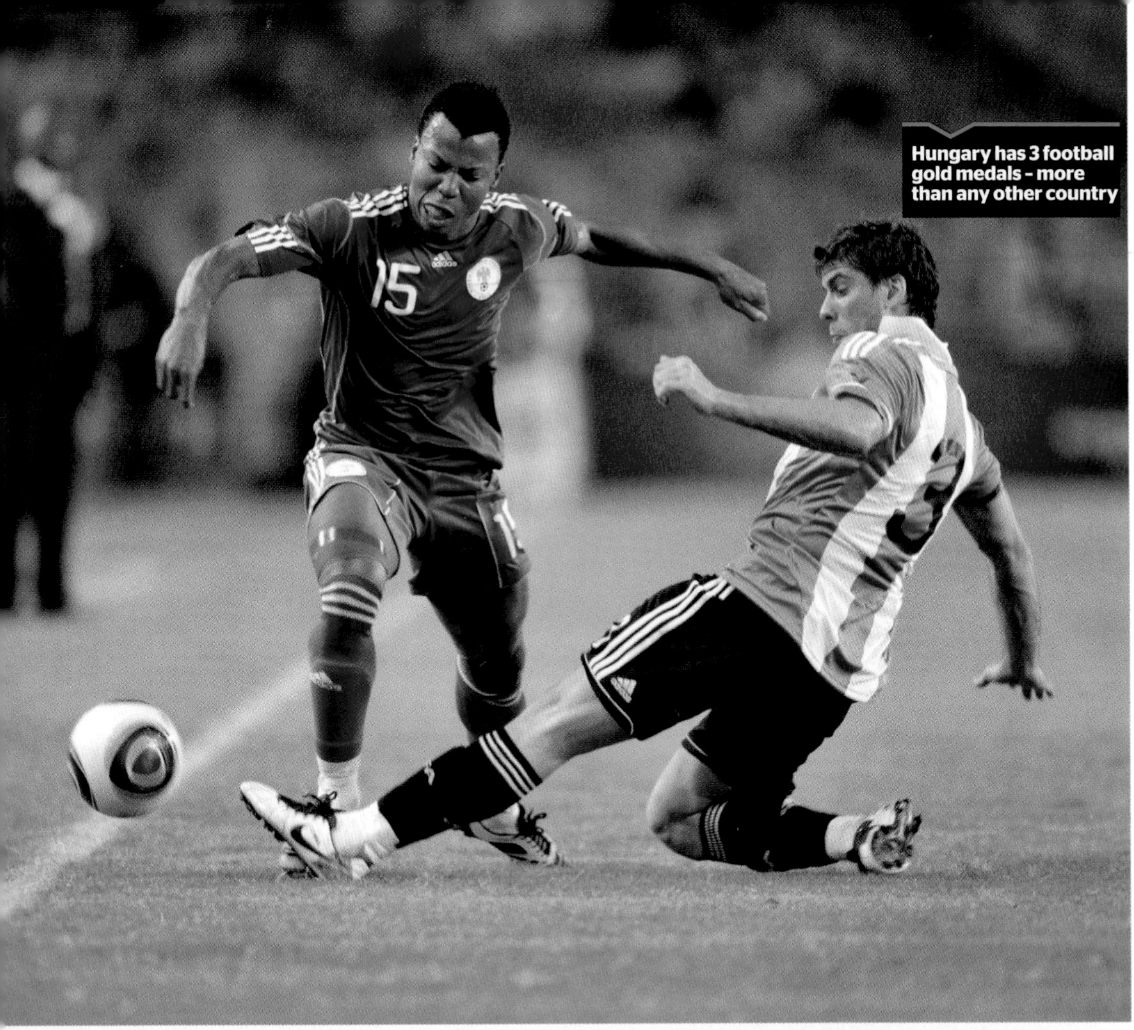

Hungary has 3 football gold medals – more than any other country

The men's 2008 final pitted Argentina against Nigeria

OVERALL MEDAL TABLE
TOP THREE NATIONS

1. USA

GOLD	SILVER	BRONZE
3	2	1

2. HUNGARY

GOLD	SILVER	BRONZE
3	1	1

3.GREAT BRITAIN

GOLD	SILVER	BRONZE
3	0	0

Factbox

Venue: City of Coventry Stadium (Coventry); Hampden Park (Glasgow); Millennium Stadium (Cardiff); Old Trafford (Manchester); St James' Park (Newcastle); Wembley Stadium
When: Wednesday 25 July – Saturday 11 August
Medal events: 2
Athletes: 504 (288 men, 216 women; 16 men's teams, 12 women's teams)

REASONS TO WATCH

1) FUTURE STAR SPOTTING
Because of the age restriction in the men's event, teams will be full of youngsters who rarely get the chance to perform on the biggest stages. With huge crowds expected, this will be a wonderful chance for them to thrive.

2) NO-STOP ACTION
With concurrent men's and women's tournaments taking place, 28 teams and all games played within 17 days, there'll be no time to take your eyes off the ball.

3) PARTY ATMOSPHERE
There's nothing better than an international football tournament to get pulses racing and the world's fans will bring their culture and singing voices to Britain.

The Ultimate Olympic A-Z

GYM – ARTISTIC

Sure to be one of the most popular sports at London 2012, Artistic Gymnastics has a rich heritage dating back to the birth of the Modern Olympics in Athens in 1896. A women's event was included 32 years later and they have been competing ever since.

The London 2012 competition will be held at the state-of-the-art North Greenwich Arena, on the River Thames, where athletes will be competing for best all-round, best team and best individual performance on each piece of apparatus.

Men tackle the floor, pommel horse, rings, vault, parallel bars and horizontal bar, while women compete on the vault, uneven bars, balance beam and the floor.

Floor exercises – performed on a sprung floor that helps athletes achieve bounce when tumbling and softens their landings – last up to 90 seconds and are choreographed to incorporate acrobatic and dance elements. These are scored higher if they correspond artistically with the accompanying music, express individual personality and, of course, are completed without fault and landed with grace.

Used only by men, the pommel horse involves a combination of single (scissor) and double leg work, the latter being the staple of each routine. Gymnasts are deducted points for not passing through the handstand position when dismounting, not using all three sections of the horse, pausing or stopping, or brushing or hitting the apparatus.

Also known as the still rings, the rings require a rather extreme level of upper-body strength and its successful proponents have big muscles in their upper arms and shoulders. Again only performed by men, ring exercises consist of swing, strength and hold elements, the difficulty and application of which determine the medals.

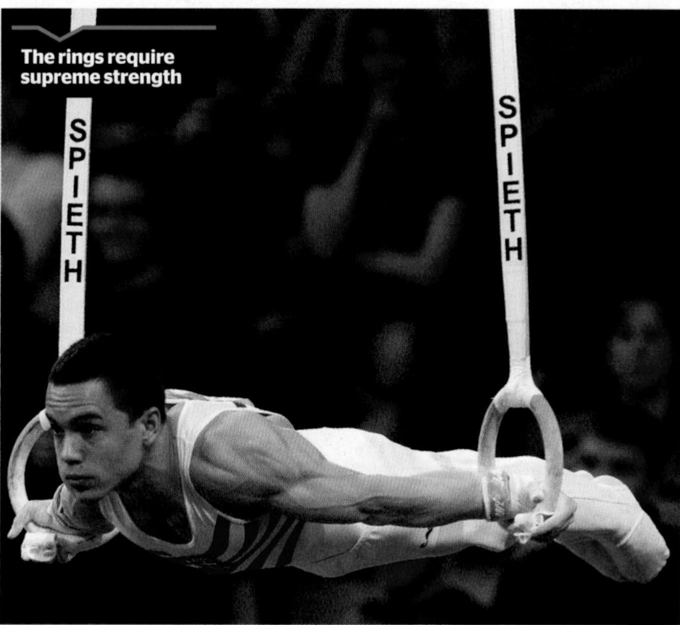

The rings require supreme strength

Only women perform on the balance beam

Men and women tackle the vault, for which speed, technique, height and distance are all looked at by the judges when considering a final mark.

The parallel bars, held in place by a metal framework, is another piece of male-only gymnastic apparatus. Typical routines involve swinging skills, a hanging position and an upper-arm position. Dismounts can occur at the end of the bars or to the side of them, and an athlete's score is determined by the skill and control he exhibits throughout.

The men-only horizontal bar throws up some of the more spectacular routines, with gymnasts executing multiple twists and flips, and eye-catching releases and dismounts. Different grips and flips are used to catch the eye of the judges.

The uneven bars are negotiated just by the women, with various spins and releases between the bars ramping up the difficulty factor. Form, technique and composition of exercises determine the medallists here.

Finally, the balance beam, as its name suggests, is a narrow beam, raised above the floor, upon which women gymnasts execute extremely difficult routines, combining acrobatics, dance elements, leaps and posing.

The huge diversity of apparatus, competitors and routines means there's never a dull moment at the Artistic Gymnastics.

DID YOU KNOW?

The pommel horse was developed to aid soldiers practising mounting and dismounting their steed. Alexander the Great is said to have had one ■ Romania's Nadia Comeneci, performing on the uneven bars, achieved the first 'Perfect 10' score in a gymnastics event, in Montreal in 1976. Scoring was made open-ended in 2006 ■ Despite breaking his kneecap during his floor routine, Shun Fujimoto went on to compete on the pommel horse and rings to help Japan win team gold at the 1976 Montreal Games

Factbox

Where: North Greenwich Arena
When: Saturday 28 July – Tuesday 7 August
Medal events: 14
Athletes: 196 (98 men, 98 women)

REASONS TO WATCH

1) IMPRESSIVE DEDICATION

The feats of human contortion, strength and flexibility are truly astounding. You will be jealous of the competitors' power and poise until you realise just how much training they have had to do to get there!

2) IMPRESSIVE VARIETY

There will constantly be something different going on in the Greenwich Arena, with each discipline offering a different array of skills, composition and execution.

3) IMPRESSIVE HISTORY

The International Federation of Gymnastics, which still governs the sport, started in Liège, Belgium, in the late 1800s.

China's 2008 gold medallist Yang Wei on the parallel bars

GYM – RHYTHMIC

Rhythmic Gymnastics is one of two women-only Olympic events (the other being synchronised swimming) and is split into two categories: the individual and team events, with two to six competitors per team.

The sport combines gymnastics, ballet, dance and apparatus use, and gymnasts have to perform a short routine, set to music, on a 13m x 13m floor area, The routines are scored by a panel of judges for leaps, pirouettes, balances, flexibility, apparatus handling, artistic effect and execution.

Scoring in Rhythmic Gymnastics used to be from nought to 10, as in artistic gymnastics but, in recent years, the sport's governing body – Fédération Internationale de Gymnastique (FIG) – changed it to a 30-point system, then a 20-point system, and, since 2008, back to a 30-point system.

The reason behind the changes is so judges can place greater emphasis on the three main areas of the sport: technical ability, artistic effect and execution. Another change the FIG have enforced is the removal of rope as an apparatus for the 2012 Games. This comes as a huge blow to the sport's fans because rope has been used to great artistic effect in previous Games and competitions.

Flexibility and a good strength-to-weight ratio are vital in Rhythmic Gymnastics, so it is more common to see young girls in this event (five of the six members of the 2008 Russian gold medal-winning team were teenagers). But the International Olympic Committee will only allow entrants who are 16 years old on 1 January 2012.

Marks are awarded for apparatus use

The 2008 individual Olympic champion Yevgeniya Kanayeva had only just turned 18 when she won gold.

Russia is the nation to beat in this sport. Apart from when the USSR boycotted the Los Angeles Games, Russia (including the USSR) has not failed to win a medal since Rhythmic Gymnastics became an Olympic event in 1984 – the same year as the boycott. However, Spain, Ukraine and Belarus are always nipping at their heels so London 2012 is set to be another competitive affair.

Rhythmic Gymnastics developed in a number of different nations – mainly Russia, Sweden and the USA – but the first official international 'rhythmic dance' competition was in Budapest in 1963, two years after the FIG recognised the sport. Russia won all three golds and seven of the nine medals at that event.

Wembley Arena, which has capacity for 6,000 spectators, will host the London 2012 Rhythmic Gymnastics. We suggest putting your money on Russia each way.

The ribbon must be exactly 7m long

DID YOU KNOW?

Only women are allowed to compete in Rhythmic Gymnastics at the Games. Synchronised Swimming is the only other female-only Olympic sport ■ The time limit for individual performances is 75 to 90 seconds and 135 to 150 seconds for team performances ■ If athletes step outside of the 13m x 13m performance area, they incur penalties from the judges. Penalties are also awarded for every second over or under the time limit they finish their routine

Russia's Yevgeniya Kanayeva won gold in Beijing in 2008

The gymnasts can use a hoop, ribbon, ball or clubs

Factbox

Where: Wembley Arena
When: Thursday 9 August - Sunday 12 August
Medal events: 2
Athletes: 96 (all women)

REASONS TO WATCH

1) SKILL AND DEXTERITY

When these gymnasts bring out the apparatus, it really is time to pay attention. The skill and dexterity on show will leave you gobsmacked.

2) INDUSTRY AND DRIVE

The sport is a mix of ballet, dance, gymnastics and apparatus use – and the competitors push themselves to the limit in each of these disciplines.

3) INEVITABLE WATERWORKS

When it comes to passion and emotion, Olympic gymnasts are unrivalled. Contrast the tears of joy and the tears of pain, and take a look at the girls' reactions to their scores to see what it means to the them.

The Ultimate Olympic A-Z

GYM – TRAMPOLINE

A relative newbie on the Olympic stage after its introduction at Sydney 2000, Trampoline has come a long way since its original use as a training tool for astronauts and acrobats.

It was invented in the 1930s by American gymnast and P.E professor George Nissen (who noted the way trapeze artists used their safety nets) and the design has, subsequently, been used all over the world – from back gardens and school gyms, all the way to the Olympic Games.

Olympic Trampoline rules state athletes must be at least 18 years old and they must perform compulsory and optional routines in the qualifying round. For the former, a prescribed set of skills must be executed in the correct order, while 10 recognised skills must be used in the course of the optional routine. The top eight gymnasts advance to the final, which is concluded with a single, optional routine.

Crucial elements, such as style, difficulty and finishing (upright on both feet), are observed by a panel of nine judges, split into three groups, awarding points for different aspects of a routine.

Some of the Trampoline elements on offer include: the wonderfully named 'Adolph', a front somersault with three and one-half twists; the 'Barani', a forward somersault with a half-twist; the 'Fliffus', a double somersault with at least a half-twist; 'Quadriffus', otherwise known as a quadruple somersault with at least a half-twist; and a 'Rudolph', (or 'Rudy'), which involves a front somersault with one-and-a-half twists.

With such an array of aerial feats, Trampoline is as impressive and physically demanding as any sport in the Games, requiring incredible strength, timing and grace from its competitors.

Style and difficulty equal good scores

Otherwise referred to as "The Russian Bouncer", male gymnast Alexander Moskalenko won gold at the inaugural Trampoline event in 2000, in Sydney, and followed that with a silver at Athens, four years later. Five world titles (1990, 1992, 1994, 1999 and 2001) have helped cement his berth as one of the symbols of the sport and his compatriots will be looking to emulate him in 2012.

The Russians do not dominate the Trampoline, though. In fact, during London 2012, the world's eyes will no doubt be focussed on the Chinese, who won gold in the men's and women's events in Beijing 2008, and who have since enjoyed a huge amount of international success.

Canada's Karen Cockburn won silver in 2004 and 2008

DID YOU KNOW?

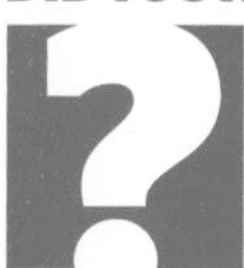

The word 'gymnastics' comes from the Greek for 'naked' – early gymnasts used to perform without any clothes on ■ The trampolines used at the London Games will be 5.05m long, 2.91m wide and 1.155m high. This leaves very little margin of error for the high-flying athletes as they attempt to use the surprisingly thin (6mm) nylon spring 'bed' to reach heights of up to 10m ■ As well as astronauts and acrobats, Trampolining was also used as a tool to help divers, gymnasts and freestyle skiers improve their acrobatic skills

Trampolinists can reach heights of 10m

OVERALL MEDAL TABLE
TOP THREE NATIONS

1. SOVIET UNION

GOLD	SILVER	BRONZE
72	67	43

2. USA

GOLD	SILVER	BRONZE
30	35	30

3. JAPAN

GOLD	SILVER	BRONZE
28	31	33

Factbox

Where: North Greenwich Arena
When: Friday 3 August - Saturday 4 August
Medal events: 2
Athletes: 32

REASONS TO WATCH

1) AUDACIOUS ACROBATICS
As close to a circus spectacle as the Olympics gets, the aerial feats of all the trampolinists have to be seen to be believed.

2) PRODIGIOUS TALENTS
Since their reinclusion in the Olympic Games, Chinese gymnasts have wowed the world with their supernatural acrobatic abilities. There will be brilliance across all the gymnastic disciplines, but especially here on the Trampoline.

3) REACHING FOR THE CEILING
There is only one gold medal available to both the women and men in Trampoline, so athletes will have one chance to shine and competition will no doubt be fierce because of it.

The Ultimate Olympic A-Z

HANDBALL

Widely considered to be a game of Danish origin (in its current format), handball is a hybrid of basketball and football in which the ball is passed and dribbled up the court, and then hurled past a keeper to score a goal. The court, measuring 40m x 20m, is the largest of any indoor ball sport at the Games and matches are played at break-neck pace, with speed, skill and stamina prerequisites for any nation's success.

Teams consist of seven players: one goalkeeper and six outfield. Typically shooters are tall and good jumpers, with a physicality similar to forwards in basketball; middle backcourt players run the show from the centre, directing attacking moves; wingers are fast and small, and shoot from various angles; and circle runners are large, aggressive types, who set up the shooters, but who can also have a go at goal themselves. No player, apart from the keeper, can enter the goal area.

Players are allowed to take three steps with the ball before they must dribble (bounce the ball) or pass, and they cannot hold the ball for more than three seconds without dribbling or passing. Such swift transfer of effort and play makes for hugely entertaining and high-scoring matches.

It is not uncommon for matches, which consist of two periods of 30 minutes, to produce more than 50 goals, the action to-ing and fro-ing as each team tries to assert their authority. Counterattacks are a common way of scoring, with fast, accurate, long-range passing and adept finishing a feature of the more successful sides.

Handball combines power and pace

Teams often score on the counterattack

Contact with an opponent is allowed if you are between them and the goal (a 'player sandwich'), but any contact from the side or from behind is considered a 'fault' and play is brought back to where the infringement occurred. Canny players commit many tactical 'faults' during a match, but anything deemed too dangerous can result in a visit to the sin-bin for a two-minute suspension.

Any foul that prevents a clear goalscoring opportunity results in a seven-metre penalty shot for the team that suffered the infringement..

A new Handball Arena has been especially constructed for the London 2012 Games, but this will not play host to the pivotal knockout matches, which will be moved the bigger Basketball Arena, also in the Olympic Park.

There are 12 teams in both the men's and women's competitions, and each event is split into two groups of six, all of whom play each other. The top four from the group stages then go through to the knock-out quarter-finals phase and compete feverishly until the gold medal match-up.

Considering its close association with the rules and physicalities of basketball, you'd think the USA would be leading medal contenders. Not so. Germany, Russia and Denmark are the leaders in worldwide handball competition. Sweden and Hungary should also give them some competition.

So there you go: Handball, one of the lesser-known sports at the Games, but one that promises to provide plenty of thrills and spills for sports enthusiasts.

DID YOU KNOW?

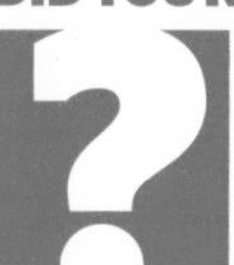

Handball is considered to be one of the oldest Olympic sports, based on a reference in Homer's *Odyssey* and a third-century bronze statuette found in Dodoni that shows a boy carrying a ball in his hand ■ The sport in its modern, indoor format first appeared in the Olympic Games in Munich, in 1972. An 11-a-side, outdoor version for men had featured in the Berlin Games of 1936, when Germany won the gold ■ The ball must be made of leather and have a circumference of 58-60cm (men) and 54-56cm (women)

The action is fast and furious, and goal tallies can be huge

OVERALL MEDAL TABLE
TOP THREE NATIONS

1. SOVIET UNION

GOLD	SILVER	BRONZE
4	1	1

2. YUGOSLAVIA

GOLD	SILVER	BRONZE
3	1	1

3. DENMARK

GOLD	SILVER	BRONZE
3	0	0

Factbox

Where: Handball Arena – Olympic Park (preliminaries, women's quarter-finals); Basketball Arena – Olympic Park (men's quarter-finals, plus all the semi-finals and finals)
When: Saturday 28 July – Sunday 12 August
Medal events: 2
Athletes: 336 (168 men, 168 women; 12 teams in each event)

REASONS TO WATCH

1) HIGH SCORING
Handball matches are played at a furious pace, and opportunities for scoring come thick and fast. So you can be sure of seeing plenty of goals.

2) ARENA ATMOSPHERE
As the tournament heads towards the knock-out phase, the atmosphere in the newly constructed Handball and basketball arenas is sure to be electric.

3) CONTINUOUS MOMENTUM
Although not officially regulated, the ball is usually resinated before games for better handling and to make spinning trick shots easier to achieve. Creating space, beating opponents and scoring from counter attacks are traits of a very watchable sport.

The Ultimate Olympic A-Z

HOCKEY

With versions of the game dating back to the Ancient Greeks, Hockey is as old an organised team sport as any that survives in modern times.

Today's game, however, has largely been shaped by 19th-century English public schools and the first British hockey club was formed in 1849, in Blackheath, south-east London, not far from where the Hockey events will take place in 2012.

It was this form of field Hockey that was introduced, for men, to the Olympic Games of 1908 – six teams entered, four from the UK and Ireland. Concerns about the lack of an international governing body led to the sport's removal from the 1924 Paris Games, but it became a fixture again four years later and has remained something of an Olympic favourite ever since.

Hockey is an intense, stamina-testing encounter, fought out over 70 minutes between two teams of 11 players, on a pitch measuring 91.4m x 55m.

Five team members are on the bench and 'rolling' substitutions can be made throughout the match.

At either end of the pitch are netted goals that stand 3.66m wide and 2.14m high, and players score by hitting, pushing, slapping or flicking the ball into this net with their hook-shaped sticks.

Another sight peculiar to Hockey is its disciplinary card system. Whereas sports such as rugby and football use two cards to keep players in check, Hockey uses three – a green card is shown for a minor offence; a yellow card requires a player to spend a minimum of five minutes in the sin-bin; and a red card means a player is permanently excluded from the game. Thankfully, this is about as complicated as it gets in Hockey.

Hockey has become an Olympic favourite

In the 40 years between 1928 and 1968, men's Olympic Hockey was so utterly dominated by India and Pakistan that no other nation won a gold medal.

However, the introduction of pitches made from Astroturf (a water-based, synthetic 'grass' that aids the ball's movement) led to a gradual decline in success for these Hockey super-nations as they failed to adapt to the new surface.

This paved the way for a number of other teams to forge a path onto the medal board, with nations such as Australia, the Netherlands and Germany excelling in recent years.

Britain memorably won the men's event in Seoul in 1988, beating Germany 3-1 in the final thanks to goals from Sean Kerly and Imran Sherwani.

In the 30 years since women's hockey was introduced to the Olympics, in Moscow in 1980, a similar picture has been painted, with Australia (three golds) and the Netherlands (two) the dominant female sides.

London 2012 will showcase Hockey across two weeks of competition, with the 12 teams in both the men's and women's events split into two pools of six, with each team playing every other in their pool. The two best teams in each pool will qualify for the semi-finals and the winners of these will face off for the gold medal.

DID YOU KNOW?

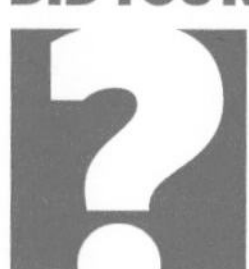

Hockey gets its name from the French word 'hocquet', which means 'shepherd's crook' ■ Olympic field hockey was first played on artificial turf at the 1976 Montreal Games, where New Zealand beat Australia 1-0 in the final to win gold ■ Goals can only be scored from inside the 'D' – a semi-circular area in front of each goal ■ There was no bronze-medal match at the 1908 London Olympics, at which Britain won gold after beating Ireland 8-1 in the final

Britain's men will be out to emulate their winning side of 1988

OVERALL MEDAL TABLE
TOP THREE NATIONS

1. INDIA

GOLD	SILVER	BRONZE
8	1	2

2. NETHERLANDS

GOLD	SILVER	BRONZE
4	4	6

3. AUSTRALIA

GOLD	SILVER	BRONZE
4	3	4

Factbox

Where: Hockey Centre
When: Sunday 29 July – Saturday 11 August
Medal events: 2
Athletes: 384 (192 men, 192 women; 12 teams in each event)

REASONS TO WATCH

1) SEEING IS BELIEVING
Many who have seen a live Hockey game claim watching it on television does not do the sport justice, with the ball often moving too fast for the cameras to pick up. The only way to really appreciate the speed and power of this exciting sport is to view it live.

2) INTENSE COMPETITION
With almost 400 athletes competing for only two medals, Hockey is one of the most fiercely contested events in the Olympic Games.

3) UNBEATABLE ATMOSPHERE
Hockey promises to be one of the most electrifying events at London 2012, with 15,000 people packed into the Hockey Centre, cheering on their teams. Just make sure you have your wits about you should a ball head your way.

The Ultimate Olympic A-Z

JUDO

Developed from an ancient Japanese art of hand-to-hand combat known as jujitsu, Judo is now one of the most popular martial arts in the world. An integral moral code that demands self-control, politeness and respect, goes some way to explaining the translation of Judo as 'the gentle way', but – with an assortment of throws and submissions that would have many a boxer wincing – this is far from a gentle sport.

Making its debut at the Olympics in Tokyo, in 1964, Judo has – bar an inexplicable omission four years later – been in every Games since. The women's event took longer to be introduced – it was a 'demonstration sport' in Los Angeles in 1984 and this paved the way for the first proper women's Judo competition at the 1992 Games, in Barcelona. Since then, seven weight classes have been introduced for both sexes, the men's ranging from 60kg to 100kg+ and the women's from 48kg to 78kg+.

The aim of Judo is for competitors to force their opponent to the floor of the eight-foot square mat (known as the 'Tatami') using regulation moves that score points.

A bout is immediately over if one of the competitors scores 'Ippon', the maximum score. This feat can be achieved in three ways; a controlled throw that lands the opponent on their back with speed and force; a mat hold of sufficient duration (25 seconds) or an opponent's submission.

If 'Ippon' is not achieved, the athlete with the greatest number of points at the end of five minutes is the winner. On occasion, an evenly scored contest will be decided by 'golden score', whereby whoever scores a point first, wins the contest.

Throws add to the drama of Judo

Unsurprisingly, the Japanese have bossed the Olympic Games medal leaderboard in the past half century, with an enviable total of 67 medals (including 35 gold), almost double that of France and South Korea, who – ahead of London 2012 – are their nearest competitors.

Despite Japan's dominance, a recent notable rise in success from Eastern European countries – not to mention the 2010 World Championships, in which a staggering 111 countries took part – means there are a fair few nations hoping to make a name for themselves on the Judo mat.

All 14 Judo events at London 2012 will use a knock-out format, with the gold and silver medals being decided in the final bouts.

The four defeated quarter-finalists in both the men's and women's events will compete in two rounds and the eventual winners of this repêchage will then battle it out with the losing semi-finalists to decide the bronze medal winners. All the action takes place at the ExCeL centre.

Despite its name, Judo is not gentle

DID YOU KNOW?

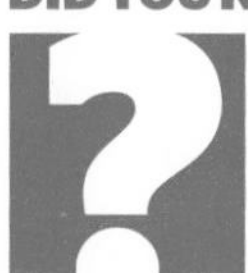

A Judo uniform is called a Judogi and a competitor is the Judoka ■ Judo rules stipulate that competitors must bow when entering and leaving the Tatami (the mat), and at the start and end of a fight ■ Judo has 13 million participants in 111 countries around the world ■ The belts in Judo are earned in the following order: white, yellow, orange, green, blue (purple), brown and black ■ The O-goshi, or the hip throw, is the first throw attempted by beginners because it is the easiest one to learn

Women's Judo made its bow at the 1992 Barcelona Games

OVERALL MEDAL TABLE
TOP THREE NATIONS

1. JAPAN

GOLD	SILVER	BRONZE
35	15	15

2. FRANCE

GOLD	SILVER	BRONZE
10	8	19

3. SOUTH KOREA

GOLD	SILVER	BRONZE
9	14	14

Factbox

Where: ExCeL
When: Saturday 28 July - Friday 3 August
Medal Events: 14
Athletes: 386

REASONS TO WATCH

1) HARD TO CALL

Few contests in the Olympics can boast competitive circumstances such as those in Judo, where a bout can be turned on its head (literally) with a single throw. You simply never know what is going to happen, making the sport a truly engaging watch.

2) RISE OF THE UNDERDOG

Japan, Russia and Cuba are historically the biggest Judo nations, but, in recent years, there has been a surge in the sport's popularity among many other, smaller countries - all of whom will be hoping to cause an upset in London.

3) CREAM OF THE CROP

The popularity of this martial art speaks for itself, with 13 million participants in 111 countries - but only an elite 386 will be battling it out for an Olympic gold medal, so London 2012 really will be simply the best.

MODERN PENTATHLON

If sports in the Olympic Games were films, Modern Pentathlon would be something of a *Gladiator*. It simply has everything, including a legendary back story that tells of a young French cavalry officer – sent on horseback to deliver a message – having to ride, fence, shoot, run and swim to complete his task. It has all the makings of a classic.

Included in the 1912 Stockholm Games after much championing by Modern Olympics founder Baron Pierre de Coubertin, the sport is a contemporary twist on the classic pentathlon of ancient times, which consisted of discus, javelin, running, jumping and wrestling.

Today, the competition is conducted over one day and fencing is the first discipline, with all the athletes competing against one another in a round-robin format. This is followed by a 200m freestyle swim and then a challenging horse-riding event over a 12-jump course.

The athletes' scores after three events are used to establish a time handicap for the (newly) combined running and shooting event, in which competitors have to shoot at sets of five targets after exhausting runs across several 1000m routes. The winner is the person who crosses the finish line first.

De Coubertin envisioned that the Modern Pentathlon should 'test a man's moral qualities as much as his physical resources and skills, thereby, producing the ideal, complete athlete'. Indeed, such are the rigours of this Olympic event, that certain European military academies have adopted the Modern Pentathlon as part of their final examination for soldiers.

The Modern Pentathlon has been a permanent fixture at the Olympic Games since 1912; a team event was even added 40 years later, but was discontinued in 1992.

Originally a four-day exhibition, it was condensed into a one-day extravaganza at Atlanta, in 1996, and the Games in Sydney at the turn of the millennium finally allowed for a women's competition.

Initially dominated by those thoroughbred athletes from Sweden, Hungary and countries from the former Soviet Union have staked their claims in the contest in recent years.

Hopes are high for Britain's women after a particularly successful first run out at the Games in 2000, when Stephanie Cook won gold – and there was a silver medal for Heather Fell in Beijing in 2008.

The 2012 competition will be held across three London venues, with fencing at the Handball Arena; swimming in the Aquatics Centre; and the riding and combined running/shooting in Greenwich Park.

Modern Pentathletes have to have a steady hand for shooting...

The event celebrates 100 years as part of the Olympics at London 2012

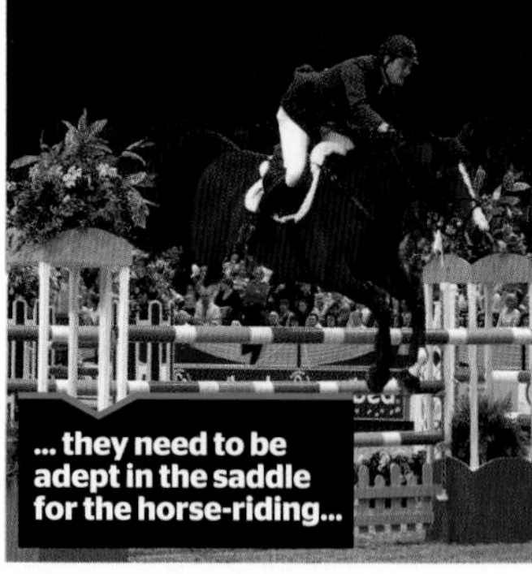
... they need to be adept in the saddle for the horse-riding...

... they must have the stamina to run several kilometres...

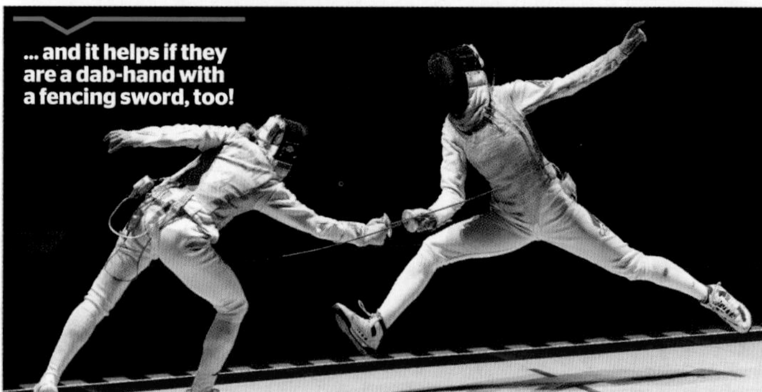
... and it helps if they are a dab-hand with a fencing sword, too!

DID YOU KNOW?

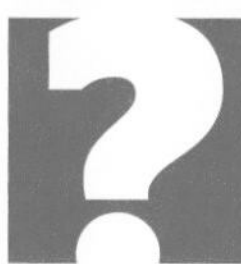

The Pentathlon was first competed for at the 18th Olympiad in 708BC, with the winner crowned *Victor Ludorum*, which is Latin for 'the winner of the games' ■ The oldest Olympic gold medallist to date in the Modern Pentathlon is Russia's Pavel Lednev, who was 37 when he triumphed in the team event at the 1980 Games in Moscow ■ The name of the sport derives from the Greek words *pente*, meaning 'five', and *athlon* meaning 'contest'

Modern Pentathlon requires skill and courage in athletes

OVERALL MEDAL TABLE
TOP THREE NATIONS

1. HUNGARY

GOLD	SILVER	BRONZE
9	8	4

2. SWEDEN

GOLD	SILVER	BRONZE
9	7	5

3. SOVIET UNION

GOLD	SILVER	BRONZE
5	5	5

Factbox

Where: Handball Arena (fencing) & Aquatics Centre, (swimming) - both at the Olympic Park; Greenwich Park (riding, combined event)
When: Saturday 11 August - Sunday 12 August
Medal Events: 2
Athletes: 72 (36 men, 36 women)

REASONS TO WATCH

1) DIVERSITY RULES
This is your opportunity to watch five separate events in one day across newly built Olympic centres and parks.

2) HOME NATION GLORY?
Britain's women have won four (one gold, one silver, two bronze) of the nine Olympic medals available at the Games in which they have been allowed to compete.

3) SENSE OF INCLUSION
Modern Pentathlon is one of the few events at London 2012 in which spectators see the start and finish of a whole contest - no heats, no semis, just straight into the action!

The Ultimate Olympic A-Z

ROWING

Originally on the programme for the 1896 Olympic Games, bad weather dictated that Rowing made its maiden splash four years later, in Paris. It has been in every Games since.

Interest in the sport was stoked after Oxford and Cambridge began their annual university Boat Race on the River Thames in 1829 – a race that is still contested today.

For a long time, only men were allowed to compete in Olympic Rowing, but women finally got their chance when events were introduced for them at the Montreal Games in 1976. A more recent addition, in 1996, has been lightweight rowing, for which there are weight limits for crews.

At London 2012, a whopping 14 Rowing events – eight for the men and six for the women – will be contested at Eton Dorney, from single, double and quad sculls to coxless pairs and fours.

Those not up on their nautical jargon will do well do familiarise themselves with the following terms – a scull is a type of boat and the coxswain, or 'cox', is the individual who sits at the stern of the boat and is responsible for steering it and directing the crew.

Before the 1912 Stockholm Olympics, races varied in length depending on the location of the Games, but now a standard is set – every race, whether for men or women, is contested over a gruelling 2,000m.

Britain was the leading nation at the Beijing Games, with six medals overall, their best performance for 100 years, and their achievements in this watery event have been impressive, none more so than Sir Steven Redgrave's. He made history in Sydney by winning an unprecedented fifth consecutive Olympic gold medal (1984-2000).

Britain's women won their first ever Olympic medal (in the coxless fours) at the 2000 Games, and added five more to that tally in Athens and Beijing.

But at London 2012 they will face strong competition in the form of the Americans and Germans, both of whom have impressive medal counts from their Olympic campaigns to date.

The format for Rowing at the London Games is simple enough, beginning with heats from which the best boats qualify for the next round – and so on until the finals.

Those that fail to do this get a shot at redemption through the repêchage round. Everyone will want to get through first time, though.

Watch out for the USA and German teams

DID YOU KNOW?

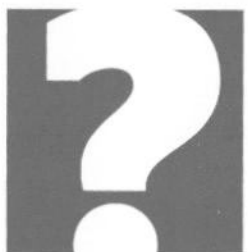

Rowing is the only sport in which competitors cross the finish line backwards ■ The youngest Olympic champion is thought to be an anonymous French boy, who coxed for a Dutch pair at the 1900 Paris Games. The boy, aged no more than 12, took part in the victory ceremony, but then disappeared ■ Baron Pierre de Coubertin, the founder of the Modern Olympics, was a competitive rower, as was famous child development expert Dr Benjamin Spock, who won Olympic gold in the men's eight at the 1924 Paris Games

The only sport in which athletes cross the line backwards

OVERALL MEDAL TABLE
TOP THREE NATIONS

1. EAST GERMANY

GOLD	SILVER	BRONZE
33	7	8

2. USA

GOLD	SILVER	BRONZE
31	31	22

3. GBR

GOLD	SILVER	BRONZE
24	20	10

Factbox

Where: Eton Dorney
When: Saturday 28 July – Sunday 4 August
Medal events: 14
Athletes: 550 (353 men, 197 women)

REASONS TO WATCH

1) THE BRITISH ARE COMING!
With 54 medals, including 33 golds, and fantastic performances over the past decade, hopes are high that the host nation will come away with some of the spoils.

2) GENUINE THRILLS
Rowing has long been one of the most exciting events at the Games – especially recent coxless fours battles.

3) RIVERSIDE ATMOSPHERE
Much as they do for the Boat Race on the River Thames, tremendously vocal crowds will gather along the waterside at Eton Dorney. Long drinks and big picnics will no doubt be the order of the day!

The Ultimate Olympic A-Z

SAILING

Beautiful Weymouth Bay is the setting for the London 2012 Sailing, in which 380 athletes will vie for 10 medals over 14 days of competition in the challenging waters of the English Channel.

Sailing races fall into two categories: match racing (between two boats) and fleet racing (mass start). In match racing, a crew only needs to beat whoever they are racing against, so strategy plays a more significant part in determining who wins. Sailors usually adopt two main tactics in match racing – 'tight coverage' and 'drawing a foul'.

Tight coverage comes into play when the lead boat wants to prevent his/her opponent from overtaking – they position their boat close to their rival's to prevent the wind reaching their sails. Essentially, they are hogging the wind and maintaining the lead.

The second tactic you will see in match racing is when the lead boat deliberately tries to draw a foul from the other boat.

The lead boat intentionally takes a bad line to force the opponent to take an even worse line (and ultimately slow them down) and, if the trailing boat fails to do so, it will receive a time penalty for their foul.

Competitors race each other in a round-robin tournament, with only the top-ranking boats making it through to the knock-out stages. Match racing is usually great to watch because its cat and mouse nature means the sailors are constantly flinging themselves around their boat to get the maximum out of it.

Fleet racing is a lot less tactical and, generally, is all down to finding the quickest route around the course while catching the strongest winds. This is particularly crucial when turning round a buoy because catching the wind before your opponent can make or break a race.

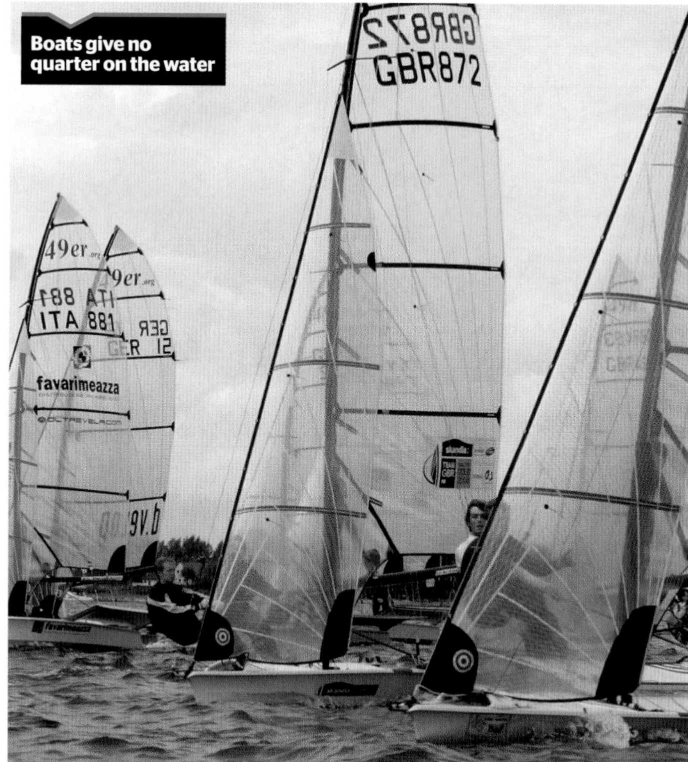

Boats give no quarter on the water

The scoring format for fleet racing is pretty complex: there are 10 races in each discipline (15 for the men's 49er) and points are awarded according to where a crew finishes in the race, with first place getting one point, second place two and so on.

The 10 boats with the lowest points total are then entered into the final (medal) race, in which the points scored are doubled. This tally is then added to a boat's existing score and the medals are determined by the combined total.

Historically, Britannia rules the waves at the Olympics, with a total of 24 gold medals – and three-time champion Ben Ainslie will become the most successful Olympic Sailor ever if he wins another gold at London 2012, his fifth consecutive Games.

Crew members rarely speak during a race

DID YOU KNOW?

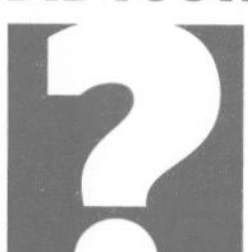

Britain were the most successful Sailing nation at the 2000, 2004 and 2008 Games ■ The sport's name was changed from 'yachting' to Sailing at Sydney 2000 ■ Denmark's Paul Elvstrøm, who won four gold medals in an Olympic career stretching from London 1948 to Seoul 1988, sailed with his daughter Trine at his last two Games – the only time a father and daughter have competed together at the Games ■ Ben Ainslie, of Great Britain, will surpass Elvstrøm as the most successful Olympic Sailor if he wins gold in 2012

They'll be no British manners assumed in Weymouth 2012

Catching the wind before your rivals is key to Sailing success

OVERALL MEDAL TABLE
TOP THREE NATIONS

1. GBR

GOLD	SILVER	BRONZE
24	14	11

2. USA

GOLD	SILVER	BRONZE
19	23	17

3. NORWAY

GOLD	SILVER	BRONZE
17	11	3

Factbox

Venue: Weymouth and Portland
Dates: Sunday 29 July - Saturday 11 August
Medal events: 10
Athletes: 380 (237 men, 143 women)

REASONS TO WATCH

1) SHREWD TACTICS
Match Sailing is extremely tactical, from start to finish. Watch how crews are constantly checking where their rivals are throughout a race.

2) READING THE WEATHER
Predicting and reacting to the weather is key in Sailing - so the English Channel, as good a place as any for strong winds and choppy seas, should keep competitors on their toes!

3) PSYCHIC SAILING
In the two- and three-man boats, sailors are so in tune with one another that hardly a word is spoken during a race.

SHOOTING

As one of the nine events staged at the very first Modern Olympic Games, in 1896, Shooting is as old as any of the disciplines you will see at London 2012.

The sport has come a long way from the antiquated period when real pigeons were used as targets (as in Paris in 1900) and its development has been helped by standardisation brought in by the International Shooting Sport Federation at the beginning of the 20th century.

Re-introduced to the Olympic Games in Los Angeles, in 1932, when it comprised only two events, Shooting has gone from strength to strength and, as a result, spectators at London 2012 can look forward to 15 events.

The three disciplines - pistol, rifle and shotgun - are split into five events, three for men and two for women, who were first allowed to compete at the 1968 Games in Mexico City. They competed alongside men in several events for a number of years and it was not until Atlanta 1996 that it was decided the sexes should be completely separated.

While undoubtedly a stern test of mental strength, all three Shooting disciplines ask different physical questions. The pistol requires just one hand, shotgun is performed standing up and rifle competitors can stand, kneel or adopt a prone position (lying on the floor) to shoot.

In the rifle and pistol classes, the competitors fire at a 10-ring target in an allocated time, from a distance of 10, 25 or 50 metres - the winner is the one who chalks up the highest score.

The shotgun category is made up of 'trap' and 'skeet', which are defined by the distinct ways in which the moving clay targets that the athletes fire at are expelled from their devices. A hit is awarded if a piece visibly falls from any of these targets and the shooter with the most hits wins.

A glance at the Olympic medal table over the years paints a telling picture. The Americans, having enjoyed long spells in the ascendancy, boast a hugely impressive 103 medals, 50 of them gold.

Arguably, their nearest competition at the London 2012 Games will come from the Chinese - and though they are some way off the USA's impressive number of medals, China will be bolstered by a fantastic outing at the 2008 Beijing Games, at which they won five golds.

In London, the five pistol, rifle and shotgun events will consist of just two rounds - qualification and finals. The scores from each round will be totalled up and medals awarded to the marksmen with the highest scores.

Shotgun is made up of 'skeet' and 'trap'

DID YOU KNOW?

Britain's shooters have to train abroad because of a ban on handguns in the UK, brought in after the Dunblane shooting in 1996 ■ Clay targets are made of pitch and chalk, not clay ■ Around 275,000 clay targets will be used for the shotgun competition at London 2012 ■ China's Zhang Shan became the first woman to win gold in a mixed-gender Shooting event at Barcelona 1992. After these Games, the sport's governing body stopped men and women competing against each other

More than 100 nations entered the Shooting in 2008

OVERALL MEDAL TABLE
TOP THREE NATIONS

1. USA

GOLD	SILVER	BRONZE
50	29	24

2. CHINA

GOLD	SILVER	BRONZE
19	11	12

3. SOVIET UNION

GOLD	SILVER	BRONZE
17	15	17

Factbox

Where: The Royal Artillery Barracks
When: Saturday 28 July – Monday 6 August
Medal events: 15
Athletes: 390

REASONS TO WATCH

1) UNIVERSAL APPEAL

Shooting is watched and participated in all over the world and more than 100 countries entered the last Olympic competition. This number is set to increase at the London Games.

2) HISTORIC LOCATION

The Royal Artillery Barracks affords spectators the unique chance to watch an Olympic event at a venue built between 1775 and 1802.

3) LATEST TECHNOLOGY

Shooting events at recent Olympic Games have borne witness to some truly remarkable firearm technology, and London 2012 promises even more revolutionary weapon designs.

The Ultimate Olympic A-Z

SWIMMING

Since people could swim, they have swum for sport. Records go back to Ancient Greek times and Swimming as an Olympic event has existed since the first Modern Games in Athens, in 1896, with women allowed to take part since 1912.

Alongside gymnastics and track & field, Swimming is one of the oldest and most popular competitions of the summer Olympics, and also one with the largest number of events and, therefore, medals.

There are four recognised Olympic strokes - freestyle, butterfly, breaststroke and backstroke - and there are an equal number of events for men and women. Deep breath, then: we have 50m, 100m, 200m and 400m freestyle; 100m and 200m backstroke; 100m and 200m breaststroke; 100m and 200m butterfly; 200m and 400m individual medley; 4x100m and 4x200m freestyle relay; 4x100m medley relay; and the 10km marathon. The men also do the 1500m freestyle and the women the 800m freestyle.

Lots of events, then, and plenty of opportunity for big medal hauls, as Mark Spitz proved by winning seven golds at the 1972 Munich Olympic Games - an achievement surpassed by his compatriot Michael Phelps, who won eight at Beijing 2008.

The first Olympic Swimming events were held in outdoor pools (in a filthy River Seine in 1900) and at London 1908 the pool was in the centre of White City stadium, in the middle of the track & field area.

In 1924, in Paris, the now standard 50m pool made its first appearance and starting blocks made their debut at the Berlin Olympic Games of 1936.

Competitors wore full-body swimsuits until they realised the drag they caused and the flip-turn was devised in the 1950s to quicken times further. In recent decades, sports science has advanced training techniques even further and more records have tumbled.

Freakishly talented Michael Phelps

Once again, Michael Phelps - the world's fastest man in water, dubbed 'The Baltimore Bullet' - will be the centre of attention at London 2012, although he has said he may try some different events and certainly won't be doing as many as he did in Beijing in 2008. But it is likely this will be his last Olympic Games and he will surely want to go out with a bang.

Every Modern Games has staged swimming

DID YOU KNOW?

Michael Phelps' unusual physique has been analysed and admired since his eight-medal haul in Beijing in 2008. He has a bigger arm span (6ft 7in) than body height (6ft 4in), size 14 feet and ankles that can extend beyond the pointe of a ballet dancer ■ There are 180,000 tiles lining the Aquatics Centre pool in London's Olympic Park ■ Until 1956, the butterfly stroke was allowed in the breaststroke races ■ Johnny Weissmuller, who played Tarzan in 12 films, won five freestyle gold medals for the USA in 1924 and 1928, and was the first man to swim 100m in less than a minute

Rebecca Adlington of Great Britain won two golds in Beijing

OVERALL MEDAL TABLE
TOP THREE NATIONS

1. USA

GOLD	SILVER	BRONZE
214	155	120

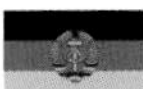

2. AUSTRALIA

GOLD	SILVER	BRONZE
56	54	58

3. EAST GERMANY

GOLD	SILVER	BRONZE
38	32	22

Factbox

Where: Aquatics Centre – Olympic Park (pool events); Hyde Park (Marathon Swimming, 10km)
When: Saturday 28 July – Saturday 4 August (Aquatics Centre); Thursday 9 – Friday 10 August (Hyde Park)
Medal events: 34
Athletes: 950

REASONS TO WATCH

1) MEDAL HAUL

Mark Spitz and Michael Phelps have broken many records in Olympic pools and we could see the birth of a new star at London 2012. As Phelps says: "Records are made to be broken no matter what they are... Anybody can do anything they set their mind to."

2) GOOD RACING

Human beings like nothing better than a good race and there'll be plenty of great head-to-head battles in the London Olympic pool.

3) MICHAEL PHELPS

Yes, we're going to mention him again, but he deserves it. The 'Baltimore Bullet' truly is a wonderfully gifted sportsman – freakishly built and freakishly talented. If you get a chance to see him in action, even if it's on the telly, you should not pass it up!

SYNCHRONISED SWIMMING

Initially referred to as 'Water Ballet', Synchronised Swimming was introduced at the London Olympics in 1948, but was not given competitive status until the 1984 Games in Los Angeles.

This women-only event was made popular in the early 20th century, when Australian swimmer Annette Kellerman toured the United States exhibiting water acrobatics. Similar forms of the sport made the spotlight a few decades later, when American film star Esther Williams performed in Hollywood 'aqua musicals'. (Williams harboured a desire to compete in the 1940 Olympic Games, but their cancellation because of World War II meant this never came to fruition.)

Up until 1996, athletes competed in duet and solo categories, but this changed to duet and team events at the Atlanta Games.

The eggbeater move in evidence

Before a 10-strong judging panel, pairs or teams of eight swimmers perform short routines to a musical accompaniment, aided by underwater speakers. The judges are separated into two groups – one awards points for technical merit, the other for artistry. Contestants are assessed on a number of things, including execution, choreography and the difficulty of their routine.

Despite being easy to watch and fantastically graceful, Synchronised Swimming is a tough, technically challenging sport that demands incredible levels of endurance. As well as being a stern test of strength and flexibility, it requires impressive displays of breath control because swimmers are often submerged for 60 seconds at a time.

Traditionally, the USA, Canada and Japan have been the strongest nations in the sport – winning every medal available from 1984 to 1996. Recently, though, it is Russia that has dominated, with its swimmers claiming every gold medal in the past three Olympic Games.

The London 2012 Synchronised Swimming will take place in the new Aquatic Centre in the Olympic Park and the duet and team events will comprise two routines – technical and freestyle.

For the technical routine, swimmers must execute specific moves in a regimented order, with routines lasting no longer than two minutes and 20 seconds in the duet event and three minutes in the team event.

For the freestyle routine, competitors perform their own material and there is a time limit of two minutes 50 seconds in the duet event and four minutes in the team event.

Holding your breath is a key skill to master

DID YOU KNOW?

Synchronised swimmers can wear nose clips, but not goggles ■ The temperature of the water must be 27°C, plus or minus one degree ■ Competitors constantly use a movement known as the 'eggbeater' – the rotation of the legs in opposite directions – to stay on the water's surface and allow them to perform arm sequences at decent heights ■ Despite being women-only now, men performed water gymnastics in flooded amphitheatres in Roman and ancient Greek times and, in the late 19th century, most synchronised swimmers were male

Heavy-duty make-up and glittery outfits add to the spectacle

OVERALL MEDAL TABLE
TOP THREE NATIONS

1. RUSSIA

GOLD	SILVER	BRONZE
6	0	0

2. USA

GOLD	SILVER	BRONZE
5	2	2

3. CANADA

GOLD	SILVER	BRONZE
3	4	1

Factbox

Where: Aquatics Centre – Olympic Park
When: Sunday 5 August – Friday 10 August
Medal events: 2
Athletes: 104 (all women)

REASONS TO WATCH

1) AN EVENT LIKE NO OTHER
As much dance as sport, performing arts aficionados will find this a true spectacle. A fantastic happy medium to take a less-than-enthused-about-sport spouse to.

2) NO BOYS ALLOWED
One of only two Olympic events (the other being rhythmic gymnastics) that limits entry to women, it avoids the potential overshadowing from men occasionally seen in mixed events.

3) COSTUMED THEATRICALITY
All of the swimmers don heavy, water-resistant make-up, giving them a strikingly glamorous appearance – even when they are submerged in the water.

The Ultimate Olympic A-Z

TABLE TENNIS

Ask a friend what the biggest participation sport in the world is and they'll probably say football, which is a reasonable response considering the number of countries in which it is played.

But the popularity of Table Tennis in China (which accounts for nearly 20% of the world's population) must put the sport right up there on the most-played list.

Table Tennis is one Olympic event that the Chinese utterly dominate and they are expected to do the same at London 2012. Since the Seoul Games in 1988, when the sport was introduced to the Olympic programme, China has won 41 medals in 24 events, including 20 golds.

But the sport wasn't born in China – it was first played by posh English families in the late 1900s. A table was cleared and books lined up across its middle as a 'net'. Books were also used as bats and a golf ball was batted between players. Later, cigar-box lids became the paddles and the balls were made of champagne corks.

From these sedate beginnings, Table Tennis has gone on to become one of the fastest spectator sports on the planet.

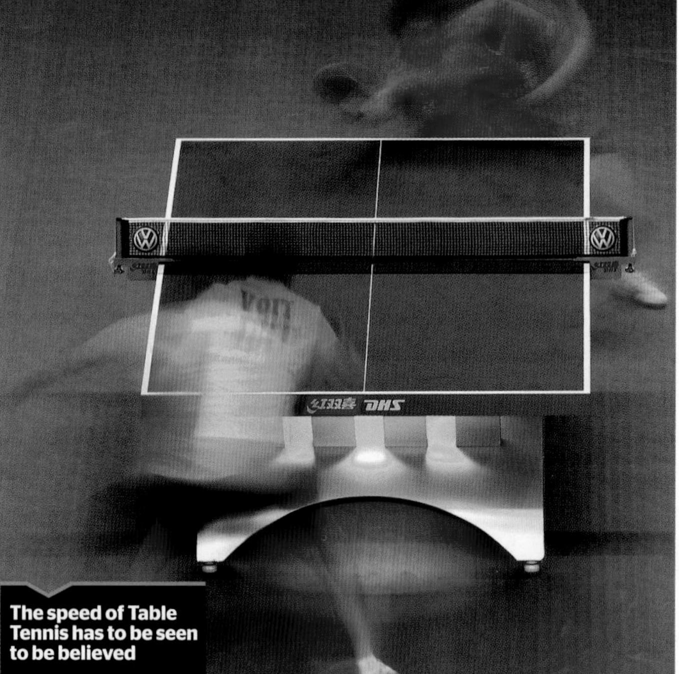

The speed of Table Tennis has to be seen to be believed

The table is 2.74m long and 1.525m wide, with a dividing net. Players can only let the ball bounce once on their side of the net and they score a point if their opponent fails to return it within the rules.

Table Tennis demands lightning movement and reactions from the players, who manipulate the ball using a lot of power and spin to limit their opponent's opportunities to attack.

As in tennis, the serve is all-important. The server throws the ball up, striking it on its descent so it hits his/her side of the court, clears the net and touches the other side of the table. The rally can then begin. The serve key is because it's by far the easiest time in a point for a player to manipulate the speed and spin of the ball.

The serve alternates every two points, regardless of who wins the point, throughout the match. The first serve of the match is usually decided by the toss of a coin.

From 1988 until 2004, Olympic Table Tennis consisted of men's and women's singles and doubles. But at Beijing 2008, the format was changed and the doubles events replaced by team competitions.

At the London 2012 Games, all of the matches will be held in the superb ExCeL arena.

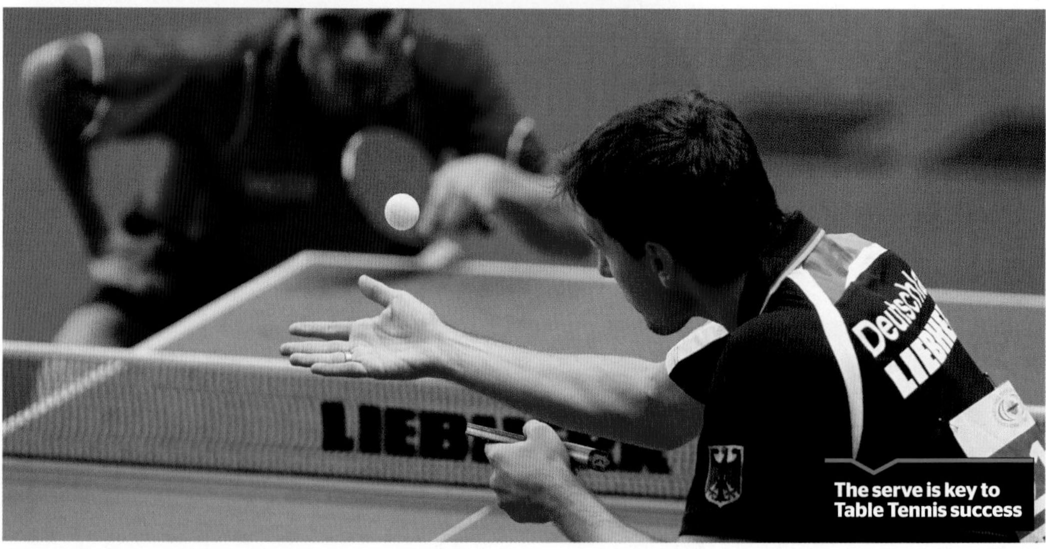

The serve is key to Table Tennis success

DID YOU KNOW?

The Table Tennis ball can travel at nearly 100mph during exchanges ■ Nicknames for the game include 'Whiff Whaff', 'Ping Pong' and 'Flim Flam', which represent the noises a ball makes when it is struck or hits the table ■ There are two grips in Table Tennis – penhold (when the fingers are positioned around the bat as if holding a pen) and shakehold (positioned as if shaking someone's hand) ■ Table Tennis was banned in the Soviet Union from 1930 to 1950 because they believed it was harmful to the eyes

Players make some incredible returns

OVERALL MEDAL TABLE
TOP THREE NATIONS

1. CHINA

GOLD	SILVER	BRONZE
20	13	8

2. SOUTH KOREA

GOLD	SILVER	BRONZE
3	2	12

3. SWEDEN

GOLD	SILVER	BRONZE
1	1	1

Factbox

Where: ExCeL
When: Saturday 28 July - Wednesday 8 August
Medal events: 4
Athletes: 172 (86 men, 86 women)

REASONS TO WATCH

1) LIGHTNING SPEED
Nothing will move quicker at the London Games than the ping-pong ball - not even Usain Bolt. You simply have to admire the quick thinking and amazing dexterity of the players.

2) CRAZY FANS
There will be a lot of Chinese fans in the ExCeL arena and they can be very vocal when it comes to Table Tennis. Sit back and drink in the atmosphere.

3) EVEN CRAZIER RALLIES
Just when you think it's impossible to get the ball back in to play, the world's top players will astound you - again and again - by managing to play a return.

The Ultimate Olympic A-Z

TAEKWONDO

Touted as the world's most popular martial art in terms of the number of practitioners (60 million people in 190 countries), Taekwondo can be roughly translated as 'the art of foot and fist', which stands to reason as powerful punches and kicks earn points in this sport.

It emerged in the South Korean military in the 1950s and 1960s, and evolved to cater for speed and competition, the elements of the martial art that have been adopted by the International Olympic Committee.

A demonstration sport at the 1988 Seoul and 1992 Barcelona Games, Taekwondo was initiated into the Olympics proper at Sydney 2000.

In 2012, there will be a single elimination tournament for each of the weight categories: men – flyweight (under 58kg), lightweight (58-68kg) middleweight (68-80kg) and heavyweight (+80kg); women – flyweight (under 49kg), lightweight (49-57kg), middleweight (57-67kg) and heavyweight (+67kg).

Men fight three rounds of three minutes, with one-minute breaks, and women contest three two-minute rounds with the same downtime.

There are 16 competitors in each discipline, who will fight in a knock-out format, the winner of each contest progressing to the next round, with the gold medal being fought for by the last two competitors. The bronze medal is decided by repêchage. In Olympic Taekwondo, all competitors who lose to one of the finalists go into the repêchage, thus ensuring they are not unduly penalised by the luck of the draw. Repêchage finalists at 2012 will each receive a bronze medal.

A spinning kick to the head is four points

Turning your back incurs a penalty

Taekwondo is known for its emphasis on kicking techniques – the rationale being that the leg is the longest and most powerful limb a human possesses, so you can strike hard, but retain distance, thus limiting the chances of retaliation.

Contests are played out on a court measuring 8m x 8m and are won by knocking down your opponent for 10 seconds or by scoring points in various zones.

One point is awarded for a valid kick or punch to the torso, two for a valid spinning kick and four for a turning kick to the head.

Hits below the waist are forbidden and strikes must be made with the foot below the ankle or by the knuckles of the index or middle fingers.

Contestants are penalised for deliberately attacking an opponent's back, attacking an opponent's face with their hands or attempting a throw. They also get punished for holding, pushing, grabbing, turning their back or feigning injury.

Coloured body padding is worn over the traditional uniform – known as a 'dobok' – to shield the competitor and to help spectators identify them more easily. The contestant wearing blue is referred to as 'chung', while the competitor in red is 'hong'.

Although there are four weight categories for each sex, each country's entry is limited to two men and two women, even the host nation.

Whatever category of Taekwondo you are watching, though, the mixture of spins, punches and powerful kicks – and an array of different attacking styles – guarantees four days of engaging combat in the ExCeL centre.

DID YOU KNOW?

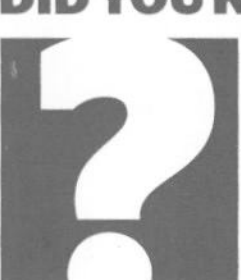

Tae means 'to kick or smash with the foot', kwon means 'to destroy with the fist' and do means 'the art or way of' ■ It generally takes three years to reach black belt status in Taekwondo, though different federations have different criteria to achieve 'dan' rank ■ Punches are used in Taekwondo but, historically, the Koreans thought hands too valuable to be used in combat, hence the larger reliance on kicking ■ Britain's first Olympic Taekwondo medal was a bronze for Sarah Stevenson (+67kg) in Beijing

Great Britain's Sarah Stevenson on her way to bronze in Beijing

OVERALL MEDAL TABLE
TOP THREE NATIONS

 **1. SOUTH KOREA**

GOLD	SILVER	BRONZE
9	1	2

2. CHINA

GOLD	SILVER	BRONZE
4	0	1

 **3. USA**

GOLD	SILVER	BRONZE
2	2	2

Factbox

Where: ExCeL
When: Wednesday 8 August - Saturday 11 August
Medal events: 8
Athletes: 128 (64 men, 64 women)

REASONS TO WATCH

1) ONE-TO-ONE COMBAT
With more ways to attack than either boxing or wrestling, Taekwondo offers an excellent alternative for fans of combat sports.

2) POWERFUL ATHLETICISM
Though at times appearing messy, the combat is undeniably impressive, with quick spinning and scissor kicks demonstrating the power, speed and flexibility of the athletes.

3) KNOCK-OUT FORMAT
There will be some big match-ups early on in each weight discipline at London 2012, so all the athletes must be switched on and ready at all times.

The Ultimate Olympic A-Z

TENNIS

Tennis at the 2012 London Games will be an odd event, taking place, as it does, just 20 days after the Wimbledon Grand Slam tournament finishes. And where is the Olympic competition being held? That's right, Wimbledon!

Athletes have been known to pull out of Games to prepare for the next major – the US Open – but don't underestimate the allure of an Olympic gold to the majority of big names in the sport. This is a competition they want to win and most, if not all, of the stars will be there.

There are five medals on offer: men's singles and doubles, women's singles and doubles, and mixed doubles.

Olympic Tennis is played in traditional knock-out format and all of the matches (for men and women) are best of three sets, except the men's final, which is a five-set game.

The one other adjustment to the rules of the majors is that tie-breaks are played on a first-to-10 points basis if one is needed in the deciding set.

Tennis was dropped from the Olympic programme after the 1924 Paris Games because of a dispute between players and the International Olympic Committee about the refusal to allow professional players to compete.

The sport was absent from the Games for 64 years until it was reinstated, with the inclusion of professional players, in Seoul in 1988.

The sport's leading Olympic medal winners, Great Britain – 44 in total, including 16 golds – have had a rough time of it since the reinstatement of Tennis to the Games, only picking up one silver medal when Tim Henman and Neil Broad finished as runners-up in the men's doubles in 1996.

Roger Federer is after singles gold

The USA have been the Olympic Tennis superpower in recent years, collecting 10 golds and 17 medals in total since 1988. However, don't be surprised if they fail to win a single medal at London 2012 because the Americans have struggled in recent grand slam events as European players have risen to dominance in both the men's and women's games.

Living legend Roger Federer has won every major Tennis event during his career – including Olympic men's doubles gold with fellow Swiss Stanislas Wawrinka at Beijing 2008 – and he has his sights on completing the set in 2012 by adding the men's singles title to his already crowded trophy cabinet.

Venus Williams has three gold medals

DID YOU KNOW?

Britain's Reginald Doherty, with three golds (Paris 1900 and London 1908) and one bronze, is the leading Tennis medal winner. Venus Williams, of the USA, can beat the record if she wins silver or better at London 2012 ■ The last time the Olympic Tennis was hosted at Wimbledon was in 1908. Britain won all of the six gold medals on offer ■ While on a trip to Athens in 1896, John Boland became the first Olympic tennis champion after a friend on the organising committee entered him in the competition

OVERALL MEDAL TABLE
TOP THREE NATIONS

1. USA

GOLD	SILVER	BRONZE
17	6	11

2. GBR

GOLD	SILVER	BRONZE
16	14	14

3. FRANCE

GOLD	SILVER	BRONZE
5	7	7

Factbox

Where: Wimbledon
When: Saturday 28 July – Sunday 5 August
Medal events: 5
Athletes: 172 (86 men, 86 women)

REASONS TO WATCH

1) GRASSED UP
Even the greatest players in the world normally only get to play the lush green courts of Wimbledon once per year, so to appear twice in such short succession is very special. It also means they will be even more accustomed to the surface's dynamics for the Olympic match-ups, giving games an even tighter edge.

2) SECOND OPPORTUNITY
If a big name gets knocked out early in Wimbledon, expect them to be double-fired up when it comes to the Olympic tournament. Andy Murray, we're looking at you!

3) IT'S AT WIMBLEDON!
Come on, it's the greatest tennis venue in the world. Oozing heritage and tradition, you know the opulent courts of SW19 will add something very special to the Olympic Games of 2012.

Spain's Rafael Nadal won the men's singles in Beijing

The Ultimate Olympic A-Z

TRIATHLON

No one seems to be able to confirm the origins of Triathlon – some say it started in France between the World Wars, some say in America in the 1970s. But what we do know is that, after two hours of competition, everyone ends up exhausted. Even the crowd!

Triathlon amalgamates three very distinct, stamina-based disciplines: swimming, cycling and running. The competitors begin with a 1500m open-water swim, then cycle for 40km and conclude with a 10km run. Olympic athletes can do all of this – plus two tricky 'transitions' in less than two hours.

Transitions are how the sport refers to the period between disciplines; the time taken to change from swimming gear into cycling gear and from cycling gear into road-running gear is included in a competitor's overall time.

There is a specified 'transition area' in which they complete their changes and if any rules are broken, or infringements made, they have to serve a time penalty on the cycling stage or the run.

An open-water swim is the first challenge for triathletes

Conservation of energy and muscle strength is key to success in the Triathlon. On the swimming leg, many competitors save their leg muscles by working more vigorously with their arms – or by swimming in another competitor's slipstream. Different strokes are also used to maximise muscle groups.

During the cycling leg, competitors must wear headgear and something to cover their torsos, and their bikes are optimised for aerodynamics.

Unsurprisingly, by the time the running begins, an athlete's muscles are very tired and newbies to the sport often report astonishing muscle weakness in their first few Triathlons. They usually train in back-to-back disciplines (i.e. cycling to running) to alleviate such marked energy drops.

There are no heats in Olympic Triathlon, just one race for men and one for women that settle the medals. More than 50 athletes will vie for the podium in each event and entries are based on world rankings, although no country is allowed to have more than three competitors.

The first Olympic Triathlon took place in 2000 and half-a-million people lined the streets of Sydney to watch its conclusion. Similar crowds will be expected in London, where the race begins and ends in Hyde Park, taking in the Serpentine and Buckingham Palace en route.

As one of the biggest 'take-up' sports in the world, Triathlon is likely to prove a popular and entertaining spectacle in 2012.

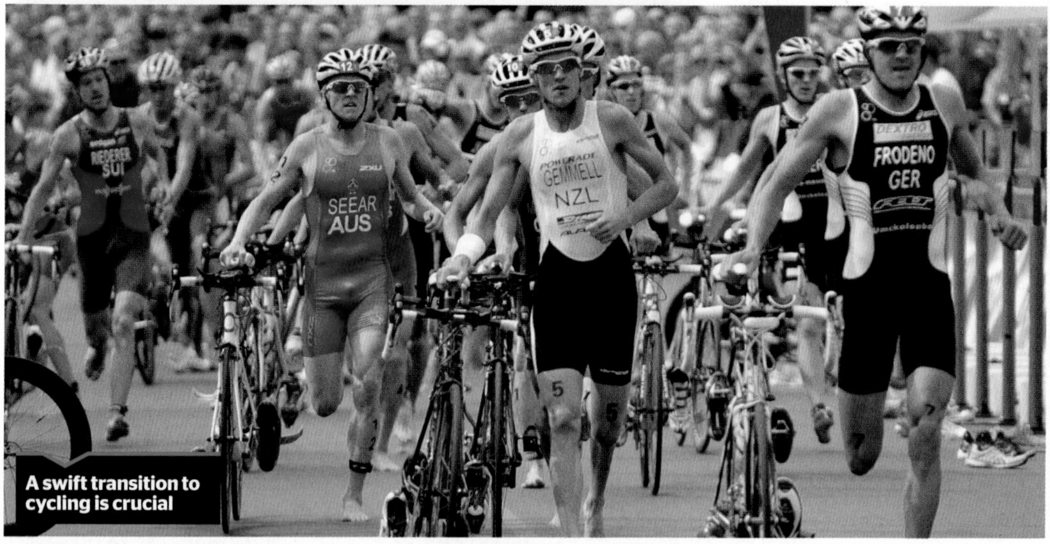

A swift transition to cycling is crucial

DID YOU KNOW?

The six Triathlon events held since its Olympic debut have been won by six different countries: Canada and Switzerland (2000), New Zealand and Austria (2004), and Germany and Australia (2008). ■ At the end of a Triathlon, organisers usually provide an aid station where athletes can get water, fruit and other refreshments. Sofas are not usually provided ■ When he's not busy trying to win grands prix, Formula One racing driver Jenson Button regularly competes in Triathlons

Tired legs tackle a 10km run

OVERALL MEDAL TABLE
TOP THREE NATIONS

1. AUSTRALIA

GOLD	SILVER	BRONZE
1	2	1

2. NEW ZEALAND

GOLD	SILVER	BRONZE
1	1	1

3. CANADA

GOLD	SILVER	BRONZE
1	1	0

Factbox

Where: Hyde Park
When: Saturday 4 August and Tuesday 7 August
Medal events: 2
Athletes: 110 (55 men, 55 women)

REASONS TO WATCH

1) PAIN BARRIERS
All endurance competitions at the Olympics are gruelling, but watching triathletes push themselves to their very limits shows how dedicated and athletic humans can be.

2) GLORIOUS HYDE PARK
One of the most beautiful open-air spaces in London, Hyde Park is the start and finish for the Triathlon – and regardless of previous interest in the event, it makes for a nice day out.

3) SWIFT TRANSITIONS
Watching someone change clothes isn't, generally, that exciting (depending on who they are) but, in Triathlon, transition timing is pivotal. Imagine trying on new jeans after running up and down the stairs twice, and you'll get some understanding of how difficult this is!

The Ultimate Olympic A-Z

VOLLEYBALL

In 1895, ageing members of a YMCA gym in Massachusetts complained basketball was too fast and physical for them, so they set about inventing a new sport that they could enjoy in their indoor gym.

They came up with Volleyball, a game that is now one of the most fast-paced and popular sports in the world, boasting more than 220 national federations and being a staple of the summer Games programme since 1964.

In Olympic Volleyball, 12 teams are entered in each of the men's and women's competitions, and these are then split into two groups of six teams that play each other once. The top four from each group qualify for the knock-out stages.

A country's entry to the Olympics depends on how well they have performed at five major Fédération Internationale de Volleyball (FIVB) competitions over the previous 24 months, with at least one nation per continent automatically qualifying.

A Volleyball team consists of six players and the action takes place on an 18m x 9m indoor court. A point is won if the ball touches the ground in the opponent's court or it is hit out of bounds by the opposing team.

Each team is allowed three touches before they have to return the ball over the net and they can only score points if they have serve. Each time a team secures serve, the server must be rotated one place in accordance with the players' shirt numbers.

The main tactic for scoring points in Volleyball is a move called 'set and spike'. A team uses one of its touches to float the ball high and close to the net, and another to quickly 'spike' the ball downwards with as much force as possible, to give the other team little chance of returning the ball.

'Set and spike' is key to scoring points

Historically, the men's and women's medal tables are strikingly different. The men's game has seen a spread of nations winning gold, with the USSR and USA topping the table with a far-from-dominant three each. Italy are currently the most successful nation in terms of medals won, but have failed to pick up a single gold.

Women's Volleyball, on the other hand, has been dominated by communist nations, with the USSR, China and Cuba winning nine out of the 12 Olympic gold medals to date. Brazil are currently the Olympic champions, however.

Returns are made in three touches or less

DID YOU KNOW?

A 'spike' in Volleyball can reach speeds of more than 130kph ■ The net in a women's game (2.24m high) is 19cm lower than in a men's game (2.43m) ■ The tallest Volleyball player to date is Russia's Aleksey Kazakov, who measures in at 2.18m (7ft 2ins) tall. He won a silver at Sydney 2000 and a bronze at Athens 2004 ■ Cuba's women won Volleyball gold at three consecutive Olympic Games, in Barcelona (1992), Atlanta (1996) and Sydney (2000)

Players must take it in turns to serve throughout a match

OVERALL MEDAL TABLE
TOP THREE NATIONS

1. USA

GOLD	SILVER	BRONZE
8	3	3

2. SOVIET UNION

GOLD	SILVER	BRONZE
7	4	1

3. BRAZIL

GOLD	SILVER	BRONZE
5	7	4

Factbox

Where: Earls Court
When: Saturday 28 July – Sunday 12 August
Medal events: 2
Athletes: 288 (144 men, 144 women; 12 teams each)

REASONS TO WATCH

1) FAST AND FURIOUS
Olympic Volleyball players have to have lightning-fast reactions and the willingness to throw themselves around the court to stand any chance of winning.

2) LOUD CROWD
Volleyball is one of the most popular Olympic sports and enthusiastic fans like to make themselves heard in the indoor venues.

3) SWAYING MOMENTUM
Keeping momentum is key to scoring points in Volleyball, but this can be won or lost in a matter of seconds. Following how it affects each team's scoring pattern is all part of the fun in this intriguing sport.

The Ultimate Olympic A-Z

WATER POLO

There is little documentation on Water Polo's origins, but it developed early in the 19th century as an aquatic form of rugby and was initially played in rivers and lakes. Early forms of the game used an inflated rubber ball stemming from India known as a 'pulu' - pronounced 'polo' by the English, hence Water Polo got its name.

Not to be confused with our Royals' favourite sport of 'polo' - a team game played on horseback by jodhpur-clad individuals with double-barrelled surnames - the version of Water Polo that survives today is akin to handball.

It has featured at every Olympic Games since Paris 1900 and, although contrasting styles developed on either side of the Atlantic, the rules of the game in Europe and America were eventually formalised, aiding the sport's Olympic development.

Teams of seven players compete in a swimming pool with a goal (3m wide and 90cm high) at each end and a match is divided into four periods of eight minutes.

When in possession, a team has 30 seconds to score or the ball is given to the opposition. Players are not allowed to touch the bottom or sides of the pool at any time during play, so this is not a game for the faint of heart, biceps or calf!

Water Polo boasts a strong Olympic heritage, with the men's competition among the very first team sports in the Modern Games and the women's event making its bow at Sydney in 2000 after much lobbying by the Australian team.

One of the most famous matches was between Hungary and the Soviet Union at the 1956 Olympic Games. As the athletes left for Melbourne, the Hungarian Revolution began and was promptly crushed by the powerful Soviet Army. With many of the Hungarian competitors vowing never to return home, an additional, political significance was attached to the upcoming match.

What transpired was one of the most brutal, bloody games of all time - a match in which the pool reputedly turned from chlorine-blue to blood-red.

With the Hungarians leading 4-0, the game was called off in the last minute after an eye-splitting fracas between two players. Hungary were awarded the victory, but the police had to be called to prevent a riot.

The men's Olympic Water Polo event has historically been dominated by Eastern Bloc countries, with the Soviet Union, Yugoslavia and Hungary, predominantly, coming away with the gold medal most often.

Indeed, the quality of the Hungary teams over the past decade has resulted in them topping the podium in the past three Olympic Games - thus, they are the bookies' favourites to win again at London 2012.

The women's competition is a lot more open, although the Netherlands look very strong in the run-in.

For the London Games, a new Water Polo arena has been constructed next to the Aquatics Centre in the Olympic Park and the format of the competition will be relatively simple.

The men's and women's events both start with group play that will see all of the nations divided into two groups, in which they will all play each other once. This will be followed by the quarter- and semi-final rounds, ahead of the final, with gold on the line.

Teams have just 30 seconds to get a goal

DID YOU KNOW?

Eight Hungarian Water Polo players were suspended in 38 seconds when Hungary played Italy at the 1972 Olympics ■ A top player will swim an average of 2.5km (1.5 miles) per match and some can throw the ball at up to 100kmh ■ The longest-running Water Polo competition is the annually held game between Oxford and Cambridge universities, played since 1891 ■ Sir Alexander Fleming (of penicillin fame) chose to attend St Mary's Medical School in London because it had a good Water Polo team

Players must not touch the bottom or sides of the pool

OVERALL MEDAL TABLE
TOP THREE NATIONS

1. HUNGARY

GOLD	SILVER	BRONZE
9	3	3

2. ITALY

GOLD	SILVER	BRONZE
4	1	2

3. GBR

GOLD	SILVER	BRONZE
4	0	0

Factbox

Where: Olympic Park, Water Polo Arena
When: Sunday 29 July – Sunday 12 August
Medal Events: 2
Athletes: 260 (156 men, 104 women)

REASONS TO WATCH

1) INTENSE RIVALRIES
As one of the oldest team sports in the Olympics, the propensity for fierce rivalries is high, especially between the elite European nations.

2) BREAKNECK TURNOVERS
With only 30 seconds of possession granted to each team at any one time, the game is played at a gruelling, non-stop pace.

3) VIRGIN TERRITORY
The action is all taking place in the never-before-used, and rather beautiful, Water Polo Arena – so athletes and spectators can revel in being the first through the door.

The Ultimate Olympic A-Z

WEIGHTLIFTING

The first thing you need to know about Weightlifting is that there are two moves each competitor has to complete, the 'snatch' and the 'clean & jerk'.

The snatch requires the bar to be lifted from the floor to above the head in one quick, fluid motion, while the clean & jerk is a two-stage lift. Athletes must first bring the bar up to their shoulders and then, in a separate movement, extend it above their head.

A lift is only considered successful if the weightlifter's arms are 'locked' above their head and the bar is fully under control.

Each lifter gets three attempts at both actions and their best lifts count towards their overall score. Weights must be nominated before they are attempted to ensure the best athletes are lifting the heaviest weights at the latter stages of the event.

Women's events first took place in 2000

Weightlifting featured at the first Modern Games in Athens in 1896, and in St Louis in 1904, but became a constant on the Olympic scene from Antwerp 1920 onwards.

The format of the Weightlifting competition at the London Games will be unchanged from that of Beijing 2008. There will be 15 categories, eight for men's weights, ranging from 56kg to 105kg+, and seven for women's weights (48kg to 75kg+).

The sport has a truly worldwide appeal, with 41 different countries having won gold medals and 67 different nations picking up a medal of some kind.

Eastern European nations have traditionally been the best weightlifters at the Olympic Games, with the former Soviet Union winning a total of 62 medals, of which 39 are gold. Even today, the USSR still top the Weightlifting medals table by 15 golds and 19 medals in total.

The heaviest individual weight lifted in Olympic competition was achieved in Athens in 2004 by Iran's Hossein Rezazadeh, who lifted 263.5kg (581lbs, 41.5st) in his clean & jerk. This is equivalent to having a baby elephant on each end of his bar.

Rezazadeh also holds the record for the total lift of snatch and clean & jerk: again at the Athens Games, he lifted a combined weight of 472.5kg (1,042lbs, 74.4st).

The current women's heavyweight record is held by South Korea's Jang Mi-Ran, who lifted 186kg (410lbs, 29.4st) clean & jerk and a combined total of 326kg (719lbs, 51.5st).

Explosive power is what it's all about

DID YOU KNOW?

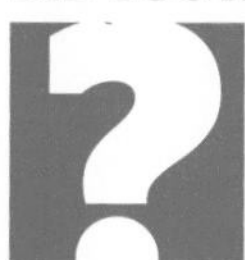

The strongest weightlifters can lift more than three times their own bodyweight ■ If two competitors are tied on weight lifted, the athlete who weighs the least is award victory ■ 1,630 weight disks, ranging from 5kg to 25kg, will be used at the London 2012 Olympics ■ With 15 minutes to go before the 1956 Melbourne bantamweight event, American Charles Vinci was 7oz overweight - but a severe haircut did the trick and he went on to win gold ■ Japan's Takashi Ichiba, who finished fourth in the bantamweight in Los Angeles in 1984, entertained the crowd by performing a backflip before each of his lifts

The weight must be under control for a lift to be successful

OVERALL MEDAL TABLE
TOP THREE NATIONS

1. SOVIET UNION

GOLD	SILVER	BRONZE
39	21	2

2. CHINA

GOLD	SILVER	BRONZE
24	11	8

3. USA

GOLD	SILVER	BRONZE
16	16	11

Factbox

Where: ExCeL
When: Saturday 28 July – Tuesday 7 August
Medal events: 15
Athletes: 260 (156 men, 104 women)

REASONS TO WATCH

1) POWER SURGE
The sheer explosive power of weightlifters is unrivalled in any other sport.

2) HUMAN DRAMA
The contest is set up so the elite compete last – and the drama of athletes trying to out-lift their fierce rivals is great to watch.

3) EXPLOSIVE EMOTIONS
Getting 'psyched up' for lifting a weight is a massive part of the sport and can make all the difference. As a result, competitors can get very emotional when celebrating success – while failure can leave them devastated.

The Ultimate Olympic A-Z

WRESTLING

Olympic Wrestling dates back to 706BC, when it was first staged in the Ancient Games. It was one of the most popular sports back then because it was seen as the ultimate test of strength, stamina and skill between two men.

It was included in the first Modern Olympics of 1896, as a bridge between old and new, and the sport proved so popular that it has remained part of the Games ever since, only not appearing at the Paris Games in 1900. Women's Wrestling made its debut at the Athens Games in 2004.

There are two Wrestling disciplines in the Modern Olympics: Greco-Roman Wrestling, which is the same as that performed at the Ancient Games, and freestyle Wrestling, which was introduced in St Louis in 1904. There are seven weight classes for men in Greco-Roman and freestyle Wrestling, and four weight classes for women in freestyle wrestling only.

The basic aim of Wrestling is to overpower your opponent and pin them to the ground. Contests are split into three rounds of two minutes, with a 30-second break in between, but a contest ends if a pin is successfully made or a wrestler wins the first two rounds. In freestyle Wrestling, a bout may also be stopped if a 10-point lead has been established.

The scoring system in Wrestling is pretty complex, but, in a nutshell, points are awarded for flips and throws – the more stylish, complex and extravagant the flip, the more points a wrestler gets. If no pin is made within the three allotted rounds, the winner is decided by the amount of points won during the contest.

Competitors get up close and personal...

In the Greco-Roman format, wrestlers are only allowed to use their upper bodies and arms, and are only allowed to attack their opponent's upper body. In freestyle Wrestling, as the name suggests, competitors are free to use their whole body to attack their rival.

Wrestling has worldwide appeal and this is reflected in the medals table, with 47 nations having Owon a gold medal in the freestyle event and 44 having picked up a medal in the Greco-Roman event.

Even so, there are still powerhouses within the sport, with Russia, Sweden and Finland dominant in Greco-Roman Wrestling, and the USA, Russia and Japan the nations to beat in the freestyle format.

...in a bid to pin down their opponents

DID YOU KNOW?

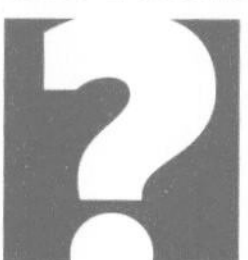

Japan's Osamu Watanabe, who won featherweight gold in Tokyo in 1964, retired from Wrestling that same year after going undefeated in 186 contests ■ Wrestling first featured at the Ancient Olympic Games more than 2,700 years ago ■ The longest Olympic wrestling match lasted 11 hours and was the semi-final at Stockholm 1912 between Russia's Martin Klein and Finland's Alfred Asikainen. Klein won, but had to pull out of the final because of exhaustion

OVERALL MEDAL TABLE: TOP THREE NATIONS

1. SOVIET UNION

GOLD	SILVER	BRONZE
68	34	25

2. USA

GOLD	SILVER	BRONZE
50	43	32

3. TURKEY

GOLD	SILVER	BRONZE
31	16	16

Factbox

Where: ExCeL
When: Sunday 5 August – Sunday 12 August
Medal events: 18
Athletes: 344

REASONS TO WATCH

1) BRUTAL EXTRAVAGANCE
Wrestlers get extra points for extravagant throws – so expect to see bones crushed with style.

2) OUT OF BREATH YET?
The ancient Greeks considered Wrestling to be the ultimate test of a person's strength, stamina and skill – which all sounds very exhausting!

3) TENSION AND INTENSITY
A contest can be won or lost in less than a second, making it one of the most electrifying sports at the Olympic Games.

A Wrestling bout can be turned on its head in seconds

PARALYMPICS

An integral part of any summer Olympic programme, the Paralympics began as a small congregation of British World War II veterans and is now one of the world's biggest international multisport contests, with competitors from around the globe. The first Paralympic Games were held in Rome in 1960.

In 2012, athletes will compete across 20 sports and in 21 disciplines (Cycling is broken into road and track), and events will take place across the capital. There are six broad categories in which athletes compete, including: wheelchair, amputee, cerebral palsy, intellectual disability, visually impaired, and *Les Autres*, which translates as 'The Others' and encapsulates athletes who don't fall into the other categories, such as those with dwarfism, multiple sclerosis, or congenital deformities.

Disabilities aside, Paralympic athletes are the same single-minded, combative beasts as their Olympic cousins and no one arriving on British soil in their country's colours for London 2012 will be there to make up the numbers.

The Paralympic programme is uncompromising, diverse and bound to make a big impression.

Archery

Archery opened the first recognised international games for the disabled in 1948, in Stoke Mandeville, which inspired the development of the modern Paralympic movement. It has been a Paralympic discipline since the first official Games in Rome in 1960 and the programme at London 2012 will include singles and team events, incorporating sitting and standing competitors. Perhaps the most famous Para-Archer is Antonio Rebollo, who lit the Olympic Torch in Barcelona in 1992 by shooting a flaming arrow towards the cauldron inside the Estadi Olímpic.

Where: The Royal Artillery Barracks
When: 30 August - 5 September
Medal events: 9
Athletes: 140 (88 men, 52 women)

Athletics

By far the biggest Paralympic event, with 1,100 competitors expected at London 2012, Athletics attracts many thousands of followers. Track events include 100m, 200m, 400m, 800m, 1,500m, 3,000m, 10,000m, marathon, 4x100m relay and 4x400m relay, while field events include shot put, discus, javelin, club throwing (for severely disabled athletes), pentathlon, and long, high and triple jumps. One of the best-known athletes is Britain's Tanni Grey-Thompson (now a baroness), who won 11 gold medals, four silver and a bronze. As a young athlete, she also competed in wheelchair basketball.

Where: Olympic Stadium (track & field); The Mall (road)
When: 31 August - 9 September
Medal events: 170
Athletes: 1,100 (740 men, 360 women)

Boccia

This unusually named sport (from the Latin *bottia*, meaning 'ball') is a 16th century Italian twist on an Ancient Greek ball-tossing game and became a recognised Paralympic sport in Barcelona, in 1992. Individuals, teams and pairs (comprising both sexes) hurl leather balls at a jack and the closest ball wins a point, with additional points awarded for every subsequent ball closer than the opposition's. Players must be seated and throw from a boxed area at one end of the playing court.

Where: ExCeL
When: 2 - 8 September
Medal events: 7
Athletes: 104

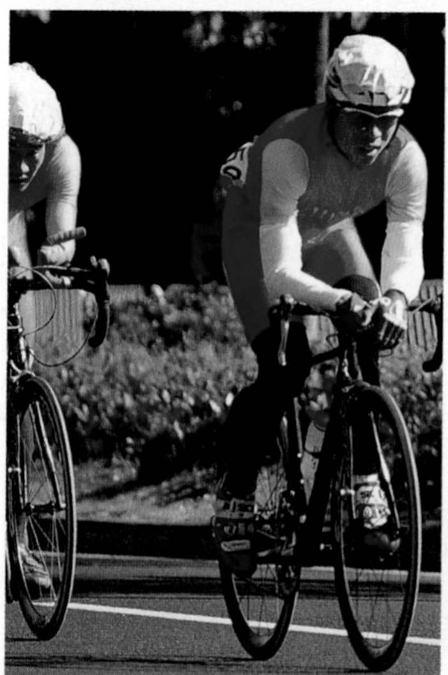

Cycling – Road

The visually impaired, who compete on tandems with a sighted team-mate, used to be the only group that took part in the Cycling at the Paralympics, but technology has opened up the sport to more disabled athletes and it is now the third-largest event at the Games. Those with cerebral palsy, amputations or other physical disabilities compete on bicycles, tricycles, tandems and hand cycles, in road races, time trials and team relay.

Where: Brands Hatch
When: 5 - 8 September
Medal events: 32
Athletes: 225 (155 men, 70 women, across road and track)

Cycling - Track

The 18 events at London 2012 (10 for men, seven for women, one mixed) make this the busiest Paralympic Track Cycling schedule to date. Power, speed and tactics will all be factors in the Velodrome.

Where: Olympic Park Velodrome
When: 30 August - 2 September
Medal events: 18
Athletes: 225 (155 men, 70 women, across road and track)

Equestrian

Equestrian activities have long been used as a means of rehabilitation and recreation for people with disabilities and Para-Equestrian Dressage developed in the 1970s. It became part of the Paralympic programme at the 1996 Games in Atlanta and, in 2012, athletes will compete in two Dressage tests: a championship test, comprising a distinct set of movements, and a freestyle test, choreographed by the rider. If the rider is unable to use their legs to communicate with the horse, other aids - such as a dressage whip or connecting bar reins - can be used. Lightness, rhythm and harmony between horse and rider will be key factors in winning gold among the beautiful surroundings of Greenwich Park.

Where: Greenwich Park
When: 30 August - 4 September
Medal events: 11
Athletes: 78

DID YOU KNOW?

The word Paralympic is said to derive from the Greek preposition 'para' meaning 'beside' or 'alongside' - thus indicating a competition being held in parallel with the Olympic Games ■ Despite making their bow at the Rome Games in 1960, the term 'Paralympic' was not officially used until Seoul 1988 ■ South African double amputee Oscar Pistorius, who competes on carbon fibre legs, has run the 400m qualifying time for the 2012 Olympics. He clocked 45.07 seconds at a meeting in Italy in July 2011

Football 5-a-side

London's new Hockey Centre will play host to eight teams of visually impaired footballers who play with a ball that has a noise-making instrument inside. Goalkeepers are fully or partially sighted, there are no throw-ins (there is a rebound wall) and there is no offside rule, so the action is almost non-stop. Games are 25 minutes each way, with a 10-minute break at half-time. Five-a-side Football made its Paralympic debut at Athens 2004.

Where: Olympic Park Hockey Centre
When: 31 August - 8 September
Medal events: 1
Athletes: 64 (all men; eight teams)

Football 7-a-side

Dramatic and fiercely competitive, 7-a-side Paralympic Football is contested by athletes with cerebral palsy. The pitch and the goals are smaller than for 11-a-side, throw-ins are taken underarm and each half lasts 30 minutes. Aside from that, though, FIFA rules are followed to the letter - so expect some play-acting and camp celebrations, too!

Where: Olympic Park Hockey Centre
When: 1 - 9 September
Medal events: 1
Athletes: 96 (all men; eight teams)

Goalball

Devised as rehabilitation for blind World War II veterans, Goalball is an indoor game for two teams of three athletes, who must try to roll a ball into a 9m x 1.3m goal as their rivals attempt to block shots with their bodies. The ball makes a noise, so the crowd is silent during play, but they go wild when a goal is scored.

Where: Olympic Park Handball Arena
When: 30 August - 7 September
Medal events: 2
Athletes: 132 (72 men, 60 women; 12 men's teams, 10 women's teams)

Judo

Visually impaired athletes compete in Judo, which became a Paralympic sport at the 1988 Games in Seoul. Women took part for the first time at Athens 2004. The five-minute bouts start in a grapple - the main difference from other top-level Judo (although the mats also have different textures to signal the competition area and zones) - and ends immediately if a competitor is awarded 'ippon', the maximum score. Otherwise, the judoka (athlete) with the most points at the end of five minutes is the winner.

Where: ExCeL
When: 30 August - 1 September
Medal events: 13
Athletes: 132 (84 men, 48 women)

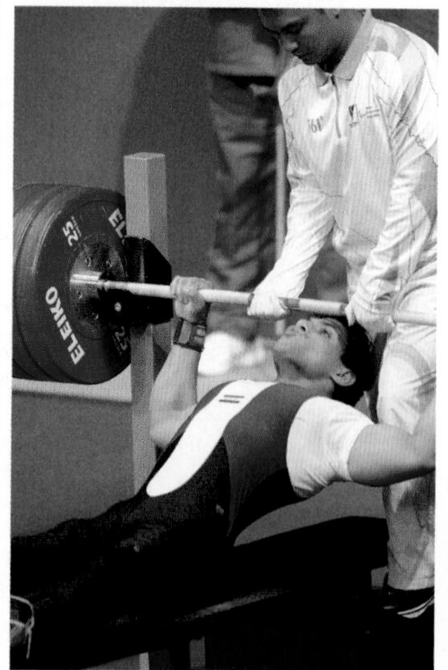

Powerlifting

Para-Powerlifting is one of the fastest-growing participation sports, with competitors in more than 100 countries, and made its debut at the 1964 Games for athletes with spinal cord injuries. It widened its scope to include other disability groups and has the same rules as able-bodied lifters. Athletes, classified by bodyweight, must complete one full press and are eliminated if they fail three times.

Where: ExCeL
When: 30 August - 5 September
Medal events: 20
Athletes: 200 (120 men, 80 women)

DID YOU KNOW?

Chairman of the London organising committee, Lord Coe, wants the 2012 Paralympics to be about more than winning gold. He has declared: "We want to change public attitudes towards disability, celebrate the excellence of Paralympic sport and to enshrine, from the outset, that the two Games are an integrated whole" ■ The most decorated Paralympian is Trischa Zorn, of the USA (who are also the most decorated nation). A blind swimmer, she has won 55 medals, 41 of which are gold

Rowing

Otherwise known as 'adaptive' rowing, Paralympic Rowing boats are designed for specific athletes, who compete in four classes over the same distance - 1,000m. Categories include men's arms only single scull (AM1x), women's arms only single scull (AW1x), trunk and arms mixed double (TA2x), and legs, trunk and arms mixed coxed four (LTA4+). Rowing made its Games debut in 2008 and will draw a big following on the magnificent waters at Eton Dorney in 2012.

Where: Eton Dorney
When: 31 August - 2 September
Medal events: 4
Athletes: 96 (48 men, 48 women)

Sailing

An event requiring nerve and skill in equal measure, Paralympic Sailing consists of single-handed, two-person and three-person keelboat competitions. Each event takes place over six days, with winners scoring one point, second-placed athletes two points and so on. After 11 races, each sailor can discard their worst score and the crew with the lowest score wins gold.

Where: Weymouth and Portland, Dorset
When: 1 - 6 September
Medal events: 3
Athletes: 80

Shooting

Introduced at the 1980 Paralympics in Holland, Shooting consists of rifle and pistol events (three each for men and women, and six mixed), and athletes compete in two classes: those who can support the weight of their weapon and those who use a support. Athletes shoot from standing, sitting, kneeling or prone positions at targets 10m, 25m or 50m away. Each event has a qualification round and a final round.

Where: The Royal Artillery Barracks
When: 30 August - 4 September
Medal events: 12
Athletes: 140 (100 men, 40 women)

Swimming

Hugely popular at the Games, the Swimming competition will take place at the new and rather marvellous Aquatics Centre. Races can start in a number of ways - from a standing start, diving from a sitting position or in the water - and swimmers are categorised according to their disability, the higher the number the lower the disability. S1-S10 includes those with physical disabilities, S11-S13 is for blind/visually impaired swimmers and S14 refers to those with intellectual disabilities. Visually impaired swimmers may use a 'tapper' to make them aware they are approaching the end of the pool.

Where: Olympic Park Aquatics Centre
When: 30 August - 8 September
Medal events: 148
Athletes: 600 (350 men, 250 women)

Table Tennis

The fourth-largest Paralympic sport behind athletics, swimming and powerlifting, Table Tennis made its debut at the 1960 Games. Matches are the best of five sets, the first to 11 points (with a margin of two clear points) winning the set. Athletes are classified in standing and wheelchair groups, and all contest a qualification stage before the knock-out phase.

Where: ExCeL
When: 30 August - 8 September
Medal events: 29
Athletes: 276 (174 men, 102 women)

Volleyball

Sitting Volleyball was introduced for men at the 1980 Paralympic Games in Arnhem, with the women's event added in 2004. Two teams of six play on a 6x10m court with a 1.15m (men) or 1.05m (women) net, and matches are the best of five sets. A set is won when a team reaches 25 points with a two-point margin. The final set is the first to 15 points.

Where: ExCeL
When: 30 August - 8 September
Medal events: 2
Athletes: 198 (110 men, 88 women, 10 men's teams, 8 women's teams)

Wheelchair Basketball

Another event borne out of the rehabilitation of war veterans, Wheelchair Basketball has been on the Paralympic programme since the first Games in 1960. Each athlete (12 per team) is allocated points - from 0.5-4.5 - depending on their functional ability and the points total for the five players on court at any one time must not exceed 14. The rules are broadly similar to Basketball and two groups of six teams (five for women) play a round-robin first phase, with the top four countries in each qualifying for the knock-out stages..

Where: North Greenwich Arena; Olympic Park Basketball Arena
When: 30 August - 8 September
Medal events: 2
Athletes: 264 (144 men, 120 women; 12 men's teams, 10 women's teams)

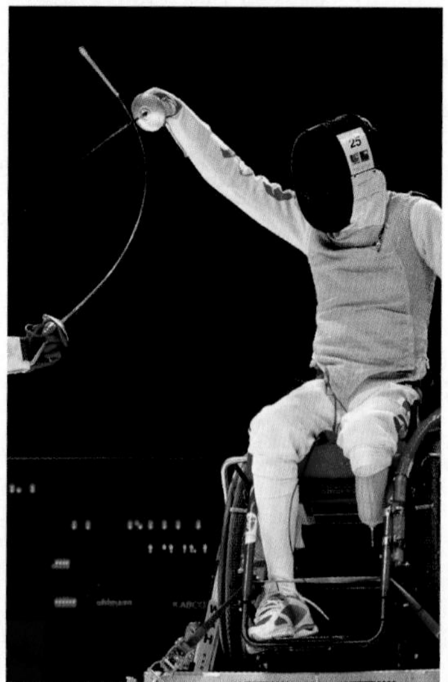

Wheelchair Fencing

A feature of the first Games in 1960, Wheelchair Fencing consists of team and individual events for men and women in foil and épée, and for men only in sabre. Wheelchairs are fixed to the floor to give athletes more freedom for upper body movement and contestants are electronically hooked up to the scoring system so judges know when a hit has been achieved. Five hits are needed for victory in the early rounds, but 15 are needed in the latter stages.

Where: ExCeL
When: 4 - 8 September
Medal events: 12
Athletes: 100

DID YOU KNOW?

Neroli Fairhall, an archer from New Zealand, was the first paraplegic athlete to compete in the Olympic Games, in Los Angeles in 1984. She came 35th and won Paralympic gold ■ 23% of the population of Great Britain watched at least some of the 2008 Paralympics in Beijing ■ South African swimmer Natalie du Toit, who won five gold medals at her first Paralympic Games in Athens, in 2004, made history when she competed in the Beijing 2008 Olympic (16th in the open water 10K) and Paralympic Games (five golds)

Wheelchair Rugby

Formerly known as Murderball, Wheelchair Rugby is the most aggressively contested of the Paralympic team sports and the fastest growing wheelchair sport in the world. London 2012 will feature eight mixed-sex teams, who will play each other, round-robin style, in two groups of four. The top two go through to the semi-finals, with the winners of this game battling it out for gold. Played indoors on a basketball court, teams of four must try to carry a ball across their opponent's goalline. Contact between wheelchairs is allowed, but physical contact is not. The result is a fast-moving sport that threw up some thrilling clashes in Sydney in 2000, when the US beat Australia 32-31 in a dazzling gold-medal game. Wheelchair Rugby will garner a massive following at London 2012.

Where: Olympic Park Basketball Arena
When: 5 - 9 September
Medal events: 1
Athletes: 96 (mixed, 8 teams)

OVERALL MEDAL TABLE
TOP THREE NATIONS

1. USA

GOLD	SILVER	BRONZE
666	586	589

2. GBR

GOLD	SILVER	BRONZE
493	470	463

3. GERMANY (1257)

GOLD	SILVER	BRONZE
433	425	399

REASONS TO WATCH

1) ADMIRABLE TENACITY
Disability? Pah! These athletes won't hear of it and are just as competitive as their Olympic counterparts.

2) ALTERNATIVE TACTICS
Many Paralympic sports are related to their Olympic equals, but require different tactics and gameplay. Sports fans will find this intriguing.

3) TOP-NOTCH TECH
More and more disabled athletes can compete at London 2012 because of the brilliantly adaptive technologies on offer. A wonderful testament to the Olympic Spirit.

Wheelchair Tennis

Having made its first Paralympic appearance at the 1992 Games in Barcelona, Wheelchair Tennis has a knock-out format and consists of men's and women's singles and doubles, plus quad singles and doubles. The Quad division is for athletes who are affected by disability in three or more limbs. The ball is allowed to bounce twice and only the first bounce has to be within the boundaries of the court. Men and women both play best-of-three-sets matches.

Where: Olympic Park Eton Manor
When: 1 - 8 September
Medal events: 6
Athletes: 112

TRIPLE THREAT

London's very own Phillips Idowu talks about special outfits, living in the zone and how everything's geared up for the 2012 Games...

-low much are you looking forward o performing in your home town n 2012?

Every British athlete has got to be wildly excited. It's a once-in-a-ifetime opportunity. Personally, being born and bred in east London, I can't think of a more nspiring Olympic scenario to be competing at.

You sound very excited.

am. But I'm also trying to remain focused. I'm taking baby steps forward and ticking the right boxes, and being careful so I'm in the best possible shape when the big one comes around.

What would be your ideal performance?

don't want to focus too hard on the performance or the outcome. just want to make sure, on the day of the final, I'm executing as well as can. Get my run-up on, get my stages correct and just be technically on-point. If I'm able to do that, I should be able to come out on top.

What is it that makes the Olympics so special for you?

t's quite simply the biggest sporting event in the world. There's only two multisport games that occur in the world – the Commonwealth Games being the other one – and this is the most prestigious and biggest.

Beijing 2008 was a really emotional Games. I'd come off an undefeated season and the only competition I lost that year was an Olympic final. It was a massive stepping stone for me, though, because, before 2008, I had suffered from a lot of injuries and not been able to perform at 100%

KNOWING HOW MUCH PEOPLE ARE WILLING YOU TO WIN URGES YOU TO DO THAT EXTRA RUN OR REP IN TRAINING

At the time, I was disappointed with silver, but I look back now and feel blessed that I got that medal because, if I'd won the gold, I'm not sure how much I'd be motivated or inspired to keep going to win the gold in London. So there are positives to take from it.

You're known for being a bit of an extrovert, Phillips...

That's what I've heard!

Do you have a specific outfit or hair colour lined up for London 2012?

No, I think it'll be quite predictable. I have spoken with my sponsors to make the London Olympics a bit more special – tweaks on my kit, or the long socks I wear, or my headband or wristband, just to portray my personality a bit more. As regards my hair: over the years, when I've performed at a major championships I've usually had it red. And I've usually won. So I doubt I'll be changing that.

How much do the crowd help you? How big a factor will they be for British athletes at London 2012?

I shut off. It's funny to say, but, in the final, I won't be aware of the crowd. It'll just be me, the runway, the sandpit and my coach. Everything else is a blur.

In the lead-up to the Games, though, just knowing the amount of support you've got and the amount of people who will be there has got to be a massive boost. Knowing how much people are willing you to win, that's the stuff that's going to urge you to do that extra run, go that little bit quicker

n training and do that extra rep in he gym. That's how the crowd and upport will help you.

Iow do you get yourself pumped ıp before competing?
'm not an athlete that needs to get pumped up. I don't need that ıdrenalin flowing through my body. I need to be chilled out and emain relaxed, that's how perform at my best. I know some people will listen to nip-hop or heavy metal to get he blood flowing, but I don't need that. The more relaxed am, the better I perform.

Aside from your own, which events are you most looking orward to at London 2012?
On the track, the 100m, which I'm sure most people will be watching! Off the track, I definitely want to see the USA basketball eam. Whether they make it to the inal will depend on who they bring and how committed they are to he Olympic Games. I'll also be supporting my GB basketball team-mates. played against a couple of the guys at school, so it's good o have them with ne on the team.

Who are the athletes you are most looking orward to seeing at London 2012?
Again, I think everyone s looking forward to seeing Usain Bolt compete, which is why all those tickets sold out so quickly. I think the men's high hurdles will be a great event. If all the contenders are 00%, you've got David Oliver, rom the United States, China's Liu Xiang and Cuba's Dayron Robles – hey're all on the verge of world ecords, so that could be quite a special race.

The women's 400m could be good, too. Christine's (Ohuruogu, nterviewed on p140) back now at 00% and she'll be keen to defend her Olympic title, so I'll look orward to seeing that

Germaine Mason is another team-mate I'm looking forward to see perform. He's had some problems with injuries and stuff, so it'll be great to have him back on the team and jumping well – he seems to have been forgotten about a bit.

What was your favourite Olympic moment as a child – and who was your hero?
I couldn't tell you which one it was, but I remember watching the Olympics as a child and Carl Lewis and Daley Thompson were the big stars – and when Carl Lewis won his fourth Olympic gold medal in the long jump it was quite special.

What level of dedication do Olympic medallists have to commit to?
The training itself is not that hard! I'm highly motivated, so regardless of how hard the sessions are, I know I'm gonna get in there and do it. The difficulty with working towards an Olympic title is how much you have to sacrifice, so the lack of free time I have, how busy my schedule is, not being able to go out with friends and see as much of your family, that's the really tough stuff.

Finally, what would you rather have: the world record or the Olympic gold?
Indoor world record in March, Olympic gold in August! Why not have 'em both, eh? ■

BUTLERS WHARF

LONDON 2012
joma
ESPAÑA
TDK
Daegu 2011

What's happening, where and when, at the XXX Olympiad? We've unearthed potential highlights so you can prepare

DAY 1
Friday
27 July 2012

What's on?

Archery

AT LAST! The London 2012 Olympic Games begin. At 19:30, the pomp and passion of the Opening Ceremony will burst into life and onto billions of TV screens across the planet, to get the London Games under way in the Olympic Stadium. Danny Boyle, the man behind *Trainspotting* and *Slumdog Millionaire*, will direct the celebrations, details of which remain confidential. A Beatles reunion was rumoured and subsequently refuted, and you can expect much more fanfare, speculation and deliberation in the run-up to the greatest show on Earth. But here, on the first Friday of competition, all those questions will be answered!

DO NOT MISS!

09:00-15:00 Archery preliminaries – the only action of the day and Lord's will be buzzing

DAY 2
Saturday
28 July 2012

What's on?

(medals contested in bold) **Archery**, Badminton, Basketball, Beach Volleyball, Boxing, **Cycling (road)**, Equestrian (eventing), **Fencing**, Football, Gymnastics (artistic), Handball, **Judo**, Rowing, **Shooting**, **Swimming**, Table Tennis, Tennis, Volleyball, **Weightlifting**

Here we go! This is the day the 2012 Olympics really explode into life, with 19 sports bursting out the starting blocks. The first medals will be competed for in cycling, with the host nation's Mark Cavendish (above) sure to be a contender on the roads of Richmond. Meanwhile, Ashley McKenzie – who won bronze at the 2007 European Junior Championships and gold at the British Open – makes his much-anticipated Olympic bow in the Judo.

DO NOT MISS!

10:00-16:15 Cycling – men's road race, London/Surrey

14:00-16:30 Judo – Men's -60kg: repêchages, semi-final contests, bronze medal contests, gold medal contest, ExCeL

DAY 3
Sunday
29 July 2012

What's on?

(medals contested in bold) **Archery**, Badminton, Basketball, Beach Volleyball, Boxing, Canoe Slalom, **Cycling (road)**, **Diving**, Equestrian (eventing), **Fencing**, Football, Gymnastics (artistic), Handball, Hockey, **Judo**, Rowing, Sailing, **Shooting**, **Swimming**, Table Tennis, Tennis, Volleyball, Water Polo, **Weightlifting**

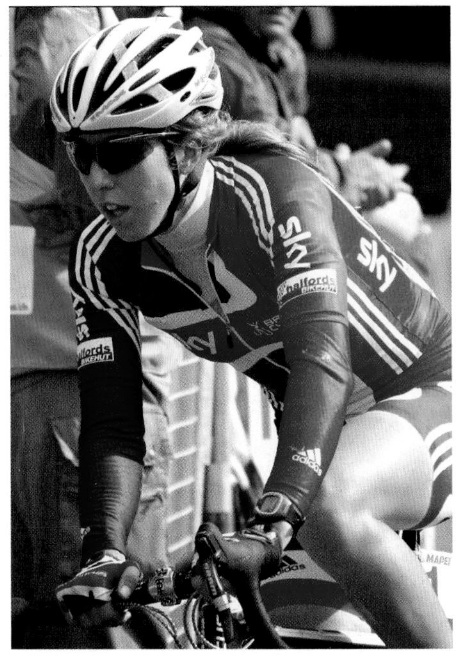

Wembley hosts its first football matches of the Olympic tournament and fans of Great Britain's brilliant Rebecca Adlington will be raising the roof of the new Aquatics Centre, gateway to the Olympic Park. There will be partying on the streets of London and Surrey as Beijing gold medalist Nicole Cooke (above) attempts to retain her Road Cycling gold and the start of the Artistic Gymnastics, always a popular event, will see more complicated shapes thrown on the floors and apparatus of the North Greenwich Arena (also known as the O2 Arena).

DO NOT MISS!

09:30-21:30 Artistic Gymnastics - women's qualification, North Greenwich Arena
19:30-21:35 Swimming - women's 400m freestyle, Aquatics Centre

DAY 4
Monday
30 July 2012

What's on?

(medals contested in bold) Archery, Badminton, Basketball, Beach Volleyball, Boxing, Canoe Slalom, **Diving**, Equestrian (eventing), **Fencing**, **Gymnastics (artistic)**, Handball, Hockey, **Judo**, Rowing, Sailing, **Shooting**, **Swimming**, Table Tennis, Tennis, Volleyball, Water Polo, **Weightlifting**

Big splash to be made in the water today, when the mighty Olympic names of Michael Phelps and Ian Thorpe (above), injury permitting, clash in the men's 200m freestyle and young Brit Tom Daley fights nerves in front of his home crowd in a bid for a medal in the 10m synchronised Diving. China's outstanding men's artistic gymnasts will be huge favourites for team gold in the North Greenwich Arena. The Games are beginning to warm up...

DO NOT MISS!

19:30-21:15 Swimming - men's 200m freestyle, Aquatics Centre
15:00-16:15 Diving - men's synchronised 10m platform: final, Aquatics Centre

DAY 5
Tuesday
31 July 2012

What's on?

(medals contested in bold) Archery, Badminton, Basketball, Beach Volleyball, Boxing, **Canoe Slalom**, **Diving**, **Equestrian (eventing)**, **Fencing**, Football, **Gymnastics (artistic)**, Handball, Hockey, **Judo**, Rowing, Sailing, **Shooting**, **Swimming**, Table Tennis, Tennis, Volleyball, Water Polo, **Weightlifting**

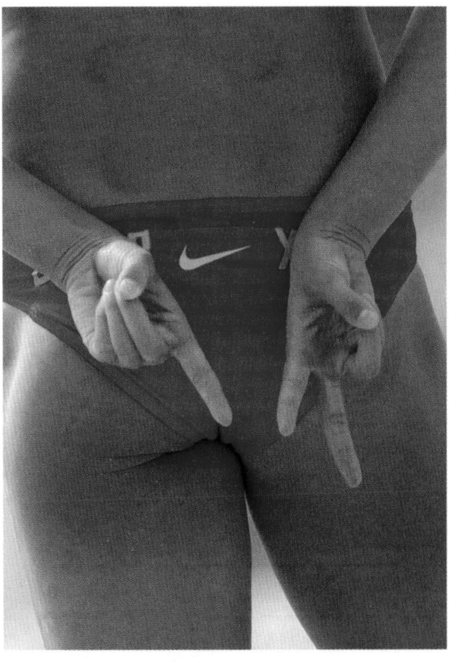

Old rivalries will be reinvigorated on the lush greens of Greenwich Park, in the Equestrian Eventing, with Great Britain trying to overthrow Germany's recent dominance. The world's eyes will also be focused on the busiest day of sailing in the natural waters around Weymouth and Portland and no doubt in the Aquatics Centre. No medals will be on offer in the Handball Arena, or at Horse Guards Parade in the beach volleyball, but both promise much entertainment for ticket-holders and television audiences alike.

DO NOT MISS!

10:30-16:00 Equestrian - team eventing, Greenwich Park
09:00-12:50 Beach Volleyball - men's and women's preliminaries, Horse Guards Parade

DAY 6 Wednesday 1 August 2012

What's on?

(medals contested in bold) Archery, Badminton, Basketball, Beach Volleyball, Boxing, **Canoe Slalom**, **Cycling (road)**, **Diving**, **Fencing**, Football, **Gymnastics (artistic)**, Handball, Hockey, **Judo**, **Rowing**, Sailing, **Shooting**, **Swimming**, **Table Tennis**, Tennis, Volleyball, Water Polo, **Weightlifting**

The irrepressible Greg Searle will be in action for Britain, bidding for a gold medal 10 years after announcing his retirement from Rowing, and the men's football group placings will be decided across the Olympic stadia. Which countries will earn the most favourable draw? We'll find out today. Also competing are Olympic hero Michael Phelps, in the 200m medley heats, and the home nation's Daniel Keatings in the Artistic Gymnastics. Drama will be unfolding all over the capital on the first day of August 2012.

DO NOT MISS!

09:30-12:50 Rowing - men's eights final, Eton Dorney
16:30-19:35 Gymnastics - men's individual all-round, North Greenwich Arena

DAY 7 Thursday 2 August 2012

What's on?

(medals contested in bold) **Archery**, Badminton, Basketball, Beach Volleyball, Boxing, **Canoe Slalom**, **Cycling (track)**, Equestrian (dressage), **Fencing**, **Gymnastics (artistic)**, Handball, Hockey, **Judo**, **Rowing**, Sailing, **Shooting**, **Swimming**, **Table Tennis**, Tennis, Volleyball, Water Polo

Within a month of Wimbledon ending, we are again reaching the climactic stages of a major Tennis tournament - at Wimbledon! There's eight hours of action on Centre Court today and Britain's track cyclists will be hoping there's more 'passing' in the Velodrome as they bid to retain gold in the team sprint. The best action of the day though might be at Eton Dorney, in the eagerly anticipated men's lightweight fours. China will also be fighting it out at lightning speed for men's Table Tennis medals at ExCeL.

DO NOT MISS!

16:00-18:30 Cycling - men's team sprint qualifying, semi-finals, finals, Velodrome
14:30-16:30 Table Tennis - men's gold-medal match, ExCeL

DAY 8 Friday 3 August 2012

What's on?

(medals contested in bold) **Archery**, **Athletics**, **Badminton**, Basketball, Beach Volleyball, Boxing, **Cycling (track)**, Diving, Equestrian (dressage), **Fencing**, Football, **Gymnastics (trampoline)**, Handball, Hockey, **Judo**, **Rowing**, Sailing, **Shooting**, **Swimming**, Table Tennis, Tennis, Volleyball, Water Polo, **Weightlifting**

London will be buzzing with Olympic-sized vibes today, with some of the host's strongest athletes in contention for medals. Competitors in 24 disciplines will be duking it out across England's capital, with Bradley Wiggins likely to be involved in the team pursuit in the Velodrome, Rebecca Adlington searching for more Swimming medals in the Aquatics Centre and Katherine Grainger (above) going for gold at Eton Dorney in the women's double sculls. The Archery also reaches a climax at Lord's.

DO NOT MISS!

16:00-18:55 Cycling - men's team pursuit, round one and finals, Velodrome
19:30-20:50 Swimming - women's 800m freestyle final, Aquatics Centre

DAY 9 Saturday 4 August 2012

What's on?

(medals contested in bold) **Athletics**, **Badminton**, Basketball, Beach Volleyball, Boxing, **Cycling (track)**, Diving, Equestrian (jumping), **Fencing**, Football, **Gymnastics (trampoline)**, Handball, Hockey, **Rowing**, Sailing, **Shooting**, **Swimming**, Table Tennis, **Tennis**, **Triathlon**, Volleyball, Water Polo, **Weightlifting**

Great Britain's best-loved female sports personality, Jessica Ennis (above), bids for heptathlon gold in front of her home crowd in the Olympic Stadium, just after the culmination of the women's 100m, in an incredible-looking day of sport in London. Swimming makes its final splash in the Aquatics Centre with the relay events, but more frenzied stroking will be undertaken in the women's Triathlon, which is sure to draw a huge crowd to Hyde Park.

DO NOT MISS!

09:00-11:40 Triathlon **- Women's triathlon, Hyde Park**
18:50-22:05 Athletics **- women's heptathlon: 800m, Olympic Stadium**

DAY 10 Sunday 5 August 2012

What's on?

(medals contested in bold) **Athletics**, **Badminton**, Basketball, Beach Volleyball, Boxing, **Cycling (track)**, **Diving**, Equestrian (jumping), **Fencing**, **Gymnastics (artistic)**, Handball, Hockey, **Sailing**, **Shooting**, Synchro Swimming, Table Tennis, **Tennis**, Volleyball, Water Polo, **Weightlifting**, **Wrestling (Greco-Roman)**

Track Athletics doesn't get bigger at 2012 than the men's 100m final. One eye will be on Jamaican sprint machine Usain Bolt (above), the other on the clock. Can he beat his 9.58-second record? East London's Christine Ohuruogo bids to retain gold in the 400m and Paula Radcliffe will pound London's streets in the marathon. The men's singles final is the showpiece at Wimbledon and sailor Ben Ainslie is in action off the coast of Weymouth.

DO NOT MISS!

11:00-14:00 Athletics **- women's marathon, The Mall**
12:00-20:30 Tennis **- men's singles gold-medal match, Wimbledon**
18:50-21:55 Athletics **- men's 100m final, Olympic Stadium**

DAY 11 Monday 6 August 2012

What's on?

(medals contested in bold) **Athletics**, Basketball, Beach Volleyball, Boxing, Canoe Sprint, **Cycling (track)**, Diving, **Equestrian (jumping)**, Football, **Gymnastics (artistic)**, Handball, Hockey, **Sailing**, **Shooting**, Synchro Swimming, Table Tennis, Volleyball, Water Polo, **Weightlifting**, **Wrestling (Greco-Roman)**

A chance to see Russian pole vault sensation Yelena Isinbayeva (above) bidding for gold and to go even higher still, alongside a fiercely contested men's 400m final and 400m hurdle final on the track. Late afternoon will see Great Britain cycling star Sir Chris Hoy trying to avoiding punctures over at the Velodrome, while Old Trafford and Wembley will be filling up for the semi-finals of the women's football.

DO NOT MISS!

16:00-18:55 Cycling **- men's sprint semi-finals, finals, Velodrome**
18:50-21:40 Athletics **- men's 400m final, men's 400m hurdles final, women's pole vault final, Olympic Stadium**

DAY 12
Tuesday
7 August 2012

What's on?

(medals contested in bold) **Athletics**, Basketball, Beach Volleyball, Boxing, Canoe Sprint, **Cycling (track)**, **Diving**, **Equestrian (dressage)**, Football, **Gymnastics (artistic)**, Handball, Hockey, **Sailing**, **Synchro Swimming**, **Table Tennis**, **Triathlon**, Volleyball, Water Polo, **Weightlifting**, **Wrestling (Greco-Roman)**

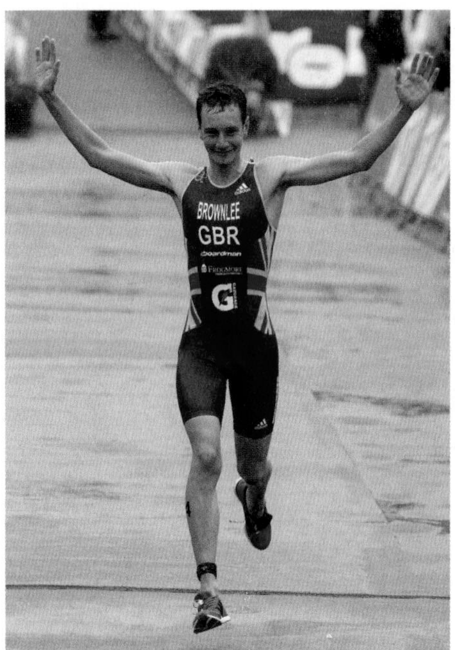

Expect Hyde Park to be heaving for the men's Triathlon, with hungry home talent Alistair Brownlee (above) hoping the crowd can propel him to victory. Sir Chris Hoy will light up the Velodrome again in the keirin and Victoria Pendleton will be in contention in the women's sprint. By the end of the day we'll know the men's Football finalists, after semis at Wembley and Old Trafford, and China's uber-dominant women's Table Tennis team will be in action at the ExCeL.

DO NOT MISS!

11:30-14:00 Triathlon - men's, Hyde Park
15:30-18:30 Table Tennis - women's team gold-medal match, ExCeL
16:00-18:30 Cycling - men's keirin, women's sprint, Velodrome

DAY 13
Wednesday
8 August 2012

What's on?

(medals contested in bold) **Athletics**, Basketball, **Beach Volleyball,** Boxing, **Canoe Sprint**, Cycling (BMX), Diving, **Equestrian (jumping)**, Handball, Hockey, **Sailing**, **Table Tennis**, **Taekwondo**, Volleyball, Water Polo, **Wrestling (freestyle)**

There will be excitement today in Horse Guards Parade for the women's beach volleyball denouement and at the BMX track as both sexes - and the venue - make their Olympic bow in the seeding phase. Canoe Sprint reaches its climax, with home favourite Tim Brabants hoping the 13th is not his unlucky day in the 1,000m kayak. Luck shouldn't play a part in the men's team Table Tennis, for which China will again be favourites.

DO NOT MISS!

09:30-11:15 Canoe Sprint - men's kayak single, Eton Dorney
15:30-18:30 Table Tennis - men's team, ExCeL
19:00-22:30 Beach Volleyball - women's gold-medal match, Horse Guards Parade

DAY 14
Thursday
9 August 2012

What's on?

(medals contested in bold) **Athletics**, Basketball, **Beach Volleyball**, **Boxing**, **Canoe Sprint**, **Cycling (BMX)**, **Diving**, **Equestrian (dressage)**, **Football**, Gymnastics (rhythmic), Handball, Hockey, **Sailing**, **Swimming**, Synchro Swimming, **Taekwondo**, Volleyball, **Water Polo**, **Wrestling (freestyle)**

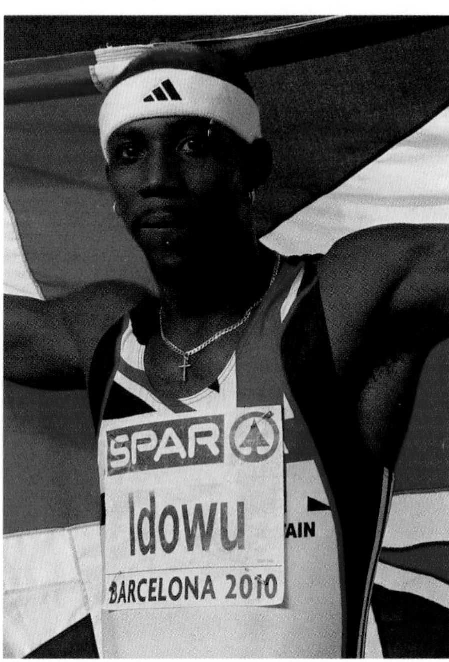

More big guns on show in the Olympic Stadium, with Usain Bolt primed to smash the field, and the world record, in the 200m and East London boy Phillips Idowu (above) ready to realise his gold-winning potential in the triple jump conclusion. We can hear the slow hand-clapping already! The women's Football final will be played out at Wembley Stadium and, through the water of Hyde Park's Serpentine, Britain's Keri-Anne Payne will be heavily backed for medals in the women's marathon swim.

DO NOT MISS!

12:00-15:00 Swimming - women's marathon (10km), Hyde Park
18:30-22:10 Athletics - men's 200m final, men's triple jump final, Olympic Stadium

DAY 15
Friday
10 August 2012

What's on?

(medals contested in bold) **Athletics**, Basketball, Boxing, Canoe Sprint, **Cycling (BMX)**, Diving, **Football**, Gymnastics (rhythmic), Handball, **Hockey**, **Sailing**, **Swimming**, **Synchro Swimming**, **Taekwondo**, Volleyball, Water Polo, **Wrestling (freestyle)**

The host nation will be focused on the BMX track, where Shanaze Reade (above), so unlucky to miss out on a medal in Beijing, will be ready to put things right on home soil. Taekwondo hero Aaron Cook will be in contention at ExCeL and the ever-dramatic Athletics relays begin. The men's Football bronze-medal match takes place in Cardiff.

DO NOT MISS!

15:00-17:20 Cycling **- women's BMX final, BMX Track**
19:00-21:40 Athletics **- men's 4x400m and women's 4x100m relay finals, Olympic Stadium**
19:45-21:45 Football **- men's bronze-medal match, Millennium Stadium**
20:00-23:15 Taekwondo **- men's -80kg gold-medal contest, ExCeL**

DAY 16
Saturday
11 August 2012

What's on?

(medals contested in bold) **Athletics**, **Basketball**, **Boxing**, **Canoe Sprint**, **Cycling (mountain bike)**, **Diving**, **Football**, **Gymnastics (rhythmic)**, **Handball**, **Hockey**, **Modern Pentathlon**, **Sailing**, **Taekwondo**, **Volleyball**, **Wrestling (freestyle)**

The Olympic men's Football final kicks off at Wembley Stadium. Can a European team break the South American stranglehold? Hockey and boxing golds are on offer, Tom Daley goes in the 10m Diving, there'll be thrills and spills in the mountain biking, and the women's Handball and Basketball conclude. It's also bye to Bolt.

DO NOT MISS!

12:30-14:30 Cycling **- women's mountain bike, Hadleigh Farm**
15:00-17:30 Football **- men's gold-medal match, Wembley Stadium**
18:45-21:30 Athletics **- men's 4x100m relay final, Olympic Stadium**
20:30-23:00 Boxing **- men's heavyweight final, ExCeL**

LAST DAY!
Sunday
12 August 2012

What's on?

(medals contested in bold) **Athletics**, **Basketball**, **Boxing**, **Cycling (mountain bike)**, **Gymnastics (rhythmic)**, **Handball**, **Modern Pentathlon**, **Volleyball**, **Water Polo**, **Wrestling (freestyle)**

It can't be over yet, can it? Afraid so, but what a day to end on. Five Boxing medals are decided in the ExCeL, the men's Handball final is sure to be brilliant and high-scoring and the USA's Basketball Dream Team should be in action. The excellent women's Modern Pentathlon will also take place across London. The Closing Ceremony starts at 19:30, when more than 14,000 athletes and thousands of spectators will bid farewell to the XXX Olympiad.

DO NOT MISS!

11:00-13:40 Athletics **- men's marathon, The Mall**
15:00-17:30 Basketball **- men's gold-medal game, North Greenwich Arena**
15:00-17:30 Handball **- men's gold-medal match, Basketball Arena**

LONDON 2012 VENUE GUIDE

The sports and the athletes are nothing without the arenas they compete in. Here are the venues for London 2012...

VENUES AROUND THE UK

1. Hampden Park

Events: Football

Where: A few miles to the south of Glasgow city centre, in Scotland

The home venue of Scotland's national football team and amateur Scottish club Queen's Park, Hampden Park is a 52,063-capacity stadium that will host eight Olympic Football matches. It is rated as a five-star venue by UEFA and was one of the venues on Take That's recent comeback tour.

Did you know? Mike Tyson headlined a boxing card at Hampden Park in 2000, fighting fellow American, Lou Savarese, and controversially beating him within 40 seconds.

2. St James' Park

Events: Football

Where: In the centre of Newcastle-Upon-Tyne in the north-east of England

The oldest (built in 1892) and largest (52,387 capacity) stadium in the north-east of England, St James' Park is the sixth largest stadium in the UK and home to Newcastle United FC. It will stage nine Olympic football matches, including a quarter-final in both the men's and the women's tournaments.

Did you know? Former England centre-forward – and now television football pundit – Alan Shearer is Newcastle United's all-time top goalscorer with 206 goals.

3. Old Trafford

Events: Football

Where: Close to Manchester City centre in the north-west of England

The 'Theatre of Dreams' is home to that little-known English football club, Manchester United, in the north-west of England. It was recently expanded to house 76,000 seats – making it the second largest football ground in the UK, behind Wembley Stadium.

Did you know? Bobby Charlton, one of Manchester United's most decorated and popular players, coined the phrase 'Theatre of Dreams'.

4. City of Coventry Stadium

Events: Football

Where: Coventry, Midlands

Home of Coventry City football club since 2005, the stadium will host 12 Olympic Football matches during the 2012 Games. The stadium holds 32,609 people, is also known as the Ricoh Arena and rock 'n' rollers Oasis, Bon Jovi and Pink have all performed there.

Did you know? Britain's double Olympic gold-medal winner Dame Kelly Holmes and Sports Minister Richard Caborn officially opened the venue on 24 February 2007.

5. Millennium Stadium

Events: Football

Where: On the banks of the Taff in Cardiff

During the building of the New Wembley, the Millennium Stadium hosted FA Cup Finals and will be the first venue used during London 2012, when the women's matches kick-off on 24 July. It will also be packed to the rafters for the men's bronze-medal match. The stadium has an impressive capacity of 74,600 and is the home of the Wales rugby team.

Did you know? The Millennium Stadium was only the second stadium in Europe to incorporate a fully retractable roof into its design.

6. Weymouth & Portland

Events: Sailing, Paralympic Sailing

Where: Dorset on the south coast of England

Some of the most scenic and natural sailing waters in the UK are to be found in Weymouth and Portland, and the marina has already hosted numerous international sailing events, including the 2006 World Youth Championships, in which more than 60 nations took part. New lifting and mooring facilities have been added to this world-class arena for the Olympic Games.

Did you know? No seats will be on offer for the Sailing. There will be sitting and standing room only for spectators.

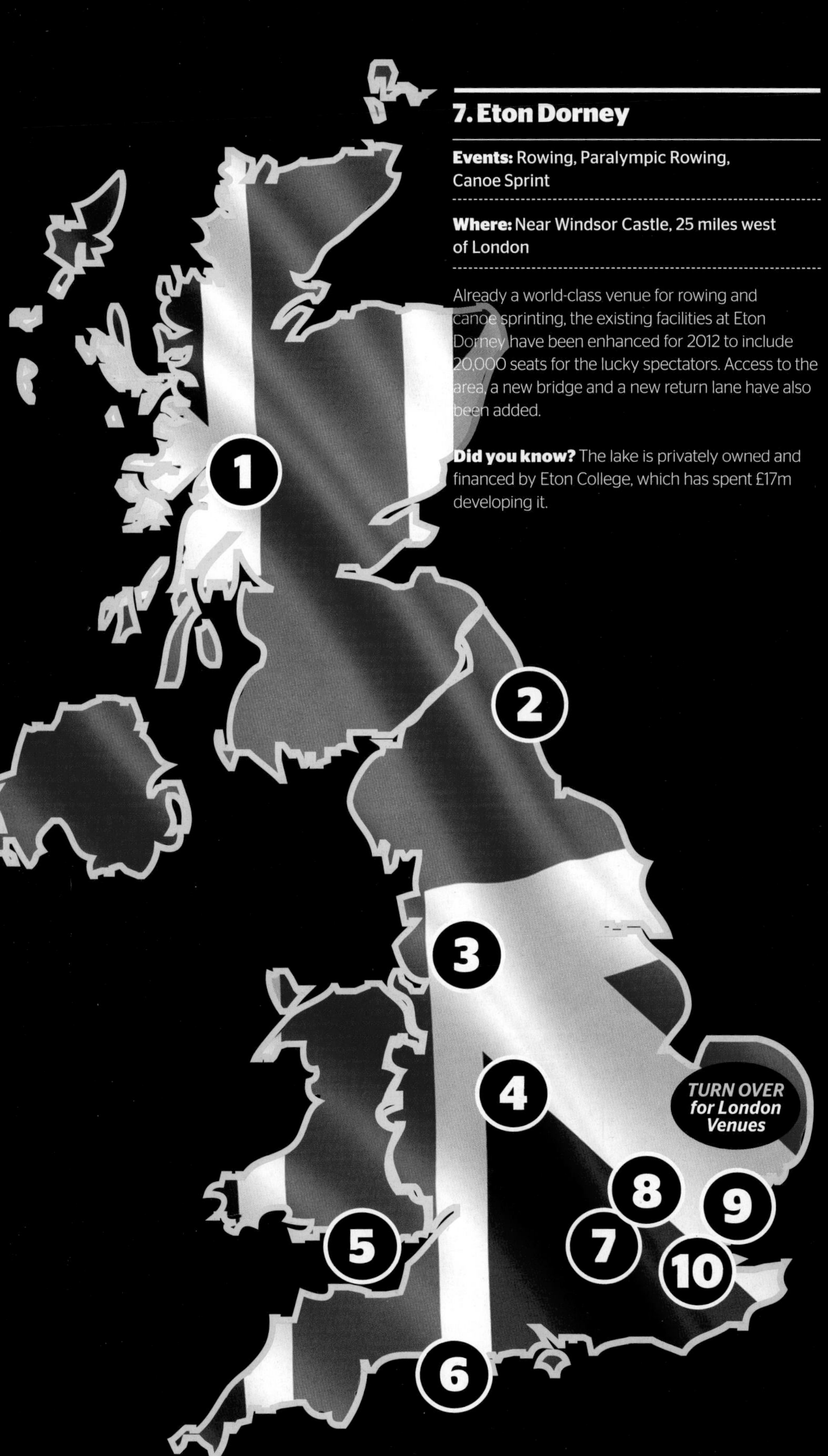

7. Eton Dorney

Events: Rowing, Paralympic Rowing, Canoe Sprint

Where: Near Windsor Castle, 25 miles west of London

Already a world-class venue for rowing and canoe sprinting, the existing facilities at Eton Dorney have been enhanced for 2012 to include 20,000 seats for the lucky spectators. Access to the area, a new bridge and a new return lane have also been added.

Did you know? The lake is privately owned and financed by Eton College, which has spent £17m developing it.

8. Lee Valley White Water Centre

Events: Canoe Slalom

Where: 30km north of the Olympic Park, on the edge of the 1,000-acre River Lee Country Park

The Lee Valley White Water Centre is the only venue that has been finished and opened to the public before London 2012. There are two courses being designed for the Games: a 300m competition course and a 160m intermediate/training course. Fifteen cubic metres of water per second will be pumped into the 300m course.

Did you know? During London 2012, temporary seating will be installed for 12,000 spectators.

9. Hadleigh Farm

NEW for 2012

Events: Mountain Bike

Where: Essex, to the east of London

Easily accessible from London, and technically challenging, Hadleigh Farm, in Essex, was the perfect venue for the Olympic mountain biking. The terrain is hilly and covered with grassland and low-lying shrubbery, and offers great viewing points for spectators. It also overlooks the Thames Estuary and connects with Hadleigh Castle.

Did you know? Temporary grandstands that can hold 3,000 people will be erected at Hadleigh Farm.

10. Brands Hatch

Events: Paralympic Road Cycling (road race and time trial)

Where: Brands Hatch, Kent

Venue for British Formula One Grands Prix between 1964 and 1986, Brands Hatch is an internationally renowned racetrack. For London 2012, it will determine the medal winners in the Paralympic Road Cycling race and time trial. The first ever race on the circuit, in 1928, was over four miles and was between cyclists and cross-country runners.

Did you know? Britain's Nigel Mansell holds the Brands Hatch Grand Prix lap record, clocking 1:09.593 in his Williams-Honda in July 1986.

VENUES IN LONDON

1. Wembley Arena

Events: Badminton, Rhythmic Gymnastics

Where: North-west London

Opposite Wembley Stadium, the Arena is a flagship entertainment facility that was refurbished at the same time as the stadium at a cost of £35m. It is London's second-largest indoor arena behind the O2 and regularly stages music concerts and sports tournaments, such as the Masters snooker and Premier League darts.

Did you know? A Square of Fame outside the Arena, where performers are invited to have bronze plaques with their names and handprints, includes Stephen Hendry, Kylie Minogue and Lionel Richie.

2. Wembley Stadium

Events: Football

Where: North-west London

Built on the site of the 1923 Wembley Stadium and the famous Twin Towers, the New Wembley Stadium is the second-largest stadium in Europe (Barcelona's Camp Nou is the biggest) with an arch that rockets 130m into the London skyline. It is one of the most expensive stadiums ever built at a cost of £798m and will host the men's and the women's Football finals.

Did you know? The first match at Wembley was played behind closed doors between Multiplex (who built the stadium) and Wembley Stadium staff.

3. Lord's Cricket Ground

Events: Archery

Where: North-west London in St John's Wood

A venue for international matches since the 19th century, Lord's is to cricket what Wembley is to football, so it's good to see the venue involved in the London Games, despite cricket no longer being a part of the Olympic programme. Instead, Lord's will host the Archery competition, with crowds of nearly 7,000 people expected to inspire the athletes.

Did you know? Lord's is the home ground of Middlesex County Cricket Club and its owner, Marylebone Cricket Club, remains the guardian of the Laws and the Spirit of the game.

4. The Mall

Events: Athletics (marathon and race walk), Paralympic Athletics (marathon), and Road Cycling (road race)

Where: Runs from Buckingham Palace to Trafalgar Square in central London

One of the grandest ceremonial routes in the world, The Mall had to play a part in the Olympics. As for Royal Weddings, the pavements of The Mall will be lined eager Olympic spectators.

Did you know? A rumour exists that, in the event of an emergency that endangers the monarch, the Mall can be converted into a makeshift runway!

5. Earls Court Exhibition Centre

Events: Volleyball

Where: West London, near the Natural History Museum

The largest exhibition centre in the middle of London and accessible from Earl's Court and West Brompton rail stations. It first opened its doors to the public in 1937 after costing £1.5m to construct, going way over budget. It will be redeveloped again after the Olympic Games.

Did you know? Earl's Court One, where Volleyball athletes will battle it out for gold, silver and bronze, has 41,811 square metres of space.

6. Hyde Park

Events: Triathlon, Marathon Swimming

Where: London's West End, very close to first-class shopping and accommodation

Open to the public since 1637, Hyde Park is one of London's largest parks and a perfect host for the gruelling Triathlon and Marathon Swimming events. There are five tube stations nearby: Hyde Park Corner and Knightsbridge (Piccadilly Line), Queensway, Lancaster Gate and Marble Arch (all Central Line), and the course will be clearly marked, so you can plan where you want to stand.

Did you know? The park is divided by the Serpentine, a 28-acre recreational lake.

7. Horse Guards Parade

Events: Beach Volleyball

Where: Central London, in the political nucleus of the country

A large parade ground off Whitehall in central London, Horse Guards Parade normally holds the annual Trooping of the Colour to commemorate the Queen's birthday, but will have its own beach built for London 2012 to host the Beach Volleyball. One of the temporary courts will have enough seating for 15,000 spectators.

Did you know? When he was Commander-in-Chief of the British Army, the Duke of Wellington was based at Horse Guards Parade.

8. Hampton Court Palace

Events: Road Cycling (time trial)

Where: In the London Borough of Richmond upon Thames

Once just one of a number of residences for Tudor King Henry VIII, Hampton Court Palace is as rich in Royal history as it is in sporting history. It houses the oldest real tennis court in the country (one of fewer than 50 remaining in the world) and the beautiful building is a mixture of domestic Tudor and Baroque stylings.

Did you know? Hampton Court Palace also has an 18-hole golf course, although it plays no part in London 2012.

9. Wimbledon

Events: Tennis

Where: South-west London near Richmond Park and Kingston-Upon-Thames

The setting for the most famous tennis tournament in the world since 1877, Wimbledon is the home of the All England Lawn Tennis and Croquet Club. Unfortunately, there will be no Olympic Croquet at London 2012, but all of the Tennis events will be held here and, with a retractable roof added to the showpiece Centre Court in 2009, there is no danger of rain stopping play!

Did you know? Wimbledon is the only remaining grass court venue in the world for Grand Slam events.

TURN OVER for Olympic Park Venues

10

11

12

13

10. ExCeL

Events: Boxing, Fencing, Judo, Modern Pentathlon, Table Tennis, Taekwondo, Weightlifting, Wrestling, Boccia, Paralympic Table Tennis, Paralympic Judo, Paralympic Powerlifting, Volleyball (Sitting), Wheelchair Fencing

Where: Near London City Airport in east London's Victoria Dock

One of the busiest venues, ExCeL will host 143 sessions across a huge variety of sports. No work has had to be done to the centre before the Games.

Did you know? ExCeL stands for Exhibition Centre London, just in case you were wondering.

11. North Greenwich Arena

NEW for 2012

Events: Artistic Gymnastics, Trampoline, Basketball, Wheelchair Basketball

Where: Just across the Thames from the mouth of the River Lee

Otherwise known as the O2 Arena, the North Greenwich Arena (rename because of IOC sponsorship regulations) was built for the millennium and is now a sports and entertainment arena with a 20,000 capacity.

Did you know? Comedian Chris Rock broke the Guinness World Record for the largest audience at a comedy show at the venue.

12. The Royal Artillery Barracks

Events: Shooting, Paralympic Shooting, Paralympic Archery

Another Olympic venue steeped in history, construction of the current Barracks building began as far back as 1776, when 'Mad' King George III was on the thrown. For 2012, four indoor ranges for pistol and rifle Shooting will be erected, as will an outdoor shotgun range for trap and skeet events.

Did you know? The shooting area was going to be built in Bisley, in Surrey, but the IOC determined too many sports were outside of the capital.

13. Greenwich Park

Events: Equestrian events – Jumping, Dressage and Eventing, Paralympic Equestrian, Modern Pentathlon

Where: On the South Bank of the River Thames in south-east London

The oldest Royal Park in London provides a fitting setting for the Olympic Equestrian events. A cross country course has been designed especially for London 2012 and the main arena will be within the grounds of the National Maritime Museum.

Did you know? James I built a brick wall enclosing the park – and most of it still exists today.

VENUES IN THE OLYMPIC PARK

1. Eton Manor

NEW for 2012

Events: Wheelchair Tennis

Where: In the north of the Olympic Park

Developed on the site of the Old Eton Sports Club, Eton Manor – with its nine competition courts and four warm-up courts – is in the north of the Olympic Park and will play host to the Wheelchair Tennis. It will also house temporary training pools for athletes in the aquatic events, including three 50m pools for swimmers and smaller ones for water polo and synchronised swimming competitors.

Did you know? After London 2012, work will begin on permanently relocating the Olympic Hockey Park to Eton Manor.

2. Hockey Centre

NEW for 2012

Events: Hockey, Paralympic 5-a-side Football, Paralympic 7-a-side Football

Where: Inside the Olympic Park

The hockey centre will house two pitches, one for competitive matches and one for warming up and practising. It makes up part of the group of centres known as Eton Manor and will have 3,000 permanent seats, but this number can be increased dramatically to around 15,000 for larger-scale events.

Did you know? Leyton Orient football club expressed an interest in moving into the Hockey Centre after the Games.

3. Velodrome

NEW for 2012

Events: Track Cycling, Paralympic Track Cycling

Where: In the north of the Olympic Park

One of the most technologically advanced and sustainable constructions designed for the Olympics, the wood for the track has been certified by the Forest Stewardship Council and the arena has a 100% naturally ventilated system, delivering the perfect climate without the need for air con. Team GB were consulted during the deign process.

Did you know? 6,000 spectators will fill the lower and upper tiers of the stadium for an event in which the home athletes are expected to do well.

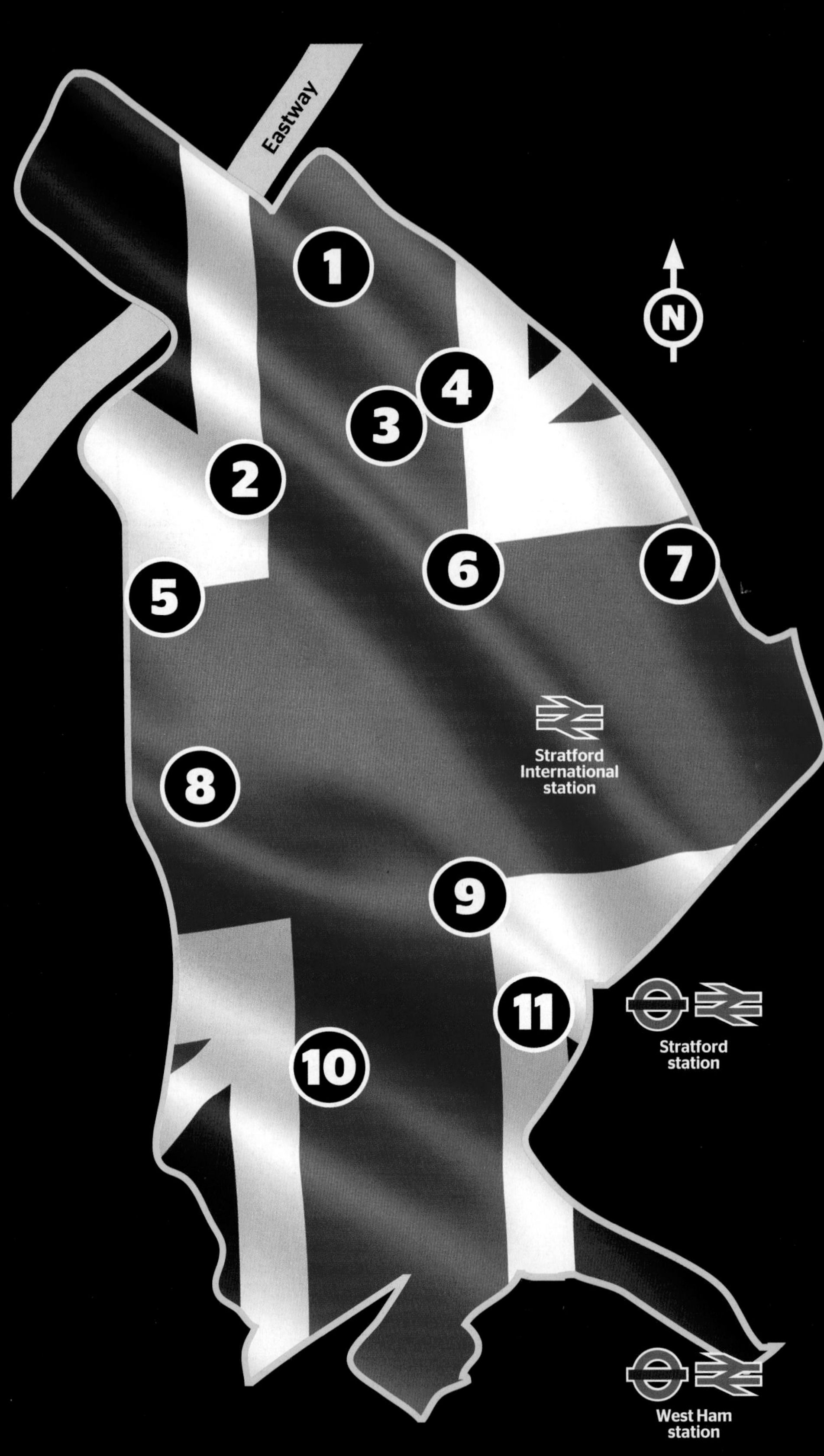

4. BMX Track

NEW for 2012

Events: BMX Cycling

Where: In the north of the Olympic Park

Located next to the velodrome in the north of the mighty Olympic Park, the 400m BMX track will have 6,000 temporary seats for fans of the newest cycling discipline, introduced at the Beijing 2008 Games. After London 2012, the track will be made suitable for BMX racers of all ages and abilities.

Did you know? 14,000 cubic metres of soil, enough to fill three Olympic-size swimming pools, was used to create a series of levels – up to four metres high – upon which the final BMX Cycling track was formed.

5. IBC/MPC

NEW for 2012

The IBC/MPC is located in the Main Media Complex and includes a 12,000 square metre catering village that will knock out more than 50,000 meals per day during the London 2012 Games. There'll also be a high street containing banks, shops, a post office, travel agents and newsagents. There is plenty of workspace, over four floors, in which journalists can write and send stories and reports, and for accredited photographers to process and send their imagery. The state-of-the-art digital technology available across the IBC/MPC should ensure no hiccups for the media during the games.

Did you know? The IBC/MPC is likely to be transformed into housing and business space after the Games.

6. Basketball Arena

NEW for 2012

Events: Basketball, Wheelchair Basketball, Wheelchair Rugby, Handball

Where: In the north of the Olympic Park

A temporary construction where the NBA's finest will be trying to spin, jump and slam-dunk their way to gold-medal glory, the Arena will be transformed halfway through the Games to cater for the fast-paced, end-to-end dramatics of Handball and then Wheelchair Rugby and Wheelchair Basketball. The staff here are going to be busy.

Did you know? The Basketball Arena is one of the largest temporary constructions ever built for an Olympic Games.

7. Athletes' Village

NEW for 2012

Events: In the Olympic Park

Home to around 17,000 competitors and Games officials, the Athletes' Village will be a hub of drama and anticipation, where the world's best will live among each other for the duration of the Olympics. Water features around the village echo the proximity of the River Lee and all rooms will have internet and wireless networking. Athletes will also be able to get to Central London in just seven minutes thanks to the High Speed 1 Javelin shuttle service. Impressive.

Did you know? After the games, the Athletes' Village will provide 2,800 new homes, including 1,379 affordable ones.

8. Handball Arena

NEW for 2012

Events: Handball, Goalball, Modern Pentathlon

Where: West side of the Olympic Park

Between 6,000 and 7,000 spectators will get to watch one of the Olympic Games' fastest-growing sports – the end-to-end, high-scoring match-ups of Handball. Despite this being a bespoke arena for one of continental Europe's favourite sports, it's not big enough for the ultimate exchanges, so the semi-finals and final will be held at the larger Basketball Arena.

Did you know? This is the only permanent indoor arena in the Olympic Park.

9. Water Polo Arena

NEW for 2012

Events: Water Polo

Where: South-east corner of the Olympic park

Adjacent to the Aquatics Centre in one of the busiest parts of Olympic Park, the Water Polo Arena shares some back-of-house facilities – such as space for broadcasters, catering and security – with the swimming and diving facilities in order to make the best use of space. It contains one competition pool and one warm-up pool.

Did you know? Despite not winning a medal since the 1920 Games in Antwerp, Great Britain are still third in the all-time medal table. Women's Water Polo was introduced in Sydney 2000.

10. Olympic Stadium

NEW for 2012

Events: Athletics, Paralympic Athletics

Where: South of the Olympic Park

The focal point for London 2012, the Olympic Stadium will host the Opening and Closing Ceremonies and all of the Athletic events. Usain Bolt and all of the other big names in world athletics will take their Olympic bow in front of a capacity 80,000 crowd, and arty concourses are planned for outside the stadium, so people can gather to watch the action on big screens

Did you know? The 1908 Olympic Stadium in London cost £60,000. The Olympic Stadium of 2012 cost £537m.

11. Aquatics Centre

NEW for 2012

Events: Diving, Swimming, Synchronised Swimming, Paralympic Swimming, Modern Pentathlon

Where: South-east corner of the Olympic Park

Designed by world-renowned architect Zaha Hadid, the Aquatics Centre has an eye-catching 160m wave-style roof, and makes a stunning entrance to the Olympic Park. It will house 50m and 25m pools, a 50m warm-up pool, a diving pool and a temporary Water Polo Arena.

Did you know? Four skeletons were discovered and removed from a prehistoric settlement discovered on the site of the Aquatics Centre.

NORWICH UNION
GBR 1
GLASGOW

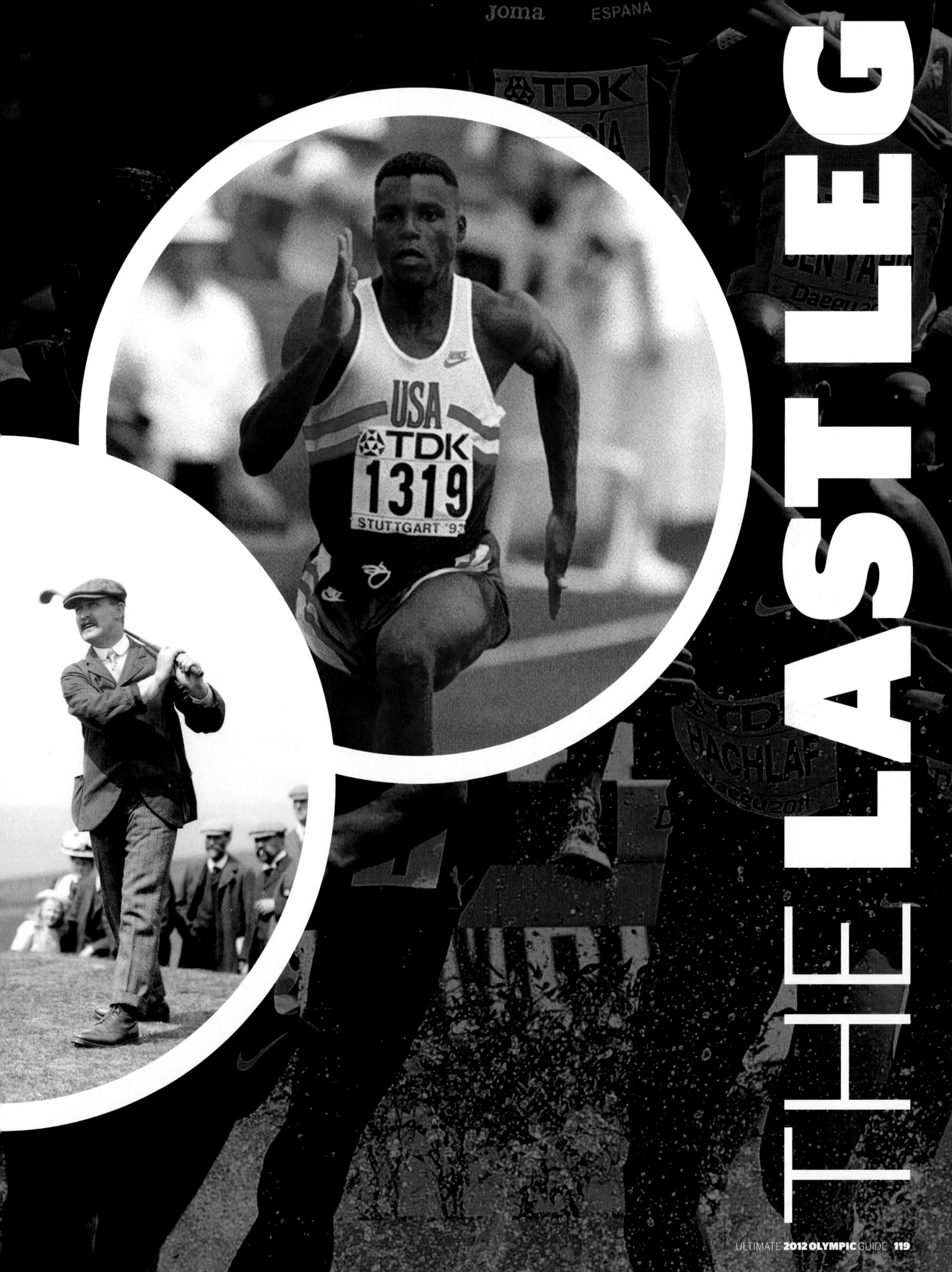
THE LAST LEG
Joma
ESPANA
TDK
USA
TDK
1319
STUTTGART
HACHLAF

LONDON 2012 MYTHS & LEGENDS

1. CALGARY '88

The Jamaican bobsled team crashed then carried their sled to the finish line

John Candy's film Cool Runnings brought the 1988 Jamaican bobsled team to the world's attention, but also took some liberties with the facts. The team were fast starters, but they weren't ever close to medal positions. They crashed during one of their four runs, and were thus disqualified, then walked alongside the sled as it was pushed to the finish line. They didn't carry it.

VERDICT: False

2. LOS ANGELES '32

A dopey lap counter cost an Olympian a world record

One of the all-time great steeplechasers, Finland's Volmari Iso-Hollo, was dominating the field in the 3,000m in 1932. When he crossed the line, no finishing bell rang, so he continued, thinking it was his error and ran an extra 460m before stopping. The idiot whose job it was to count 'laps completed' had been distracted by the decathlon and Iso-Hollo was robbed of a world record. In 1936, Iso-Hollo retained the gold and broke the world record.

VERDICT: True

3. ST LOUIS '04

A one-legged gymnast won six medals

George Eyser was an inspired German-American artistic gymnast, who tragically lost his left leg after being run over by a train, of all things. But, not one to be deterred, he competed in the 1904 St Louis Olympic Games with a prosthetic limb, winning six medals in one day of competition, including three golds in the vault, rope climbing and parallel bars. He also competed in the athletics triathlon, but finished last.

VERDICT: True

4. LONDON '48

A 17-year-old American won the decathlon despite barely training for it

You can't really make this up to be honest. Bob Mathis was a teenage athletic prodigy who only learnt some of the decathlon events three weeks before the 1948 Olympics in London. It didn't matter, though. He finished third on the first day, rose to first on the second and comfortably maintained his lead on the third. He remains the youngest athlete to win an Olympic gold medal in track & field history.

VERDICT: True

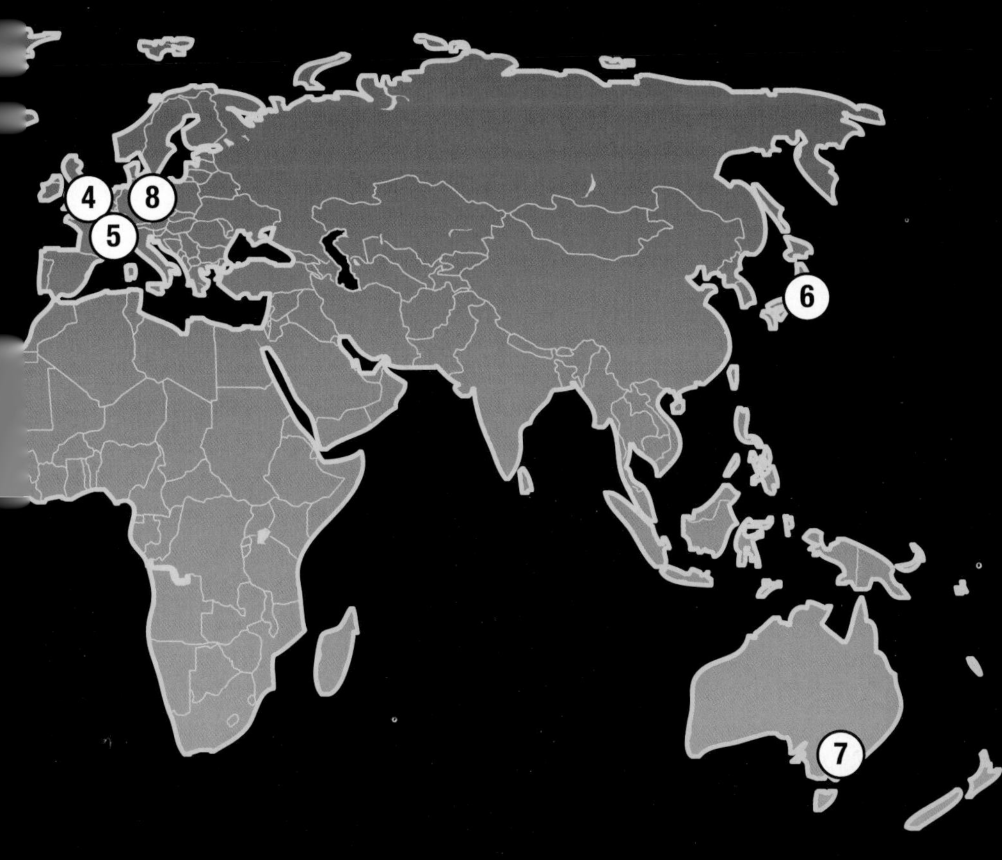

8. BERLIN '36

A German man competed as a woman in 1936

Obsessed with proving his Aryan mob were, like, the best humans ever, Hitler wanted Germany to top the medal table in 1936, which they did, winning 89 golds to the USA's second-placed 56. However, asking 18-year-old Hermann Ratjen to compete as Dora Ratjen in the women's high jump proved desperate, not astute. The deep-voiced German competitor only finished fourth, leaving Hitler red-faced and embarrassed.

VERDICT: True

8. BERLIN '36

The Nazis started the Olympic Torch relay

In the Ancient Olympic Games, flames would be kept lit throughout the festival, but torches didn't make a comeback in the Modern Olympic movement until 1928, when the practice of lighting was reborn. The current relay format, though, was not invented until 1936, by Dr Carl Diem. Hitler believed the Ancient Greeks were forebears of the Aryans and a flame relay from Olympia to Berlin would echo this. Good addition, bad reason.

VERDICT: True

5. AMSTERDAM '28

An Olympic rower stopped still during a race to let a family of ducks swim past

Henry 'Bobby' Pearce was the ultra-talented lone rowing representative for Australia in Amsterdam, in 1928. While racing against a cumbersome Frenchman, he indeed stopped to let a family of ducks pass his boat before going on to win the race and, later, the gold medal...which he retained in 1932, and in the process became the first the first single sculler to win back-to-back gold medals.

VERDICT: True

6. TOKYO '64

Joe Frazier qualified for the 1964 Olympics despite defeat in qualifying to Buster Mathis

Buster Mathis was a 300lb human wrecking machine, unfortunately for him, his bones still broke. His finger proved this while he was defeating Joe Frazier in the US qualifiers for the Tokyo games. He was subsequently forced to pull out of the 1964 Games and Frazier went on to become Olympic champion, despite breaking his thumb in his second-round bout (he didn't tell anyone!).

VERDICT: True

7. MELBOURNE '56

A female equestrian Olympian won two silvers despite not being able to feel her legs

Lis Hartel was a two-time silver medal winner at the 1952 and 1956 Olympic Games. Impressive, sure, but even more so when you realise she lost the use of her legs below her knees after a bout of polio while pregnant. She wasn't deterred, though. She gave birth to her child and went on to become one of the most remarkable Olympians and a bit of a celebrity in her native Denmark. True grit.

VERDICT: True

8. BERLIN '36

Hitler snubbed Jesse Owens in 1936

Hitler made a point of only congratulating German winners on his first day at the Olympic Stadium and was told this wasn't in the spirit of the Games. The next day he congratulated no one, including Owens – he did not single Owens out. Hitler did leave the stadium after African-American athlete Cornelius Johnson won gold in the high jump. When Owens became a motivational speaker in the 1950s the story was amplified, to please his audiences.

VERDICT: False

ULTIMATE **OLYMPIC**

LEGENDS

The Olympic Games is a stage where the truly great perform, a place where the ultra-talented few cement their names in history – forever

Carl Lewis

Country: USA
DOB: 1/7/1961
Olympics: 1984, 1988, 1992, 1996
Medal haul: 10 (9 gold)

The Greatest Track and Field Athlete Ever
Frederick Carlton Lewis dominated sprinting and long jump for more than a decade, becoming the only man to successfully defend Olympic 100m and long jump titles (winning in Los Angeles in 1984 and Seoul 1988).

At the 1996 Atlanta Games, Lewis's third-round leap of 8.50m won him the gold by a margin of 21cm and he became one of only three Olympians to win the same individual event four times, sharing the honour with Danish sailor Paul Bert Elvstrøm and American discus thrower Al Oerter. In 1991, Lewis also recorded a then world record time of 9.86secs for the 100m, at the age of 30.

Did you know?
After hanging up his spikes, Lewis became an actor, but never really hit the Hollywood big-time, mostly appearing in cameos as himself. Lewis Carl Hamilton, the British Formula 1 driver, born soon after the 1984 Los Angles Olympics, was named after Lewis.

Sir Steve Redgrave

Country: Great Britain
DOB: 23/3/1962
Olympics: 1984, 1988, 1992, 1996, 2000
Medal haul: 6 (5)

The Shoulders of a Giant
Dubbed 'Britain's Greatest Olympian' for very obvious reasons, Steve Redgrave competed at five consecutive Olympic Games and came home with five gold medals, the only Olympian to have achieved such a feat.

After his Atlanta triumph in 1996, he memorably declared: "If anyone sees me get in a boat ever again they have permission to shoot me!" But he came back four years later to win in the coxless fours with Matthew Pinsent, James Cracknell and Tim Foster – the so-called 'Oarsome Foursome'. A truly indomitable Olympian.

Did you know?
Redgrave was a member of the 1989-90 British bobsleigh team.

Larysa Latynina

Country: USSR
DOB: 27/12/1934
Olympics: 1956, 1960, 1964
Medal haul: 18 (9)

Greatest Olympian Ever
Such a title can be measured in so many ways, and has been over the years, but it's hard to dispute the facts: gymnast Larysa Latynina has won more Olympic medals than any other competitor, male or female, in any sport and, therefore stands alone, in our eyes, as the Greatest Olympian Ever. A painstaking trainer and obsessive perfectionist, she single-handedly established the Soviet Union as a mighty force in gymnastics and holds the record for most individual medals (she has 14 outside of team events) in Olympic history. Dispute that!

Did you know?
Latynina's nine Olympic wins puts her joint second on the list of athletes with the most gold medals – alongside Mark Spitz, Carl Lewis and Paavo Nurmi – behind only Michael Phelps, who has 14.

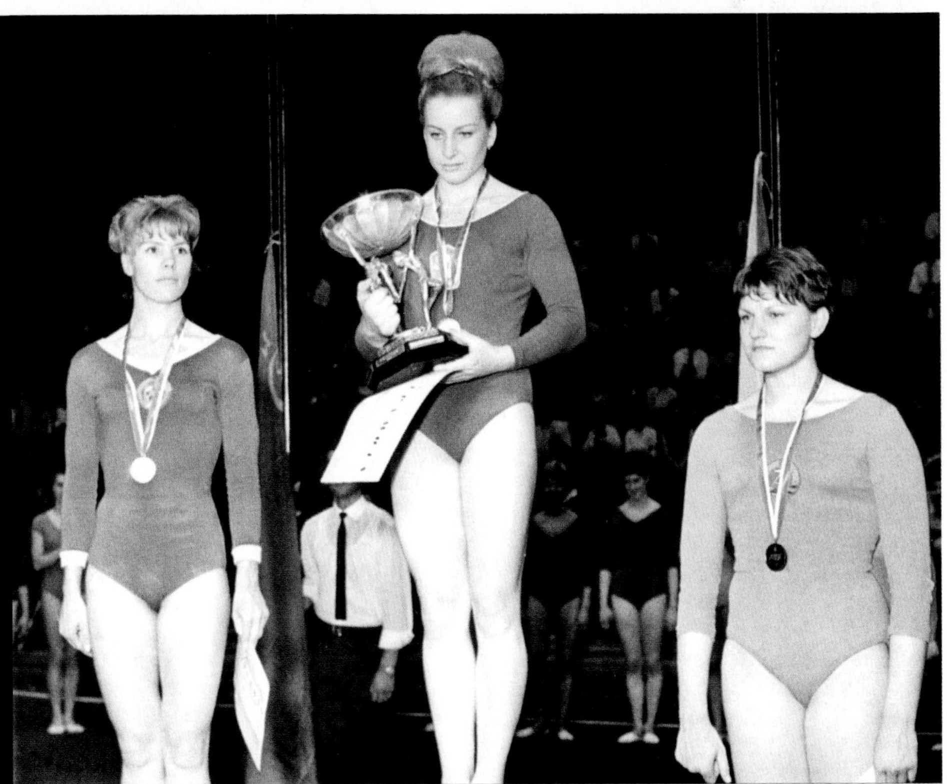

Jesse Owens

Country: USA
DOB: 12/9/1913 Died: 31/3/1980
Olympics: 1936
Medal haul: 4 (4)

Hitler's Symbolic Nemesis

"I let my feet spend as little time on the ground as possible. From the air, fast down and from the ground, fast up." The seventh of 11 children, Jesse Owens was born with a gift for speed across a track and flight across a long-jump pit, and came to the world's attention when he bagged four gold medals in front of Adolf Hitler in Berlin, in 1936. Hitler's Nazi propaganda machine promoted the ludicrous concept of Aryan racial superiority and Owens' incredible triumph flew directly in the face of it.

Did you know?

Honouring his legacy, the Jesse Owens Award is USA Track & Field's highest accolade and is presented to the outstanding US performers. It was first awarded in 1981, after Owens' death, to hurdler Edwin Moses.

Dawn Fraser

Country: Australia
DOB: 4/9/1937
Olympics: 1956, 1960, 1964
Medal haul: 8 (4)

Greatest Living Female Water Sports Champ

One of the, if not *the*, greatest female swimmers and one of only two (Hungary's Krisztina Egerszegi being the other) to have won the same event at three successive Olympics. The 100m freestyle record was Dawn Fraser's for 15 years – from 1 December 1956 to 8 January 1972 – and in an illustrious career she won eight Olympic medals.

Did you know? Fraser broke the one-minute barrier for 100m freestyle in October 1962.

Jeannie Longo

Country: France
DOB: 31/10/1958
Olympics:1984,1988,1992,1996,2000,2004, 2008
Medal haul: 4 (1)

The Cyclist Who'll Never Say Die

A stalwart of world-class cycling for more than 20 years, Jeannie Longo often competes against riders who weren't even born when she first rode in the Olympics, in Los Angeles in 1984. Twenty-eight years later, will she make London 2012? It would be foolish to count her out.

Did you know? Longo has a degree in maths and was an alpine and cross-country skier before she got into cycling.

Teófilo Stevenson

Country: Cuba
DOB: 29/3/1952
Olympics: 1972, 1976, 1980
Medal haul: 3 (3)

Best Boxer Never to Win Heavyweight Title

Teófilo Stevenson is one of only three boxers – alongside Hungarian László Papp and fellow Cuban Félix Savón – to win three Olympic golds. In 1976, American promoters offered him a $5million clash with Muhammad Ali, but Stevenson refused, asking: "What is one million dollars compared to the love of eight million Cubans?"

Did you know? During his career as a boxer, he won 302 fights and lost only 22.

Bob Beamon

Country: USA
DOB: 29/8/1946
Olympics: 1968
Medal haul: 1 (1)

"My Goodness Me, It's An Enormous One!"
Sent to live at his grandmother's as a child because his violent father was threatening to kill him if his mother brought him home, Bob Beamon fought his early demons to make *that* long jump at the Mexico Olympics of 1968. His leap of 8.9m bettered the then world record by a whopping 55cm and remained the global mark to beat for 23 years.

After this, many sports reporters began to use the expression 'Beamonesque' to describe feats of almost unimaginable spectacle and *Sports Illustrated* recently listed Beamon's 1968 jump as one of the five greatest sporting moments of the 20th century.

Did you know?
Beamon's 23-year holding of the record is not the longest time a long-jump mark has stood without being broken; Jesse Owens' jump of 8.13m held for 25 years, from 1935-1960.

Sebastian Coe

Country: Great Britain
DOB: 29/9/1956
Olympics: 1980, 1984
Medal haul: 4 (2)

Lord of the Manor

Alongside fellow Britons Steve Ovett and Steve Cram, Sebastian Coe dominated middle-distance racing for much of the 1980s, winning gold in the 1,500m at the 1980 and 1984 Olympic games. He is the only person to win successive Olympic 1,500m titles.

A hero on the track, it was Coe - as head of the London bid to host the 2012 Summer Olympics - who did most to help secure the International Olympic Committee's go-ahead for the sporting spectacle that lies ahead. A British legend in more ways than one.

Did you know?

If you ever see Lord Coe in a sandwich shop he won't be having a tuna melt - he's allergic to fish. He was a Conservative MP from 1992-1997 and was made a life peer in 2000.

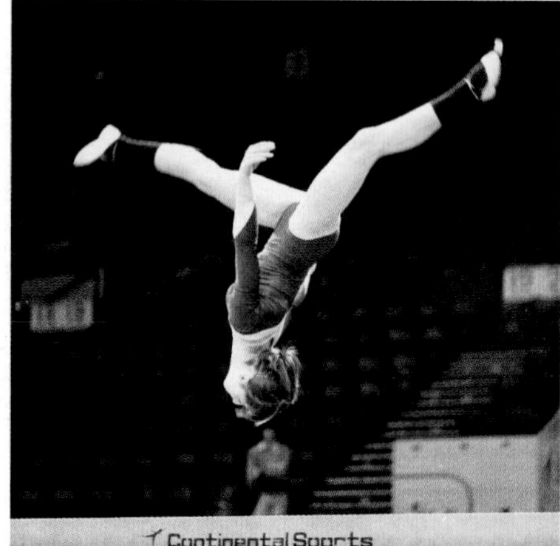

Nadia Comaneci

Country: Romania
DOB: 12/11/1961
Olympics: 1976, 1980
Medal haul: 9 (5)

The Perfect 10

At 14 years old, gymnast Nadia Comaneci achieved the first perfect 10 score on the uneven bars in Montreal 1976. It caused a good deal of confusion because the scoreboards weren't equipped to display the extra digit. Incredibly, she scored an additional six scores of 10 during the Games.

Did you know? Comaneci is the youngest all-round Olympic gymnast ever and a cat in the TV series *Lost* was named after her.

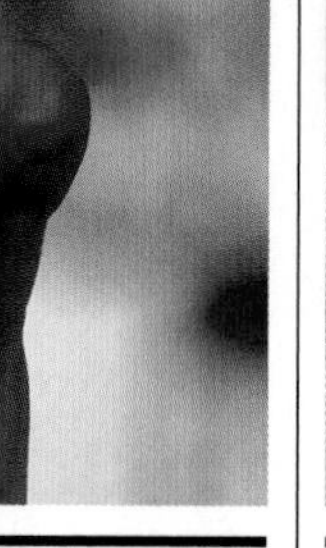

Marie José Perec

Country: France
DOB: 9/5/1968
Olympics: 1992, 1996
Medal haul: 3 (3)

French Swan

Only the second woman ever to win the 200m and 400m events at the same Games (1996), Marie José Perec also set an Olympic record for the 400m in Atlanta. She would have competed in Sydney 2000 for the ultimate showdown with Cathy Freeman, but claimed she was harassed by the Australian media and decided not to take part.

Did you know? In 1996, Perec beat Michael Johnson to the 200/400m double by 20 minutes.

Yoshinobu Miyake

Country: Japan
DOB: 24/11/1939
Olympics: 1960, 1964, 1968, 1972
Medal haul: 3 (2)

Greatest Oriental Weightlifter Ever

With a style described as 'unique' and 'impeccable', Yoshinobu Miyake won a silver medal in the bantamweight class at the 1960 Games in Rome, but won gold as a featherweight at Tokyo 1964 and Mexico City 1968.

Did you know? Miyake set 25 weightlifting world records and the 'Miyake Pull' - a technique by which lifters keep their heels close together and toes pointed out - is named after him.

Michael Johnson

Country: USA
DOB: 13/9/1967
Olympics: 1992. 1996, 2000
Medal haul: 4 (4)

Reshaping the Science of Sprinting
Recognised as the greatest long sprinter in the history of track and field, Michael Johnson's brilliantly conditioned, apparently unorthodox, style gifted him the accolade of being the only male athlete to win the 200m and 400m events at the same Olympic Games (Atlanta 1996).

Did you know?
Johnson's medal haul could and should have been larger. Before Barcelona 1992, he contracted food poisoning and, losing strength and conditioning, came sixth in his semi-final.

Florence Griffith Joyner

Country: USA
DOB: 21/12/1959 Died: 21/09/1998
Olympics: 1984, 1988
Medal haul: 5 (3)

The Fastest Woman in History
The most remembered name of the 1988 Olympic Games in Seoul, 'Flo-Jo' won the women's 100m in an incredible world record time of 10.49 seconds - which has not been bettered - and earned another two golds in the 200m and 4x100m relay, plus a silver medal in the 4x400m relay. Constantly deflecting accusations of using performance-enhancing drugs during her career, she died in her sleep in 1998 from a congenital brain abnormality at just 38 years of age.
Did you know?
DJ Jazzy Jeff & the Fresh Prince, and Ludacris, have both paid homage to Flo-Jo in hip-hop recordings.

Mark Spitz

Country: USA
DOB: 10/2/1950
Olympics: 1968, 1972
Medal haul: 11 (9)

Seventh Heaven
In 1972, Mark Spitz's haul of seven gold medals was an Olympic record (only usurped in 2008 by Michael Phelps' eight in Beijing) and his total of nine gold medals overall equals that of Olympic greats such as Carl Lewis, Larysa Latynina and Paavo Nurmi. He was named World Swimmer of the Year in 1967, 1971 and 1972, and sported a wonderful moustache during his most successful periods.
Did you know?
Spitz broke his first world record in the pool at the age of 10, in the 100m butterfly.

Félix Savón

Country: Cuba
DOB: 22/9/1967
Olympics: 1992, 1996, 2000
Medal haul: 3 (3)

King of the Olympic Rings

The finest in a long and illustrious line of amateur Cuban boxers, Félix Savón dominated the heavyweight division for 14 years, competing in three Olympic Games (in Barcelona, Atlanta and Sydney) and never looking like coming away with anything less than a gold medal.

His first Olympic gold, in Barcelona, came after he beat Nigeria's David Izonritei 14-1; four years later, Savón annihilated David Defiagbon, of Canada, 20-2. A brutal punching machine, he won his third successive Olympic gold at the 2000 Games – beating Russia's Sultan Ibragimov 21-13 – and then promptly announced his retirement, at the age of 33.

Did you know? In February 2001, Welsh band the Manic Street Preachers – who became the first western rock group to play in Cuba for more than 20 years when they appeared at the Teatro Karl Marx in Havana – dedicated their song *You Love Us* to Savón.

Iolanda Balas

Country: Romania
DOB: 12/12/1936
Olympics: 1960, 1964
Medal haul: 2 (2)

It's Not All Win, Win, Win...

...unless your name is Iolanda Balas, the Romanian high jumper who chalked up 140 consecutive victories between 1957 and 1967 in all competitions and consecutive gold medals in Rome 1960 (winning by 14cm) and Tokyo 1964 (winning by 10cm). A pre-Fosbury, preternaturally long-legged, springboard phenomena.

Did you know? Balas went on to become head of the Romanian Athletics Federation.

Birgit Fischer

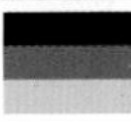

Country: Germany
DOB: 25/2/1962
Olympics: 1980, 1988, 1992, 1996, 2000, 2004
Medal haul: 12 (8)

Canoe Believe It?

Birgit Fischer's record is so sprawling and complete it is barely believable. Born in the early 1960s, Fischer was a phenomenally talented kayaker, who won eight gold medals over six Olympic Games, and was the first woman in Olympic history to win gold medals 20 years apart.

Did you know? Fischer holds the records for oldest Olympic canoe champion (42, in 2004) and youngest Olympic canoe champion (18, in 1980).

Muhammad Ali

Country: USA
DOB: 17/1/1942
Olympics: 1960
Medal haul: 1 (1)

Simply 'The Greatest'

Muhammad Ali began his boxing career as Cassius Clay and his hard work as an amateur boxer (100 wins, 5 losses) brought him a light-heavyweight gold medal in Rome in 1960.

Did you know? Fuming over the theft of his bicycle, a 12-year-old Cassius Clay was comforted by a police officer and boxing trainer called Joe E Martin. His boxing career stemmed from this childhood incident.

Matthew Pinsent

Country: Great Britain
DOB: 10/10/1970
Olympics: 1992, 1996, 2000, 2004
Medal haul: 4 (4)

Much More Than Just 'The Other One'
Winning three of his four consecutive gold medals alongside (or rather, in front of) Sir Steve Redgrave, Matthew Pinsent's record at the Olympics reads four out of four out of four – four golds from four events in four Olympic Games. Not bad, eh?
Did you know?
Pinsent, at one time, had the largest lung capacity recorded for a sportsman, at an incredible 8.5 litres.

Alexander Dityatin

Country: Soviet Union
DOB: 7/8/1957
Olympics: 1976, 1980
Medal haul: 10 (3)

1, 2, 3, 4, 5, 6, 7, 8...
Perhaps not the best-known Olympic legend, but Russian gymnast Alexander Dityatin won eight medals in front of his home crowd at the 1980 Moscow Olympics, setting the record for the most medals, of any type, at a single Games (now equalled, twice, by Michael Phelps).
Did you know? Dityatin is the only athlete to win a medal in each of the eight men's gymnastics events at one Olympics.

Kelly Holmes

Country: Great Britain
DOB: 19/4/1970
Olympics: 2000, 2004
Medal haul: 3 (2)

A Force To Be Reckoned With
Ex-army PT instructor Kelly Holmes was inspired by Sebastian Coe to take up middle-distance running and surpassed his achievements by winning the 800m *and* 1,500m titles at one Games, Athens 2004. It is thought to be one of the only times in her career when she was fully fit.
Did you know? In claiming the double in 2004, at 34, Holmes became the oldest woman to win either race at the Games.

Aladar Gerevich

Country: Hungary
DOB: 16/3/1910 Died: 14/5/1991
Olympics: 1932, 1936, 1948, 1952, 1956, 1960
Medal haul: 10 (7)

The Greatest Olympic Swordsman
Despite his sports career being interrupted by WWII, fencer Aladar Gerevich is the only Olympian to have won the same event (team sabre) six times – and is one of only two (the other being Birgit Fischer) to win medals at six different Games.
Did you know? Gerevich won Olympic golds an unprecedented 28 years apart (in Los Angeles 1932 and Rome 1960). His wife, father-in-law and son also won Olympic medals in fencing.

Usain Bolt

Country: Jamaica
DOB: 21/8/1986
Olympics: 2008
Medal haul: 3 (3)

The Fastest Human Being

Defying logic, reason and even sports science, Usain Bolt's 2008 sprint season culminated in world and Olympic records in the 100m and 200m events in Beijing. He ran 9.69secs and 19.30secs respectively, smashing two of the hardest-to-break records, becoming the fastest human being ever and the first man to hold the 100m and 200m world and Olympic titles at the same time.

Did you know?

When he smashed the 100m record, one of his shoes was untied.

Linford Christie 

Country: Great Britain
DOB: 2/4/1960
Olympics: 1988, 1992
Medal haul: 3 (1)

The Old Man of Sprinting
In 1992, at the age of 32, Linford Christie, who only started taking athletics seriously at 19, won a gold medal in Barcelona to become the oldest Olympic 100m champion by four years and the most famous sportsman in Britain.

Christie was the first European sprinter to break 10 seconds for the 100m, but his track career ended in 1999 when, after an indoor athletic meeting in Germany, he was found guilty of using the performance-enhancing drug nandrolone.

Explanations offered by Christie's team included eating avocado. He received a two-year ban and the British Olympic Association said he would not be accredited for future Games.

Did you know? Much to Linford Christie's apparent dislike, his genitalia, or 'Linford's Lunchbox', have become a part of modern British lexicology.

Fanny Blankers-Koen 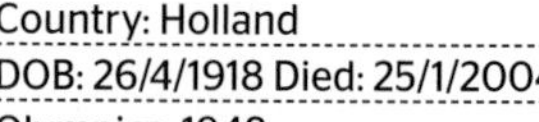

Country: Holland
DOB: 26/4/1918 Died: 25/1/2004
Olympics: 1948
Medal haul: 4 (4)

The Flying Dutchwoman
A 30-year-old mother of two when the Olympics began in London in 1948, Fanny Blankers-Koen sprinted away four gold medals from the Games, in the 100m, 200m, 80m hurdles and the 4x100m relay – while she was pregnant with her third child. A dramatic achievement that is unlikely ever to be surpassed.

Did you know? Blankers-Koen also set world records in the high jump and long jump.

Derartu Tulu 

Country: Ethiopia
DOB: 21/3/1972
Olympics: 1992, 2000, 2004
Medal haul: 3 (2)

Little Lady With Large Lungs
Despite being one of the biggest names in women's distance running, Derartu Tulu is a mere 1.56m tall. The only woman to win two long-distance (10,000m) Olympic golds – in Barcelona in 1992 and Sydney in 2000 – Tulu was also the first African woman to win Olympic gold.

Did you know? In the Sydney 10,000m final, Tulu ran the final 400m in 60 seconds to win in 30mins 17.49secs, a new African and Olympic record.

Al Oerter 

Country: USA
DOB: 19/9/1936 Died: 1/10/2007
Olympics: 1956, 1960, 1964, 1968
Medal haul: 4 (4)

King of the Discus
The first track and field athlete to win gold in the same individual event at four consecutive Games – and, while doing so, becoming the only athlete to set four consecutive Olympic records – Al Oerter is to discus what James Bond is to Aston Martins.

Did you know? Oerter continued to use the discus in his post-athletic career – by creating abstract art. He'd cake the equipment in paint before hurling it at canvas.

Michael Phelps

Country: USA
DOB: 30/6/1985
Olympics: 2004, 2008
Medal haul: 16 (14)

The Baltimore Bullet

Okay, deep breath: Michael Phelps is an American swimmer who holds the record for the most gold medals won by an athlete at a single Olympics (eight). His overall Olympic medal haul is second only to Larisa Latynina, he was the most successful athlete at the Athens (2004) and the Beijing (2008) Games, and holds the record for most individual gold Olympic medals (nine). He has also set more records in his career than any other swimmer.

Did you know?

Phelps's arms span 6ft 7in – which is disproportionate to his height of 6ft 4in – his ankles can extend beyond the *pointe* of a ballet dancer and he has size 14 feet.

Paavo Nurmi

Country: Finland
DOB: 13/6/1897 Died: 2/10/1973
Olympics: 1920, 1924, 1928
Medal haul: 12 (9)

The Flying Finn
The incomparable 'Flying Finn' Paavo Nurmi set 22 official and 13 unofficial world records across a huge array of running disciplines, including the 1,500m, 3,000m, 5,000m, 10,000m, steeplechase, cross-country and marathon. Nurmi's exhaustive and uncompromising training system, and mastery of pace, brought him medals galore and the adulation of his home nation.

Did you know?
There are three statues of Nurmi in Europe: one in his hometown of Turku, one outside the Olympic stadium in Helsinki and one in the park of the Olympic Museum in Lausanne.

Edwin Moses

Country: USA
DOB: 31/8/1955
Olympics: 1976, 1984, 1988
Medal haul: 3 (2)

Nine Years, Nine Months and Nine Days
This is the length of time in which Edwin Corley Moses did not lose a 400m hurdles race. Remarkable, eh? At his peak, he was simply unbeatable – not bad considering he began his athletics career as a 120-yard hurdle and 440-dash merchant.

Did you know? Moses still holds nearly a quarter of the 100 fastest times in the 400m hurdles. A fierce anti-drug campaigner, he also developed out-of-competition and random drug-testing programmes for sport.

Daley Thompson

Country: Great Britain
DOB: 30/7/1958
Olympics: 1980, 1984
Medal haul: 2 (2)

Ten Disciplines But a Single Mind
The Great British public's favourite all-rounder, Thompson endeared himself to the nation after winning gold in Los Angeles in 1984 and casually whistling *God Save the Queen* on the medal podium. He was awarded the MBE in 1982, the OBE in 1986 and the CBE in 2000.
Did you know? In the 1990s, Thompson played professional football for Mansfield Town and Stevenage Borough.

OLYMPICS IN NUMBERS

10 million
number of tickets that will go on sale for the London 2012 games

302 number of gold medals to be won

900,000
different items of sports equipment that will be used in the games, including footballs, towels, trampolines, hurdles, basketballs and shuttlecocks

5 the number of rings in the Olympic logo: they represent the five continents that come together to compete – Asia, Africa, the Americas, Europe and Oceania

330
tonnes of fruit and vegetables the athletes will consume over the 17 days

245
number of athletes who took part in the first Modern Games in 1896

108,500m²
area the Olympic Stadium covers

1mm
the maximum amount by which the Olympic running track can deviate

14,700
number of athletes competing at London 2012 (10,500 in the Olympics, 4,200 in the Paralympics)

21,000
number of journalists and broadcasters at the event (to be served 50,000 meals per day)

75,000
litres of milk the athletes will consume over the 17 days of competition

10,000
tonnes of steel used to build the Olympic stadium

17,500
capacity of the Aquatics Centre

6,000
capacity of the Velodrome

27°C
the temperature of the pool in the Aquatics Centre

3

the number of times London has hosted the Games, more than any other city

30,000

the number of people gathered in Trafalgar Square to cheer the London bid victory in 2005

60,000

the number of spectators who watched the first Modern Olympic Games in Athens, Greece.

70,000

the number of volunteers involved in London 2012

120,000

number of people that will pass through Stratford Regional train station every morning of the Olympics

3 out of 4

number of people in the world who watched at least some of the last Olympic Games

776BC

the date the first Olympic Games were held in Ancient Greece

12

the number of years there wasn't an Olympic Games because of World War II

14

number of countries who took part in the 1896 Games

26

number of Olympic sports

20

number of Paralympic sports

17

number of days London 2012 will last

30

number of bridges spanning the rivers and railways of the Olympic Park

11

number of days the Paralympics lasts

205

number of countries involved in the London 2012 Olympics

4.7billion

number of people who watched the Beijing Olympics on the telly

10 DISCONTINUED OLYMPIC SPORTS

Motor boating at the Olympics? Sometimes officials of the Greatest Event on Earth don't have the Greatest Ideas on Earth...

1) Golf

Should make a re-appearance in 2016 in Rio de Janeiro where a 72-hole stroke-play competition for men and women, with 60 players in each field is being proposed. Charles Sands won gold in 1900 and returned in 1908 as a Jeu de Paume competitor. The 1900 women's champion, Margaret Abbott, was the first ever US woman to win a gold medal. 1904's champ, George Lyon, didn't pick up a club until he was 38, preferring baseball, tennis and cricket.

2) Cricket

In 1900, cricket made its only Olympic appearance and was contested solely between Great Britain and France after the Netherlands and Belgium pulled out. It wasn't much of a spectacle or much of a sport. A British report observed that: "We found the French temperament is too excitable to enjoy the game and no Frenchman can be persuaded to play more than once," even though the French side consisted mainly of British expatriates living in Paris!

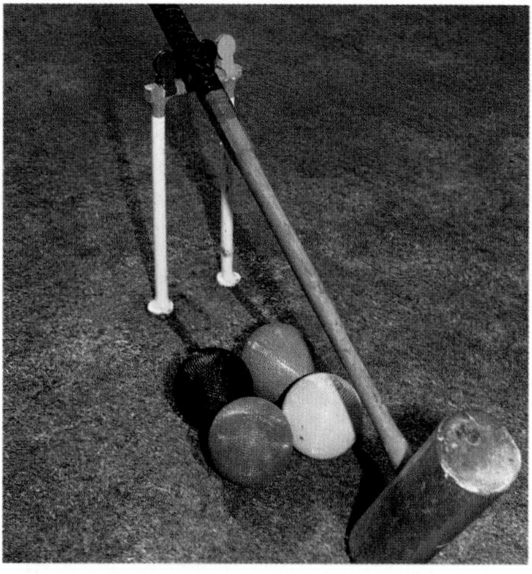

3) Croquet

Its sole appearance at the Olympics came in Paris in 1900 where nine out of the ten competitors (seven men and three women) hailed from the home nation and the token Belgian couldn't be bothered to finish the first round of competition. That and the fact that only one paying spectator, an English gent, paid to watch, meant Croquet with "hardly any pretensions to athleticism" was ditched in St Louis in 1904 .

4) Jeu De Pame

To anyone who isn't French, Jeu de Paume means "game of palm" and was essentially tennis but using your hands (or small paddles) instead of rackets. Also known as "court tennis" or "real tennis" it was an Olympic medal event only in London 1908, when the USA's Jay Gould beat a string of capable Englishmen to the gold medal despite being behind in every set in his eventual straight sets victory.

5) Lacrosse

A male-only event at both the Games of 1904 and 1908, Lacrosse didn't set the world's imagination alight but one country in particular seemed to enjoy it. In 1904, three teams from only two nations competed with Canada winning gold and bronze. Great Britain represented Canada's only obstacle in 1908 and were eventually beaten 14-10. Did we mention: Lacrosse is the national summer sport of Canada.

6) Motor Boating

There were three events: Class A – Open to all boats; Class B – under 60 feet; and Class C – 6.5-8 metres. Each class had multiple competitors (though only from two nations) and were tasked with completing 5 laps of an 8 nautical mile course. However, thanks to a prevailing gale only one boat finished each race so only the three gold medals were ever awarded. After 1908 the IOC decided motorised sport should not be included in the Olympic programme.

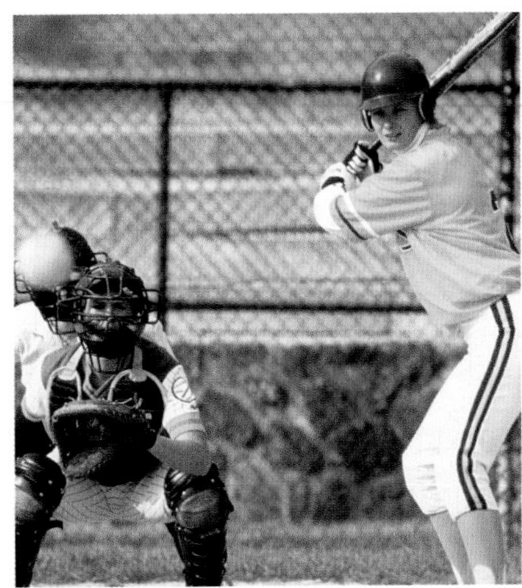

7) Softball

Introduced at the Atlanta 1996 Summer Olympics for women-only and contested for the next three Olympic games, the IOC voted to drop baseball and softball from the Olympic Programme for 2012 despite a keen interest from countries who like softball, whoever they are. The International Baseball and International Softball Federations are not having any of it though, and are proposing to revive both at 2020. A softball, by the way, is harder than a baseball.

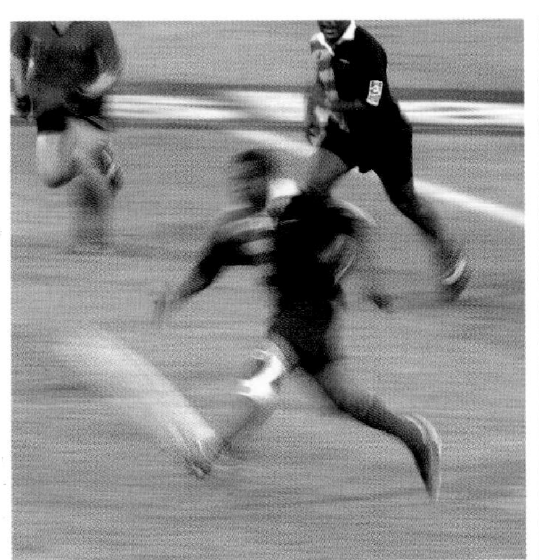

8) Rugby

Bizarrely, the USA is the most successful Olympic nation when it comes to rugby, having won gold in both 1920 and 1924, the Star-Spangled Banner being drowned out in 1924 by the booing of beaten French fans in Paris. A pitch invasion at the latter tarnished the sport's image and a lack of interested nations spelt the death knell for the event in the Olympics. A seven-a-side version for both men and women has been proposed for inclusion in 2016.

9) Rackets

In 1908 in London, two rackets events were contested, the men's singles and the men's doubles, exclusively by seven athletes from Great Britain. It was the precursor to squash and was played in a 30 x 60ft (9.14m x 18.28m) enclosed court, with a 30ft (9.14m) high ceiling. Matches are typically best of 5 games and in the olden times no rests were allowed between games.

10) Tug of War

The 1900, 1904, 1908, 1912 and 1920 Games all hosted the ancient Olympic sport of Tug of War. The event was open to club teams meaning several teams from one country could compete for the medals, resulting in a clean medal sweep for the USA in 1904 and Great Britain in 1908. The first team to pull the other one 5ft was the winner and if this didn't happen in the allotted five minutes, whomever had pulled the farthest.

LAP OF THE GODS

Christine Ohuruogu talks about her pride and excitement at being afforded the chance to defend her Olympic 400m title in her home town

How much are you looking forward to performing in, essentially, your own back yard in 2012?
I'm very excited. It's something that can only happen once in a lifetime. I'm really looking forward to being part of the experience and having lifelong memories of the whole thing.

Are your friends, family and community especially excited about seeing you perform?
They are excited about the Games full stop. I think I'm just a bonus!

What would be your ideal performance?
Obviously, I want to win. But I know it's not going to be that easy. I haven't given it too much thought. Once the season's out of the way, I can start prepping for the Games.

Why do all athletes claim not to be thinking about it yet?
It doesn't help on a day-to-day basis right now, so I don't give it too much energy.

What, for you, is so special about the 2012 Olympics?
It being so close to home. I grew up in Stratford – I love my borough, I love London and I love sport, and for those things to be married at such an important time in my career is just brilliant. I'm very happy for Newham and I'm happy for London. This is my home, I could never live anywhere else, and I'm very happy my community has this once-in-a-lifetime experience. They couldn't have written the script better, to be honest.

How much do the crowd help you when you are competing? How big a factor will they be for the British athletes at London 2012?
It's great for the British, who are keen lovers of sport, to experience an event like this so close to home. All of the athletes are competing on behalf of the public and we are all very appreciative that they support us.

How do you get yourself pumped up before competing?
I don't really get too pumped. I don't need to work on that kind of extreme level for my event, I just try to keep myself as calm and as focused as possible. Some people like to be extremely pumped – I don't need to be.

Aside from your own, which events are you most looking forward to at London 2012?
I want to take in as much as possible and experience as much as I can. We are all in it together, so it'll be good to go around and support the other athletes. There's nothing specific I have my eye on, I just want to see and support as

nuch as I can. When I was in Beijing didn't really get the chance to vatch anything, so I'll just be appy to watch whatever's appening!

Who are the three athletes you are nost looking forward to seeing at he Games in 2012?

bviously, the men's 100m is going o be special. I will certainly be vatching to see how Usain Bolt gets on – and I'm really looking orward to seeing how Phillips Idowu, interviewed on p106] gets on. Aside from them, I just want to get to as many events as I can and end as much support as I can.

s the team spirit better at the Olympic Games?

here is a special sense of ogetherness at the Olympics, yes. You're all going on this journey ogether. No matter what your houghts or stance in life, you are all pretty much going through the same thing and you realise, whatever your differences, you are all very similar.

What was your favourite Olympic noment as a child?

didn't really watch any of the Olympics – I'm the worst person to nterview about this! I followed it, but I wasn't really on it, if you know what I mean? I loved participating n sport, but I didn't really watch it. The Olympics went over my head as a child.

Did you have a hero, though?

When I was a kid, people used to called me 'Linford Christine', which was quite nice. I did have a ot of admiration for Linford, so always felt very proud to be compared to him.

What levels of dedication do Olympic medallists have to naintain? How will you be preparing for the London 2012 Games?

won't do anything different to what I did last year – or the year before that or the year before that eally. I'll just be focused on what need to get done and do it to the est of my ability.

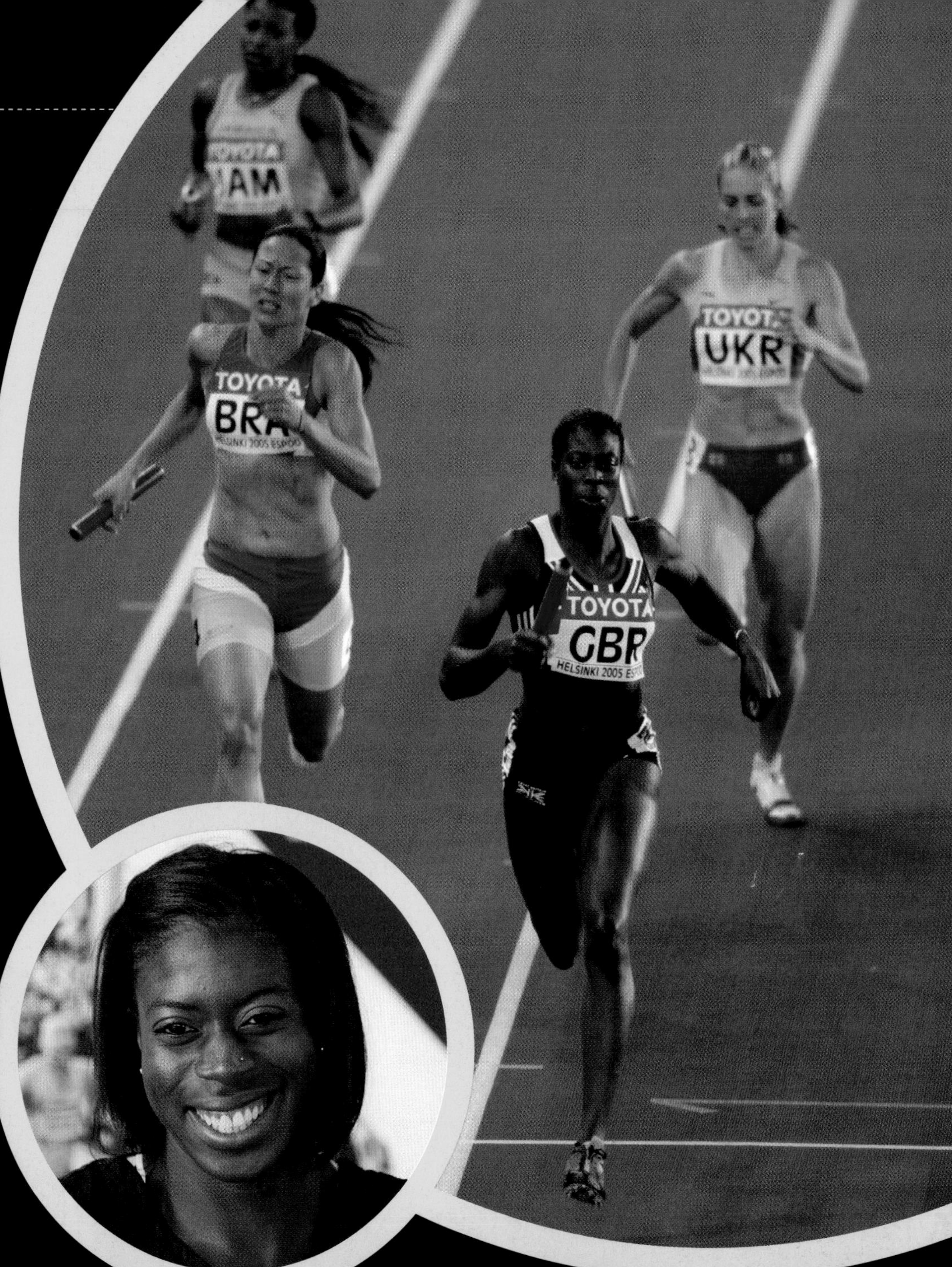

"THIS SPORT IS VERY TOUGH. HAVING A GOLD MEDAL DOESN'T MAKE LIFE EASIER, IT MAKES LIFE VERY HARD"

What has been your career highlight so far?

I guess it has to be winning gold at the Beijing Games, in 2008. But my bronze medal in the European Junior Championships [in 2003, in Tampere, Finland] was also very special. It might not seem like a big thing, but, for me, winning that bronze medal was one of the biggest things that shaped me as a person. That sort of thing doesn't make the headlines, but it was a real milestone.

What will you do after the London 2012 Games?

Everything hinges on what happens in 2012, I think all of the athletes will attest to that.

Your victory in Beijing was the 50th Olympic gold medal for Britain in athletics. What milestone/benchmark do you want to set next?

This sport is very tough. I want to get back to the level I was at in Beijing. When I won there, everything seemed so wonderfully easy, but then you realise it's not. Having a gold medal doesn't make life easier, it makes life very hard. ■

10 OLYMPIC ECCENTRICS

The Olympic Games have taught us mere talent and results are not always enough to achieve sporting immortality. Sometimes, you have to have something a bit extra, something a bit, well, 'different'...

1) Usain Bolt

An eccentricity of character that is only surpassed by his prodigious talent on the running track, Usain Bolt became a household name in Beijing 2008 when the world stood up to watch his chest thumping figure smash the 100m record to pieces, despite pulling up at the end to celebrate. With an indulgent celebration only the fastest man in the world could attempt to pull off, and dance moves that would have MJ turning in his grave, all was forgiven for a man who's future is set to dazzle brighter than the shoes he so regularly champions.

2) Florence Griffith-Joyner

It was not just the flamboyance of 'Flo Jo' that grabbed worldwide attention when she burst onto the scene at the 1984 Olympics, but a talent as bright as her psychedelic spandex unitards. Famed for her extremely long and colourful fingernails, Flo-Jo's pioneering fashion sense transcended the Games and she went on to design basketball uniforms for the Indiana Pacers. She died in 1998, aged just 38, but her records for the women's 100m and 200m still stand.

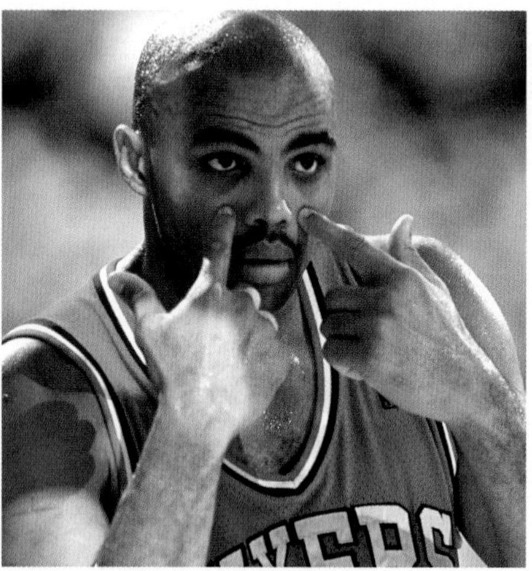

3) Charles Barkley

Part of the all-conquering 1992 USA's Basketball "Dream Team", which beat every opponent on their way to gold by an average of 44 points, Charles Barkley was as controversial as he was effective. During his 17-year career he enjoyed a scrap both on and off the court and in March 1991 he mistakenly spat on a young girl fan cheering courtside. In 2008, he announced he would run for Governor of Alabama in 2014 but he changed his mind two years later. Bit of an odd one.

4) Dick Fosbury

Hailed as one of the most influential athletes in the history of track and field, Dick Fosbury irrevocably changed the high jump with his revolutionary technique. His 'back first' execution was labelled the 'Fosbury Flop' and has since been adopted by almost all high jumpers, the antiquated 'straddle' technique practically relegated to obscurity. Far from being a flash in the pan fad, Fosbury employed his new technique in clinching gold, with an Olympic record height, at the 1968 Games.

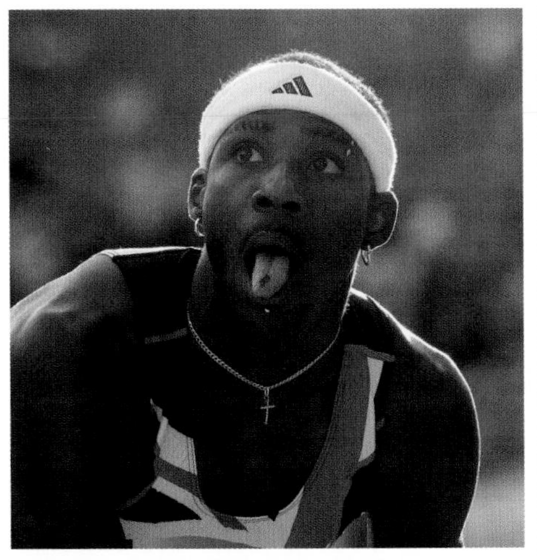

5) Phillips Idowu

Despite a brash hue of a red hair, a rebellious range of piercings and a swagger that has attracted criticism from some quarters, world champion triple jumper Phillips Idowu remains one of the most popular characters among his British team-mates. Love him or hate him, he is keeping his feet firmly on the ground until he throws them in the air in search of gold at the London Games in 2012 – a feat that could see larger-than-life Idowu being hailed as one Britain's great Olympians.

6) Eric Moussambani

Equatorial Guinea's Eric 'the Eel' Moussambani swam his way to fame – and the record books – in Sydney, in 2000. Having only learned to swim eight months earlier, and having never before seen a 50m pool, Eric's 100m freestyle caught the world's attention. Two other swimmers were due to compete in his heat, but both false started leaving Moussambani to 'swim' on his own. A spluttering struggle saw him complete the distance in one minute 52.72 seconds – a full minute off a competitive time, but a national record nonetheless.

7) Abebe Bikila

A shepherd's son from a remote Ethiopian village, Abebe Bikila is not only remembered for being the first athlete to win the Olympic marathon twice – but also for the eccentricity and grace he displayed while doing so. Drafted into the Ethiopian team at the very last minute for the 1960 Rome Games, Abebe won the race barefoot, having not found the regulation Adidas shoes comfortable. Four years later, he won again, in a world record time, and finished with some routine exercises in front of an astonished crowd, explaining he could happily have run 10km more!

8) Muhammad Ali

As eccentric and talented as any of the names on this list, Ali's rise to boxing fame was springboarded by his winning gold at the 1960 Olympics in Rome. But after a dispute in his hometown, Ali threw his prized medal in the Ohio River. It found its way back to him in 1996, when the great champ – now diagnosed with Parkinson's – travelled to Atlanta to light the Olympic torch. Shaking as he did so, because of the onslaught of his illness, it remains one of the most poignant moments in Games history.

9) Daley Thompson

Possibly the most eccentric athlete of the lot, Daley Thompson's long list of misdemeanours endeared and alienated him from the public in equal measure. From performing a lap of honour in a T-shirt emblazoned with the slogan 'Is the world's 2nd greatest athlete gay?' (a thinly veiled dig at Carl Lewis), to the public admission of wanting to bed Princess Anne, it's not hard to see why Thompson had his critics and his admirers. Still a great character today.

10) Mark Spitz

Before Michael Phelps, the majority of swimming plaudits and, indeed, medals belonged to the tall, moustachioed form of Mark Spitz. No stranger to an outlandish statement, Spitz cawed that he would do what no man had done before and win six golds at the Olympic Games in 1972 – a cocky disposition he justified by winning seven, which, at the time, was the greatest performance by an Olympian. Spitz followed his swimming career with a less-impressive stint in showbiz.

The First Awards

Winners in 1896 were presented with a silver medal, a crown of olive branches and a diploma. Second-placed athletes were given a bronze medal, a crown of laurel and a diploma.

OLYMPIC FIRSTS

1896

Baron Pierre de Coubertin was the first president of the International Olympic Committee (and inventor of the Modern Olympic format)

APRIL 6 – THE DATE THE FIRST MODERN OLYMPICS BEGAN

The first **race of the Modern Olympics** is the opening heat of the 100m dash, still one of the most popular events.
Spiridon Louis is the first **marathon winner**.
Fencer Leonidas Pyrgos becomes the first **Greek** Modern Olympics **champion** by winning the masters foil competition.
John and Sumner Paine become the first **siblings** to finish first and second in the same event – the men's Military Pistols.

1900

Women make a first appearance in the Modern Games in Paris.
The first **female champion** is in tennis: Charlotte Cooper of Great Britain.
First place in Paris doesn't earn the athletes medals, rather cups and trophies.
The first **football champions** of the Olympics are the London amateurs of Upton Park FC.
Constantin Henriquez de Zubiera, the Franco-Haitian centre in the rugby tournament, is the first **black gold medallist**.

1904

Gold, silver and bronze medals are first awarded at the Olympic Games in St Louis.
The marathon includes the first **black Africans** to compete in the Olympics; two Tswana tribesmen named Len Taunyane and Jan Mashiani.
The first appearance of **boxing** and **freestyle wrestling**.

1906

First and last 'intercalated' Games held in Athens

1908

First appearance of **diving** and **field hockey**.
First summer Games to include **winter events**.
The **Olympic Creed**, that 'the most important thing in the Olympic Games is not to win but to take part', is publicly stated for the first time.

1912

First use of a **public address system**.
Japan are the first participating **Asian nation**.
Decathlon and **pentathlon** introduced, along with art competitions [erased in 1948!].
Portuguese marathon runner Francisco Lázaro is the first **athlete to die during competition**, suffering a heart attack while running.
Electric timing devices are first used in athletics.

1916

First Games to be cancelled because of war, World War I

1920

Introduction of the **Olympic Flag**.
First time the **Olympic Oath** is recited, by Belgian fencer/water polo player Victor Boin.
Ice hockey is included in the summer Olympic Games for the first – and the last – time.

1924

The **Olympic Motto** Citius, Altius, Fortius (Swifter, Higher, Stronger) is introduced.
The **closing ceremony ritual of raising three flags** – the Olympic flag, the host nation's flag and that of the next host nation – starts in the Stade Olympique Yves-du-Manoir.
First Games to use the now standardised **50m** (55yd) **pool** with marked lanes.

1928

First lighting of the **Olympic Torch**.
Greece first, **hosts last** became a part of opening ceremony protocol in at the 1928 Games
First gold medals won by **Asian athletes**.
First Games to last **16 days** (the duration has since been between 15 and 18 days).

1932

Los Angeles is the first Games to turn a considerable **profit** ($1m).
First time all of the male athletes stay in designated **Olympic Village**.
Liu Changchun becomes the first person to represent the 40m people of **China** in the Olympics.
First Games to use a **victory podium**.

1936

First Games to be awarded by a **bidding process**.
Introduction of the **torch relay** and the first time it is run from Olympia to the host nation.
Berlin is also the first Games to **broadcast on television** and produce the first **official film**: *Olympia* by Leni Riefenstahl.
Basketball, **canoeing** and team **handball** make their first appearance at the games.

1948

The first summer Olympic Games since Berlin because of World War II.
First Games to be shown on **home television**.
Pictograms introduced, one for each of the 20 sports.
First time **swimming events** at an Olympics are **held undercover**.
Women's canoeing introduced.

1952

Soviet Union enter for the first time.
Lis Hartel, of Denmark, is the **first woman to be allowed to compete against men**, in the equestrian dressage (despite being paralysed below the knee!).
Lars Hall becomes first **non-military gold medallist in modern pentathlon**.

1956

First games to be held in the **southern hemisphere** (also the first outside of North America and Europe).
Laszlo Papp of Hungary becomes the first **boxer to win three golds**.
First time **butterfly stroke** is separated from breaststroke.
First **false start in the marathon**.
First time **athletes enter closing ceremony stadium together** – a suggestion by John Ian Wang to symbolise global peace and unity.

India lose their first **field hockey final**, 1-0 to Pakistan, who win their first ever Olympic gold medal.
Ghana's Ike Quartley, becomes the first **black African medallist** and Abebe Bikila the first **black African gold medallist**.

1960

1964

First **Games** held **in Asia**.
First Games from which **South Africa** are **barred** because of apartheid.
Judo and **volleyball** introduced.
Adebe Bikila first person to **retain marathon crown** (and probably the only person who'll ever do it in bare feet)
Hungary suffer **first defeat in team sabre** in 40 years.

1968

First Olympic Games hosted by a **developing country**.
First hosted by a **Spanish-speaking** country.
First summer Games to include **sex testing** for women.
Al Oerter becomes the first track and field athlete to win **four consecutive gold medals** in an individual event.
Eulalia Rolinska, of Poland, and Gladys de Seminario, of Peru, are the first **women to compete in the shooting**.
Debbie Meyer becomes the first swimmer to win **three gold medals** at **three separate individual events** at the same Olympic Games.

1972

MARK SPITZ BECOMES THE FIRST PERSON TO WIN **SEVEN GOLD MEDALS** AT ONE OLYMPIC GAMES.
WALDI BECOMES THE FIRST **OFFICIALLY NAMED OLYMPIC MASCOT**.
SLALOM CANOEING INTRODUCED.

1976

First time the **host country fails to win any gold medals**.
Women's rowing, **basketball** and team **handball** introduced.
Gymnast Nadia Comeneci achieves the first **perfect-10** score on the parallel bars.
First **women's volleyball team** (Japan) to **win all of their matches in straight sets**.
First **200m/400m double** victory by Alberto Juantorena of Cuba.
Miklos Nemeth is the first **son of a track and field gold medallist to win a gold medal** (his father was 1948 hammer thrower Imre Nemeth).

1980

First games to be staged in **Eastern Europe**.
Teófilo Stevenson becomes the first boxer to **win the same weight division at three separate Olympics**.
Gerd Wessig (East Germany) becomes the first person to set a **world record for high jump** at an Olympic Games.

1984

Women's marathon is finally added to the Olympic programme, the first winner is Joan Benoit of the USA.
Synchronised swimming, **road cycling** and **rhythmic gymnastics** also introduced.
Nawal El Moutawakel of Morocco becomes the first **woman from an Islamic nation to win a gold medal**.
Sebastian Coe becomes the first man to **retain the 1,500m title**.

1988

Table tennis introduced.
For the first time, the **equestrian dressage podium is occupied only by women**.
American diver Greg Louganis asserts his dominance by becoming the **first man to win both diving disciplines twice**.
Ben Johnson becomes the first Olympic megastar to be branded a cheat and stripped of his medal after a **positive drug test** (Carl Lewis, therefore, becomes the **first man to win the 100m twice**).

1992

Basketball is opened up to professionals for the first time, instigating the formulation of the American 'Dream Team'.
Chinese athlete Zhang Shan becomes the **first female to win a mixed-sex shooting** event.
Derartu Tulu, a 10,000m runner from Ethiopia, becomes the first **black African female gold medal winner**.

1996

Palestine is allowed to compete in the Olympics for the first time.
After winning the super-heavyweight Greco-Roman wrestling category, Aleksandr Karelin, of Russia, becomes the **first wrestler to win the same division three times at three different Games**.
Hubert Raudaschal, the Austrian yachtsman, becomes the **first person to compete at nine different Olympic Games**.
Professional riders permitted into cycling events.
Beach volleyball, mountain biking, **lightweight rowing** and **women's softball** and **football** introduced.

2000

Steve Redgrave becomes first rower in history to win **gold medals at five different Olympics**.
Michael Johnson becomes the first **repeat winner of the men's 200m**.
First time the **USA fail to win a medal** in the men's long jump.

First time since 1896 that the Olympics are held in **Greece.**
For the first time the **Olympic Flame** tours the world.
Internet coverage of events allowed for the first time.
Birgit Fischer becomes the first woman in any sport to win **gold medals in six different Olympic Games**.
Women's wrestling allowed for the first time.
Liu Xiang's gold in the men's 110m hurdles is **China's first gold** in men's track and field
Swimmer Michael Phelps from America becomes the first athlete to win **eight medals in a non-boycotted Olympics**.

2004

2008

FIRST GAMES TO BE FILMED AND BROADCAST ENTIRELY IN **HIGH DEFINITION**
CHINA WON 51 GOLD MEDALS, **THE HIGHEST OF ANY NATION AT THE OLYMPICS,** BECOMING THE FIRST NATION OTHER THAN RUSSIA OR THE USA TO DO SO SINCE THE 1936 SUMMER OLYMPICS

2012

London is first city to officially host the Modern Olympic Games three times